"If I wasn't laughing, I was crying. Felt ALL the feels reading this book."

—**Jessica S.**
Beta Reader

My Mountains

Our family's story of adventure, mysteries, and tragedy

CHRIS SMITH

LUCIDBOOKS

My Mountains
Our family's story of adventure, mysteries, and tragedy
Copyright © 2025 by Chris Smith

Published by Lucid Books in Houston, TX
www.LucidBooks.com

All rights reserved. No part of this publication may be reproduced, stored in a retrieval system, or transmitted in any form by any means, electronic, mechanical, photocopy, recording, or otherwise, without the prior permission of the publisher, except as provided for by USA copyright law.

Unless otherwise indicated, scripture quotations are taken from the Holy Bible, New International Version®, NIV®. Copyright ©1973, 1978, 1984, 2011 by Biblica, Inc.™ Used by permission of Zondervan. All rights reserved worldwide. www.zondervan.com The "NIV" and "New International Version" are trademarks registered in the United States Patent and Trademark Office by Biblica, Inc.™

Scripture quotations marked (ESV) are taken from the ESV® Bible (The Holy Bible, English Standard Version®), copyright © 2001 by Crossway, a publishing ministry of Good News Publishers. Used by permission. All rights reserved.

ISBN: 978-1-63296-859-3 (Paperback)
ISBN: 978-1-63296-860-9 (Hardback)
eISBN: 978-1-63296-861-6

Special Sales: Most Lucid Books titles are available in special quantity discounts. Custom imprinting or excerpting can also be done to fit special needs. Contact Lucid Books at Info@LucidBooks.com

*For my six children,
a legacy of their mother*

Table of Contents

Chapter 1: Standing up Smiling — 1

Chapter 2: The Girl with the Green Eyes — 21

Chapter 3: When Miracles Happen — 53

Chapter 4: Camp Life — 72

Chapter 5: The Blessedness of Family — 87

Chapter 6: The Call of the Mountains — 106

Chapter 7: Angels in the Making — 131

Chapter 8: The Weight of a Son — 162

Chapter 9: Uphill in the Dark — 175

Chapter 10: Above Tree Line — 197

Chapter 11: Questions in the Shadows — 217

Chapter 12: When the Leaves Fall — 234

CHAPTER 1:
Standing up Smiling

"Have either of you heard from Keagan? He's not responding to my texts," Cheyenne texted Michele and me.

It was a beautiful July day in the Rocky Mountains. Summer in Pagosa Springs, Colorado, is spectacular. Surrounded by the North Range views and the East Range mountains, it is an idyllic, small town, mountain paradise. This is where our son, Keagan, and his wife, Cheyenne, along with their two young boys, lived. We cherished having our oldest son's family living in our mountain town. For five years, we got to share in Keagan and Cheyenne's growing family while they lived in our house, with a three-month-old, Kai, and later the joyous arrival of his little brother, Liam. After those years, they finished building their own custom home and finally owned their first home together.

"No, but I'll try," I replied.

"I tried earlier and didn't get a response either."

I texted Michele, at home alone, while I was at work, trying not to get annoyed by these interruptions.

Michele followed up, "I'm worried this time."

We hadn't seen or spoken to Keagan in four days, which was unusual. Keagan was alone at his home because Cheyenne had divorced him to protect herself and their sons, Kai and Liam. For the past few years, following a horrific auto accident which had left him confined to a wheelchair Keagan had been addicted to pain medicine and illegal drugs. Back when they were just dating, Cheyenne and Keagan were a super cute and adventurous couple. They loved the outdoors and spent a lot of time hiking, rock climbing, and four-wheeling. But the accident had changed everything. Before the accident, and before the drugs took over, Keagan was a fantastic father to their boys. And Cheyenne recognized his importance in their boys' lives, doing everything to have Keagan spend time with them.

"I'm not getting any response, either," I texted Cheyenne and Michele.

"I talked to Blake, and he is going over to knock on the door and see what's up," I followed up.

Blake was married to Kassidy, our daughter. They lived next door to Keagan. Blake was home and was glad to go check. He had gone over on a few other occasions when Keagan didn't respond, and we were concerned.

We felt so blessed to have four of our six children and their families living in our mountain town of Pagosa Springs.

It was more work doing things in the mountains and on lakes, with Keagan in a wheelchair. But it never occurred to any of us to just leave him behind. He was essential; his passion was being outdoors. Our family did things together. We always tried doing an activity with as much of our family as we could get.

I was worried that Michele was worried. I wasn't especially worried that something was amiss because this had happened several times before. But Michele had mastered intuition. She was tight with every member of our family. She was the hub that our entire family communicated through. Despite the kids leaving our house and moving into their own homes, she maintained meticulous communication with all of them. Michele remembered every birthday, anniversary, grandchild's birthday, birth weight, middle name, favorite book, special child toy, and whatever else was important to each person in her family. Words were Michele's most cherished objects on earth. Both to give and receive. She wrote cards for everything, texted everyone regularly, and posted anything she could smile about regarding her kids and grandchildren.

I often went and checked on Keagan. If he wasn't responding to calls, it was usually some little thing like misplacing his phone. Maintaining a home and life order presents challenges for wheelchair users. Sometimes he was just wrapped up in a crazy art project in his garage. He loved making things out of metal and used loud grinders and welders. Sometimes Keagan's phone died, or he passed out from his medication, or simply slept. Keagan rarely slept at night, so he often dozed during the day on and off. Keagan's fight against pain was a battle. It was physical, emotional, and mental. He really was a warrior. Throughout, his pain rarely subsided to less than moderate, especially at night. I'm not talking about needing an extra Tylenol. He was on the maximum dose of OxyContin, a narcotic drug. His doctors told us that without this high dose, Keagan would die of a stroke or heart attack, brought on by the intensity of his pain. Most days involved his body convulsing in fits of muscle spasms. Spasms that looked like he would break out his teeth or pop blood vessels in his arms. Nights were even worse, with little to distract his mind in between episodes, and he would sit alone in his wheelchair in the living room away from Cheyenne, dreading the next episode of convulsions. From upstairs, we would hear him. It was excruciating to wake up multiple times in the night, only to hear him still trying to conceal his gasping breaths. This was most nights.

Blake called me back.

I was no longer feeling interrupted.

Blake was silent for a very long time.

A massive panic was quickly developing in my body. Nausea swept over me as if I were about to throw up, but nothing came out.

Blake didn't want to talk, and he knew I didn't want him to. He actually couldn't talk. He tried a couple times to get the words out but couldn't. For years, we met regularly for breakfast and Bible study. We discussed careers, construction—our shared profession—and faith. In that precipitous moment, I wanted everything to stop, just freeze. I didn't want to go any further. No words had been spoken, leaving room to possibly turn back time and prevent any unfortunate events.

"I knocked, but nobody answered. All the doors were locked. I started going around looking in any windows I could," he described.

"I saw in through the bathroom window and... He's gone," Blake finally said.

"He's lying in the shower and has fallen out of his chair. His body has no color. It looks like it's been quite a while," he added.

Cheyenne and Michele were the ones who asked me to find out what was going on. They were waiting for me to tell them what I had found out. I didn't want to tell them. I didn't want to tell anybody what was going on in my day. I wanted to sit in anonymity at my desk and let everything around me go on normally. Maybe then this would evaporate magically. My brain was frantically trying to recall if there really was a way to freeze time and just stop this whole thing. From my desk, I walked through my office building. I kept my head down and ignored everyone there. All I wanted was to become invisible. I beelined it to my CEO, who takes care of everything for me. Everything was a blur to my eyes. Nothing seemed real. I told her the horrific news. She rarely displays panic or shock. She must daily manage many decisions and significant challenges. Instantly, she gasped and began crying. She understood why I came right to her. She caught my attention, then reminded me of my responsibility to inform Michele and Cheyenne. I couldn't just sit by myself in shock indefinitely. There was no magic spell that could freeze time while things moved back to before. I went through a checklist with her to think if everything at work was OK for me to leave for the day, or forever maybe. My minor tasks at work weren't just petty. Suddenly, they didn't matter at all. I definitely was not OK. Nothing was OK. How was any of this going to be OK?

I've heard that making yourself do hard things when you don't want to is a great habit and helps your brain to develop grit. Like when you make yourself get up and exercise or climb a tough mountain. This time, I didn't care what it did. I didn't want to do this. Surely this was in a different category of things to avoid at all costs. This was beyond "hard." This was miserable, awful, horrible. I would be intentionally causing life-changing, catastrophic injury to the most cherished person in my life. My mind was bouncing all over, trying to grasp why this happened. It seemed so unnecessary. Why did a young man, a father, have to die? What a waste! All that life and potential. Keagan was a great father. Now his two boys would not have him around. Keagan loved them, he loved Cheyenne, he loved the outdoors, he loved work, he loved God. He impacted many people around him in the world. How can something so good just end?

That day, a wound opened in me that would never heal. I wasn't angry with God. Somehow, I knew He was in charge of all of this. I was just completely stunned and perplexed. Not even so much wanting to know why but wondering how any good could come of this. I am optimistic. Generally speaking, I trust the people I meet or work with. I live my life knowing Jesus is looking out for me and my family. I believe the Bible verse that says our Heavenly Father only gives good gifts to His children. But my eldest son's lonely death after constant suffering for eight years completely stunned me. He didn't write a book about his suffering or speak at church or start a foundation to help people with chronic pain. His story was now one of not making it through. Until now, my family's story was mostly typical with some grand adventures. We faced our fair share of trials. But now somebody died!

I didn't even call Cheyenne or text her or go visit her. My thoughts were numb and scattered. I called the police to gain entry into the house for the coroner to conduct his investigation. It seems inconceivable that I didn't go to tell her. Thankfully, since the police still had Cheyenne as Keagan's emergency contact, they contacted her right away. There were so many things to do. I couldn't just tell Michele, "Something happened. I'll explain it later." Her premonition was correct, and I knew she would be worrying sick until she got word. The longer it went, the more she would worry.

The hardest thing I had ever done was before me—to tell Michele her son was dead.

Coming home early in the workday was already way suspicious. I couldn't sneak in the back. That would scare her to death. I was going to have to let her see me drive up. She was going to know it was bad when she saw me. She was going to want to freeze time, too. Maybe she was going to tell me to go away and not say anything. I had nothing to go on about how to approach Michele. I got ahold of our dear friend Peg and asked if she would meet me at the house. Peg was one of Michele's dearest friends who lived across the highway. Peg was a licensed biblical counselor. I knew she had helped many people through really hard things. This time, it was one of her closest friends who needed her help. I was sick to my stomach, dreading having to tell Michele the awful truth that Keagan was gone. Keagan, who was so full of adventure, even in a wheelchair. Our son, our family's most artistic member, was a wonderful father who deeply loved his two young sons.

Michele was very suspicious seeing Peg and me come to the front door. Upon entering, I swiftly placed my arms under her arms, recalling the doctor's actions with Cheyenne in the ER when Keagan was airlifted to Denver at the beginning of this ordeal. I cried as I confirmed Michele's suspicion that Keagan was gone. I don't know how to cry, though. It doesn't sound like me. But Michele knows how to weep from her soul, and she just wailed. Just like I wish I could have. She wailed in my arms, then she kind of dove onto the stairs we were standing next to and lay out on them and renewed her wailing. She let it out loud and for a long time.

I knew I had wounded her deeply by delivering such horrible news. I felt like it was the most unkind thing I had ever done in my life to anyone. The pain of hurting her was unbearable. Michele had always been so strong of spirit. She was the most cheerful person you'd ever met. Losing her eldest son was a life-changing blow. She longed for Keagan. She wanted him back. Her hope in finding a solution for his pain had always been bright. She didn't fail at things in her life. Surely there was still a solution, not this, not death, not yet.

Keagan died of a drug overdose. The coroner found needles lying around him in the shower. He called us a week later and told us the result of the autopsy showed heroin and fentanyl. There was no suicide note this time. We had suicide notes from previous scares, but not this time. Many suspected Keagan wouldn't survive many more years. We don't really think he wanted to die this time, though. Over the years, Keagan tried alcohol, cocaine, mushrooms, and lots of marijuana. He knew how to find anything he wanted on the "streets." We didn't know he was shooting up heroin, though. He didn't like alcohol, as it made him angry. Although he found mushrooms amazing, they did not ease his pain. He couldn't live without constantly taking pot. He was mixing all this with the maximum doses of OxyContin. As time went on, the prescription drugs lost their effectiveness. So, he was self-medicating and in a downward spiral. We all agonized with him but had no answers.

"Lord, why would this kind of pain ever be part of your plan for someone? What could be the purpose? I know you care, OK, and I believe in your love, but none of this makes sense to me. I mean, you let Keagan suffer more than even Jesus did. Blasphemy? Maybe, but Jesus died on the cross in less than a day. Keagan suffered for eight years. Eight years, Lord! You allowed this pain and suffering. You let it into our family. And it defeated my son. It broke him down, and it took him away forever."

"Ah, but it didn't."

"What? Yes, it did. He's gone. He died in pain and alone."

"He wasn't alone. I was there."

"Then why didn't you heal him?"

"I did heal him. He is now whole. Forever."

"You could have spared him and everyone else from eight years of suffering."

"And now I have."

"What? Why?! I can't fathom a reason for that!"

"Just because you cannot fathom a reason does not mean there isn't one."

"That's cold comfort, Lord."

"Cold comfort that I am God, and you are not? My child, comfort and ease in this life are not the goal. The goal is finding me, walking with me, trusting me, and loving me. Is it not during trials that you are the closest to me?"

"Well, I . . . I know what I'm supposed to say."

"Keagan understood this. Why can't you?"

"Because I had to watch him suffer. I remained helpless. I just stood by and watched."

"I had to watch my son suffer, too, and I couldn't even stand by him. I had to turn away and abandon him. My son was utterly alone. Yours never was and never will be. Your son ran down the road home, straight into my arms. My son's broken body was the path beneath KEAGAN'S feet."

For many sleepless nights, this was my midnight conversation with God. It kept me going. I often feel like I can just talk to God. It gives me solace. Now, when I fall back into despair all these years later, I picture Keagan running down his road home.

Family support sustained us. Belonging held us together when things fell apart.

For years, our lives with Keagan had been a mixture of joy and sorrow. Michele, Cheyenne, and I, and all of Keagan's siblings had grown accustomed to helping him out. For every trip the family took, we spent tons of time arranging logistics to ensure everything would be wheelchair accessible so he could join us. But we all wanted to journey together.

One of the best vacations our family ever had was to Hawaii in 2018. This trip included the entire clan—Michele's family. Michele's parents, Linda and Louis, dreamed of this journey; however, Louis's death left Linda to fulfill their wish.

And she did it big. I'm sure every one of the forty-two of us would agree it was the best vacation ever. That is, except for the whole we're all going to die thing. I'll tell you about that in a bit. Linda and Louis had three daughters, Michele, her twin, Minette, and their older sister, Melissa. These three girls shared a close bond. Think of the book, Little Women. The sisters' lives intertwined deeply. Every sister was "required" to attend each other's childbirth. There were weekly FaceTime chats. And Minette and Michele, being identical twins, infrequently missed daily calls. They also sent cards of encouragement to each other, birthday cards and anniversary cards, and Christmas and Easter cards, even if they were going to spend the holiday together. If they were breathing, they might as well use that breath to produce words of encouragement for each other. Being identical twins, Minette and Michele also shared the same number of children. Six, similarly aged. Melissa and her husband Joel had just three. These fifteen cousins grew up with their moms sharing homeschool ideas together, having their every little new skill shared abroad, and doing everything together as they grew up.

Extensive planning ensured all families could enjoy a ten-day Hawaiian vacation. There were kids in college and grandkids in school who could only go during a break. The adults with jobs had to get approval for vacation time. Those who had their own businesses had to make arrangements for their customers and employees while they were away.

Some were having babies or had just had babies. Some were not married but had a significant other they wanted to bring. And what if they didn't end up getting married? Some hurried up their marriage so they could go.

Keagan was in a wheelchair and had to stay somewhere with accessibility. Bliss—our dear niece with special needs—well, Bliss just couldn't do it. Bringing her would've been too dangerous for her. So Tony, Minette's husband, stayed home with Bliss and let Minette go with the rest of their kids. We very much missed Tony and Bliss on that trip. Bliss is the most endeared person of the entire clan and the youngest cousin. Bliss was born with Hydrocephalus, water on the brain. It caused severe developmental delays. Bliss has never eaten food via her mouth. She has always had a feeding tube and has had dozens of brain surgeries, many of them life-threatening. She breathes out of a tracheotomy and struggles to walk. There are many other diagnoses I can't spell and don't even know about. Each day, Minette and her full-time, in-house nurse dose dozens of vials and syringes, which keep Bliss from having seizures and worse. She has only traveled away from home a couple of times in her life. Hawaii was too far. Air travel is improbable for Bliss.

Linda chose Disney's Aulani Hotel on the island of Oahu. True to Disney, the Aulani resort was an absolutely magical place. Just the anticipation of vacationing in Hawaii excited everyone. Few had ever visited Hawaii. Tony and Minette's family were all pastors' kids and never thought of traveling to Hawaii because of the expense. Bliss was also the final vote on them ever traveling anywhere, pretty much. Joel and Melissa went to Hawaii on their honeymoon because Joel was a lifelong surfer. Their honeymoon was the last time they could afford Hawaii after that. The Aulani is beautiful and grand with all the Hawaiian culture plus some. I lived in Hawaii during my stepfather's Navy posting. Upon exiting the plane, perfect weather greeted us. Coming from Colorado or the Midwest, winter in February and disembarking directly outside to perfect weather was a lovely shock. Seeing my family at the airport exceeded expectations. Imagine going to "paradise" with all your lifelong, favorite people. The boy cousins were Jordan, Keagan, Sawyer, Sully, Clancy, Dawson, Hudson, and Cooper. I have never seen nut slapping at an airport before, but the excitement was contagious as they greeted each other in that manner. Keagan's wheelchair height was perfect for getting a lot of hits without receiving any payback.

We were all still giddy, splitting up in vans to get to the resort and check in. Stepping into your lavish rooms and then sharing everything with each other. Linda had the command center suite. The Lakers were in the playoffs, and all the grandkids had to catch the game with her that afternoon. You wouldn't think it, but Linda is a diehard Lakers, Dodgers, Angels, Rams, and now Chiefs fan. She watches all their games. And her grandsons love it! She is a trove of information on all the players and stats, too, just to make sure her progeny keeps up with it all.

I love getting in the water. Lakes, oceans, pools, rivers, all of them. So, I pleaded with all my kids to let the grandkids go swimming with me as soon as we arrived. I got Kai and Liam, Keagan and Cheyenne's boys, to float around the lazy river with me. My most memorable activity was playing Spikeball with my brother-in-law, nephews, and sons. Fun Spikeball games need players of relatively equal skill. Spikeball is a bit like volleyball. Tony, Joel, and I used to play in volleyball tournaments together. Tony was always way better than Joel and me but would drop a level sometimes to play with us. Clancy and Dawson, Hudson and Cooper are always up for anything with a ball that involves competing. Sawyer and Sully were good for a laugh and got better on that trip. We had epic games every day of the trip.

Did I mention Dole Whip drinks? The Dole Whip drinks were the most-sought-after treat the entire time. If you can believe it, even the ladies substituted their coffee/creamer time for the Pineapple Dole Whip treats.

We booked excursions to go zip lining and horseback riding and got to see giant waves on the North Shore. While zip lining, Michele, Minette, and Melissa could exercise their rare and attention-grabbing ability to squeal. Minette was ready and eagerly waiting to zip up. I'm not sure what happened, but she ever so slightly started losing her balance, and just slowly started going before she was told to go. She was still hooked up to her safety tether, thank goodness. This is the lanyard that made sure she didn't go until you finished your safety check, and the cable was safe to go on. She began to squeal lightly as she slowly tipped off the platform and rolled out until her tether caught her about ten feet away from the platform and flipped her upside down.

Now she was upside down, hanging over a 100-foot drop, and couldn't get back. The squeal immediately elevated to its highest level on the squeal meter. We had forty-two family members on that trip, so most of the people at the zip line park were family. Although we were in separate groups, everyone heard Minette freaking out about something. Minette did a little variation of save my life squealing and gut laughing. It went back and forth a few times as she tried to decide if she was about to die or had broken some rule that would get her ejected from the park. The zip line guide enjoyed the dilemma and took his time enjoying Minette's little upside-down dance, scream, yell, and laugh skit.

Our daughter Kailey found an exciting spear fishing excursion we could sign up for. Kailey, her husband, Kyle, and Tad, husband to our daughter, Sydney, were all going and invited me along. I love water, so that is why I agreed, but I don't really like the middle of the ocean, mile deep, scary ocean. And that is where we ended up. There was no bottom to see underwater. It was pure blue and made us all have a sense of vertigo when we were snorkeling way far from shore. We also got seasick on our tiny little boat. Someone contacted us the day before the trip to meet at a certain dock, but we couldn't find it on our maps. We had to call the company back to get directions a couple of times. The boat captain kept explaining it to us, but we couldn't figure it out. Turns out, Kailey, helping Linda, had booked a spear fishing trip on Hawaii, the Big Island, not just in Hawaii. We were in Hawaii on the island of Oahu. But Linda wasn't about to let that ruin things; she bought us seats on a cheap flight that arrived just in time to fish.

One magical morning, Michele, Minette, and I went on an early walk down the beach. We went a little over a mile while talking, praying, and enjoying every minute together. This was the trio from our college days at Biola University. Sharing the same major, we attended many classes together. We always sat together in the daily Chapel time and lingered afterward to discuss the service if we ever had time. We often jogged in the evenings and played volleyball when our schedules would permit. Then later, as we started our families, we'd have play dates for the kids. For years, Minette and Tony's family vacationed with ours. We never tired of each other. We craved time together with their family. They could show up at our house anytime, and we would gladly rearrange whatever was going on to accommodate them. Even now, when I travel to visit them, all their adult children with spouses and children of their own make time to come over for a BBQ with us.

There were some other people out this beautiful morning for a relaxing stroll, some with their babies in strollers. It was still a bit too early for volleyball and Spike ball games, but sunbathers were walking up to the edge of the sand to look for their spot for the day.

As we thought about turning around to head back, all three of our cell phones blared a loud alert, the same as those Amber alerts for missing children. We looked around and saw everyone along the beach looking at their phones, too, so we took ours out. We live in the country and get those child abduction alerts, but always realize we can never help, as we are hundreds of miles away from whatever incident is happening. Something looked different this time as we looked at our phones, about to silence the alert.

It wasn't an Amber alert. It was an alert for an INCOMING BALLISTIC MISSILE! Yeah, this was the 'we're all going to die thing I mentioned. We didn't see these every day in our remote mountain town in Colorado. Minette's family, living in Missouri, didn't see these in their sheltered Midwest town either. I mean, it is easy to understand those words, but this wasn't real, right? Surely it was a test. All three of us reread it and said to each other, "It's not saying it's a test." In fact, it clearly says it is not a test. Does that mean it's real, and it's not a test? It's saying it is NOT a test. What a crazy thing to pop up on our phone. We were thinking, why are they telling us this? These alerts never apply to us. Wait, what's on a Ballistic missile? I'm pretty sure it's a nuclear warhead. We're on a tiny little island. If they hit it, we're all goners! What did we ever do to anyone with a Ballistic missile? What did our politicians do to piss somebody off, so I have to get blown up today? Everyone we were looking at would be dead in minutes. We would be dead!

We had brought our family to Hawaii to die. This was the end. Minette would never see Tony and Bliss again. No one was ever going to see home again. Our grandkids were going to die today. The nuclear holocaust was beginning. All three of our family's lineages would end here. Michele, Minette, and I felt we had to do something. Hurry, let's rush back, we decided. I thought we may not make it, and what does it matter? Maybe let's just sit here and get blown up, I thought. Michele can't "rush" anyway. Minette was too bullheaded to just sit there and die, so we "rushed" back. Minette and I piggybacked Michele to hurry back and maybe find someone in our family to hold hands with as we evaporated in the nuclear explosion. Other people along the beach started reacting, getting hysterical, and running. Mothers were screaming and scrambling to pack up their babies.

Fifteen minutes later, the alert sounded again, giving us just minutes until impact! We were leaving the paved path on the approach up to the resort, trying to run through the sand, piggybacking Michele, with her cheering us on, and holding back her tears. All we wanted was to get to our family so we could be together when we died.

When we finally arrived at the hotel, it was exactly like the Godzilla movies: 4,000 people were running around wildly. Loudspeakers were telling us to run outside to the front of the hotel. A few minutes later, we were told to get to the basement. It was all chaos. And it was not a drill. It was impossible to find any of our family. I think right before a nuclear bomb, you can't really know how catastrophic it will be. You'll be dead in an instant. Maybe it really isn't such a bad way to go. It's fast. I remember thinking, what if it strikes closer to downtown Honolulu? That was 20 or 30 miles away. We would be in the fallout perimeter. I think it would be worse for us, living with radiation poisoning, burns, cancers, trying to survive those first days and weeks without water, food, transportation, communication, and electricity. Yes, that was going to be worse. I just wanted to be evaporated. I was hoping the missile would be a little off target and hit us directly. I also wondered, what if their target was Kauai, and we escaped unscathed? We only got the Missile warning because we were in the same state after all.

Keagan and Cheyenne scrambled to get out of their room and followed the loudspeaker instructions. Keagan was not fully dressed, but he had no time to waste. He threw his son, Kai, on his lap to cover up and zoomed out into the hall and onto the elevator. Despite grabbing his bag of pain medications, it fell from his lap in the chaos and was lost. He figured it didn't matter, as they were all about to die.

After a little under an hour, people were calming down a bit as rumors went around that it may actually have been a false alarm, although the two alerts both said it was not a test or false alarm. After more time passed, authorities announced it was a false alarm, a mistake made by the government. A mistake that supposedly could never happen because of safeguards against it. To this day, we all say it was real, but our military was able to shoot down the missile in time.

It's fascinating how different people react in an emergency. It's certainly not always logical, and this time, it was downright comical. True to form, Joel and Melissa's son, Jordan, slept right through the whole thing. When he didn't reconvene at Linda's command center suite, my son Sawyer told us he already knew Jordan had slept through it. Linda wasn't about to leave her room without putting her makeup on, so she just stayed put. Nobody faulted her for it either. We would have been ashamed and in disbelief if she had run out without her makeup on.

Michele, Minette, and I began rounding up our family. We reconvened in Linda's command center suite. She was still in her robe but had managed to get her makeup on; she was ready to die beautifully. Jordan was the last to stop by, still groggy from his blissfully unaware nap. When he heard what happened, he shrugged it off and said if he had woken up and seen the Alert, he would have known it was a hoax, then asked if they were still serving breakfast. Another nephew, Hudson, struggled to move past it. Hudson was Minette and Tony's third son. He was still single and hoping to become a nurse. His whole life was still in front of him. It took a long time to get the panic and anxiety out of his system.

Later, some went out for a swim in the ocean. It felt surreal to see them splashing around in the water after narrowly missing mass destruction. Everyone had earned their Dole Whip that day.

But Keagan and I didn't join the Dole Whip party or any swimming. After, our entire clan gathered in Linda's command center suite and had a prayer of thanksgiving for avoiding the apocalypse. (That was the first time I ever prayed that one.) Keagan and I jumped into an Uber to the local emergency room. He was completely without his pain medications now.

I had seen his blood pressure spike to double the normal levels before when he went off his meds. And his heart rate would rise to his maximum heart rate while sitting at rest. He needed to take his meds every several hours, and the clock was ticking.

Doctors don't prescribe narcotic painkillers like an antibiotic for a cold. Understandably, the regulations are very strict. The opioid epidemic is a national crisis. In 2019, 125,000 people died of prescription opioid overdose. 2.5 million people became addicted to opioid pain medication in 2021. Keagan was an addict by design. If he was off his medications for too long, he got sweaty and panicky, just like any addict would. These ER doctors and nurses were picking up on the signs that he was clearly an addict. They dealt with people regularly coming in claiming they needed pain meds. If that didn't work, they would beg for it. If that didn't work, they went out on the streets to find it illegally. We were trying desperately not to seem like one of "those people," but they would not give him any medication.

We were in a different time zone. His Colorado doctors had gone home for the night and could not verify that he was a legitimate patient needing those medications. The whole "we lost them in the ballistic missile panic" was one of the best excuses the ER doctors ever heard. As Keagan and I were becoming increasingly irrational with panic, we had to employ every ounce of diplomacy and rational negotiation tactics to convince them this was a legitimate need. The Hawaii ER doctors remained unconvinced until Keagan's Colorado doctors returned to work 8 hours later. Keagan was in agony. This life of being chained to pain medications went on for years. In that ER, Keagan talked to me about how difficult it was going to be for him to live out his life that way. He said if it weren't for his boys, Kai and Liam, he wouldn't be able to make it. We talked about why he even survived his accident. It really was horrific, and nobody thought he would have made it. Modern medicine is really remarkable in being able to save people's lives, but at what cost?

We put together a memorial service for Keagan up on top of Reservoir Hill in our town of Pagosa Springs. When I say "we," I mean Michele. She didn't get crazy bossing everyone around like a psycho bride at a wedding. Michele had often said, if people are going to show up for an event like a wedding or funeral where they sacrifice to get there, you have to give them an event worth coming to. We had done a bunch of weddings. Each time our kids would question why we went to so much trouble to make the wedding so nice. By now, they understood. Rez Hill is a lovely forested "park" with trails all over it. I used to go hiking up there in the afternoons once our business had a few employees to man the office. I'd rarely see other people while I listened to podcasts and books. Up on the main hill, there is a grass meadow and gazebo where they hold lively music festivals. It was obvious to everyone who knew Keagan that outside was where Keagan grew up and always longed to be. This was going to be an outside service. Still being the summer monsoon season, the threatening dark clouds were building on the North range for the afternoon show again. Part of our service was going to be provided by those up in Heaven. Hundreds of people meandered slowly and tearfully up Rez Hill. They were coming in pairs and small groups, clinging to the loved ones they had with them. Someone hung pictures around the large white tent to remind everyone of Keagan's intentional outdoor life. I don't recall pictures of Keagan being inside. Maybe a Christmas photo was about it. Other tear-stained faces who knew Keagan's struggle surrounded his grandparents, uncles and aunts, cousins, and a slew of nephews and nieces. Hundred more watched online from around the world as we broadcast the service. Kailey and the rest of the family all helped a bunch, too. Uncle Tony preached the sermon. Auntie 'Nette (Minette) was one of the few who could get up and get the words out we all wanted to say. One day, a few months prior, Keagan brought us a suicide note he had penned. He confessed he couldn't pull the trigger and leave his boys fatherless that time. We pulled out that note and read it to the crowd.

"I had a wonderful life, amazing family, awesome friends.
I'm not walking through those gates into Heaven,
I'm crashing through the gates, skidding and rolling in
all bruised and broken, standing up smiling.
But anyways, life has been awesome!
I love you all. I couldn't have ever asked
for a better life. Don't forget me guys,
I love you all so much.

CHAPTER 2:

The Girl with the Green Eyes

"Oh, hi! Is this seat taken?"

The two young ladies looked up at me with striking emerald-green eyes and matching brown hair slightly past their shoulders. They gave me a thorough once-over from head to toe before responding. Many awkward college freshmen attended the Freshman ice cream social. The cafeteria table they were sitting at had six open seats, and all the tables next to theirs were vacant.

"No," they replied in unison, turning to look at each other like they were looking into a mirror, with a tone and smirk signaling some kind of inside joke.

The other freshmen were across the dining hall. I never really liked the cliques in high school and in the youth group at church. These two had the same feelings, I thought. All three of us liked to be a little separate from the crowd. These two had a little group of their own going, and adding one more person appeared easy enough. I suppose I wasn't too intimidating for them. After all, at a mere 155 pounds and sporting a mullet of shock blonde hair, I looked far more like a high schooler who snuck out of the group campus tour to sneak an ice cream.

I sat down and remained quiet for a beat, using the ice cream cone I was eating as an excuse not to say anything. With equal commitment to their ice cream, they stayed silent as well, and nobody said anything for an uncomfortable amount of time.

"I'm Minette, and this is my sister, Michele," one of them finally blurted out.

The silent one turned into her mirror again and replied to the other, "No, I'm Minette, and she's my sister, Michele."

The two glared at each other now, no longer in conversation with me, but with each other, while licking their ice cream cones a little more. Then they sneered at each other, wondering what the heck the other was saying, and were embarrassed that the other one was so silly.

Are these girls OK? I thought. I stated my name, Chris, pleased to be in control of the conversation since I remembered my name.

It really wasn't a joke, either. Michele just got the names mixed up as she introduced herself and her twin sister. For the rest of the conversation, I avoided using names so I wouldn't have to worry about getting it wrong. They didn't dress alike, but I honestly could not tell who was whom.

"What's your major?" I asked.

This is the go-to question when you're in college, and asking it makes you feel like a big college guy. It's really not; it just shows you're pretty uninteresting and unskilled in casual conversation or engaging meaningfully with another person.

"Missions," they responded in continued unison, which made it easier for me to continue to address them as one person and not mess up whatever their names were.

"Great, me too!"

I was not clever enough with pick-up lines to say this like some kind of smooth talker. I was far too naïve. It really was my major. Wow! The first people I met were in the same major as me. It didn't hurt that they were super cute—a little mischievous, perhaps, but cute. It was pretty exciting. These two would probably be in some of my classes; they were not hanging on some guy here, already, and said 'Hi' to me. Michele and Minette were the first two people I met at Biola University. Within a few weeks, we were spending a bunch of time together in classes, at chapel, running together, and in the dining hall. I was seventeen and had kissed one girl in high school, and thought she was my girlfriend for about a month. Between my on-campus job, a full class load, and playing soccer on the school team, there was no way I had time for a girlfriend. Even saying that feels like a joke now, as I felt so completely immature in those regards. Minette always had outside activities, many of which I later discovered involved her boyfriend, Tony. The cool thing was, even with me having no time for a girlfriend, Minette already with Tony, it worked out so well for the three of us to be great friends. I entertained the thought of Michele and me being together one day, perhaps when I got old enough. It wasn't just that Michele was beautiful, or that she seemed to always know the right thing to say. It was something deeper—the way she cheered me on, her kindness, and how effortlessly she made me feel like I belonged. I had never known someone who made me feel so accepted. Somewhere during our friendship, I couldn't help wanting to be more than just friends. I hadn't made a checklist of wife qualities yet, but as I started spending more time with Michele, I was seeing the ones I wanted in her. It took about 3 weeks, as I recall, to decide that I should marry her.

Thankfully, making casual friends was easy for me. The problem was that I never had experience keeping friends. As I sat there, watching the other freshmen talk and laugh, I couldn't help but feel the pull of hope. Maybe this time, things could be different. Maybe I could build the kind of friendships that lasted—not the transient ones I had in my past. College offered a chance to stop moving and make my own life.

My parents divorced when I was seven. I was subsequently stuck in the middle of the custody dispute. And for many years, it was an actual battle. I remember my dad pounding on the door of my stepdad's car, demanding I unlock it and go with him. This was in the parking lot of the courthouse when he lost the custody decision. No matter. A couple of months later, he came and kidnapped my sister and me and took us to live with him in another state. My toe-headed, blond little sister, Carolyn, always went with me. This wasn't the only time this scenario happened. In between kidnappings, because my dad and Stepdad were both naval officers, the navy transferred us every year or two. This meant moving to a different place—sometimes multiple places—every year. By the time I was seventeen, I had moved twenty times. I always felt loved by my parents, but they couldn't figure themselves out for most of my childhood. I always felt that a part of me was missing—like I never belonged anywhere. Moving so often, changing schools, never being able to truly settle into a place, left me constantly searching for something to hold on to. And now, even in college, with new people around me, I couldn't shake that feeling of being unmoored, like I was always one step away from being left behind. Because my time in any place never lasted long, I didn't have lasting friendships, and I couldn't keep up with so many past friends who were now far away. During high school in Johannesburg, South Africa, my peers bullied me for being the dumb American. Upon my return to the States, people teased me, calling me the "African boy." People always asked where I was from, and I could not say any one place. I couldn't even narrow it down to where I spent the most time.

I made some good friends as a child, but I couldn't keep in touch with them when I moved to the other side of the world. And the only way to keep in touch would have been by letters. There was no internet, cell phones, or social media. Even my own parents felt distant from me. It was hard to bond with a parent whom you move away from every year or two. When I graduated from high school, my stepdad told me I had to move out of the house, and I wasn't allowed to come back, even for Christmas. All this fighting, and back and forth, and now they didn't want me, I felt. By the time I got to college, I was very lonely. I've heard that missionary kids and kids adopted from foreign countries call themselves third culture kids because they might have been born American, raised in China, but never felt like they were from either place. I ended High School with one friend I kept in touch with through life, Steve, a third-culture missionary kid. At that time, though, he went to the East Coast to college, and I stayed in Southern California. I expected that friendship to dissolve as well. Thankfully, it didn't. I was comfortable in casual situations and enjoyed meeting people, but my commitment to them never got much further than that. I developed into a bit of a loner. But I longed to be among people and do life together.

Being a college student offered a glimmer of hope, though. I was on my own now and in control of my life. Adulthood was on the horizon for me. I could develop deeper friendships because I didn't have to move away if I didn't want to—well, unless I ran out of money for school.

Biola University accepted me because I got pretty good grades in high school, and I had a strong desire to go into ministry work. My father wanted me to go to the Naval Academy in Annapolis, where he graduated from. He made it clear that my choice of Bible college disappointed him. My stepfather, although he was working in the ministry for World Vision, also expressed his disapproval. He was very clear that he wouldn't be taking part in paying for anything after kicking me out of the house.

My grades got me a few scholarships, but I was still way short of funds. I figured I'd get through one semester and have to leave. Once I made it through the first one, every semester after, I felt like Westley in *The Princess Bride* when the Dread Pirate Roberts would tell him, "Good night, good work, sleep well, I'll probably kill you in the morning."

The twins had very supportive parents. Home wasn't too far away. They had lived in the same area around Walnut, California, their whole life. They were involved in their local church and went to the same summer camp every summer with all their friends. Minette commuted from home her first year, but Michele made the bold decision to live on campus. Thankfully, my dorm was along the way Michele walked from the girls' dorm to all her classes. I don't think I ever sat there looking out my dorm window, waiting for her to pass by so I could watch her. I don't recall, but I might be wrong about that one.

All three of us applied ourselves right away in college. We were excellent students in High School and were now going to apply ourselves to something we really wanted to learn. I took a full load because I thought every semester would be my last. Biola only charged for the first thirteen credits in a semester, so anything over that was free. Michele and Minette took a full load because they were excellent students, and their parents expected them to remain so.

Even though we hadn't been friends for long, the twins and I quickly saw the same convictions and sincerity in each other, which began a very strong mutual respect. We attended every chapel service we could together. The chance to sit by them was a major motivator for me to show up, but I also came because I genuinely found value in those services.

Biola had amazing chapel speakers. We got to see and hear from people like Richard Wurmbrand, a Romanian Evangelical Lutheran priest who faced imprisonment and torture at the hands of the

Communist government, and Elisabeth Elliot, a missionary who ministered to the Huaorani people of Ecuador despite tribal members killing her husband on the first day he made contact with them.

These speakers introduced us to a world beyond our limited experiences as young American Christians and helped ignite in us a passion for sacrificial service to God. We would leave chapel reminded we were at Biola to learn more about God and how to serve Him for life.

The first Bible class we took was Old Testament. It was a required course, but the twins and I were thrilled. We were grateful for this incredible opportunity to actually study the whole Old Testament.

"How many of you have read the entire Bible cover to cover?" our professor asked on day one.

Out of 350 students, Michele, Minette, and I, and maybe one or two others, raised our hands. We were shocked they hadn't all read it yet. We were at Biola because we sincerely wanted to study the Bible.

I think the twins were perhaps a tad more eager than I was. To sit with them meant always sitting in the front row of Sutherland Hall, a large auditorium with seating for several hundred students. They wanted to get every word from that Old Testament professor, so only the front row would do.

One day, they got a little lost as new freshmen and were very late for class. You would think they would choose seats in the back of the auditorium so as not to draw too much attention, but nope. As they walked into the room, they headed toward their usual front-row seats, which were still unoccupied.

The mood was awkward as they sneaked in on tiptoe, thinking they weren't interrupting too much. But even if they had fooled some people with their sneaky approach, their giggling and giant grin certainly drew the attention of every person in the room. And don't forget, they were identical twins and very cute, which also drew attention to themselves.

The professor kindly paused to allow them to complete their spectacle and sit down. However, it didn't end there; after the professor resumed, Minette and Michele began giggling. It wasn't just one of them chuckling under her breath; it was two distracting laughs in increasing volume. Why the continued commotion? They realized they were in the wrong class.

Finally, the professor stopped and glowered at them, giving them a chance to admit their mistake. With bright, blushing red cheeks, they repeated the tiptoe prance out of the row, like they were really trying to be subtle, and started high-stepping up the aisle to escape the most embarrassing moment of their lives.

Later in our freshman year, Minette was getting more serious with Tony, a guy she had known from summer camp at Angeles Crest Christian Camp. Tony had a sports car and played professional doubles beach volleyball. He had turned down volleyball scholarships to the top Southern California universities to pursue a Bible degree and career in ministry. In Southern California, if you're getting full-ride scholarship offers for volleyball, you are cool. Football or basketball scholarships to USC or UCLA aren't bad, but men's college volleyball and professional beach volleyball are super cool. He was already working too, for an architect while finishing up college, and was the youth pastor at a church.

Meanwhile, I was cleaning toilets on campus for a work-study program. During four years of college, I never found a job that paid more than $3.50 an hour, which was minimum wage. Someone stole my really cool 10-speed bike during my freshman year. Tony was driving a Fiat X19 convertible. I couldn't have been more outclassed. Tony had been the California 5A State champion in multiple sports. I did sports my whole life, not because I was good, but because I loved to play. Recess was my best subject throughout school. I didn't feel like an athlete like Tony. Because I moved around so much, I never had the chance to mesh with a team or engage with any single sport, program, or league. I walked onto the Varsity soccer team at Biola. The reason they took me was that I liked to run around outside. I was no prima donna by any means. I just wanted to have fun.

Just hearing about Tony made it clear to me how unlikely I was to have a shot at a romantic relationship with Minette's twin sister. Surely Michele would aim higher than the likes of me. And Tony absolutely had friends who were cool like him. He and Minette encouraged Michele to date them. And she did. It was too late for me to catch up to these guys, I thought. I had no idea how I could fit into their group of friends. It was laughable. I am an optimist, but even I could see I was just a kid and completely outclassed—not just by their coolness, but by their success. Most of them were already working in proper jobs, and I was about to drop out of Bible college because I was broke. It was no surprise when Minette got engaged to Tony later in our freshman year and married him when she was nineteen.

One episode really brought clarity to my lesser status. At Chapel time one morning, as I approached where the twins and I usually sat together for chapel, I stopped dead in my tracks. One seat right next to Michele was open. Minette wasn't at school that day, and Heidi hadn't arrived yet, so here was my chance to sit right next to Michele. Grabbing the seat right next to Michele was an ongoing contest between me and Heidi, and I had won that day. Heidi was Michele's roommate and was one of her best friends in college. She was also one reason Michele was always busy. Michele took time for you if you were her friend. She invested in her real friends. And Heidi wanted all she could get of Michele, her time and friendship. I was the teenager who impeded a genuine friendship between them; I felt.

Filled with smug glee, I slid into the red velour seat next to Michele. It almost felt like I was showing up on a date with her that day, despite being surrounded by a couple of hundred other students.

When Heidi finally arrived, she was more than displeased that the only seat available was on the other side of me. As she sat down, she barely acknowledged me, instead leaning over to tease some information out of Michele. But chapel had already started, so Michele would not answer. Pouting, Heidi pulled back into her seat—only temporarily deterred, though.

Throughout the whole service, Heidi kept looking past me to get Michele's attention, showing there was something exciting she really wanted to talk about. As chapel ended, she practically pushed us out of Crowley Hall. She stopped us just outside the door while hundreds of other students parted to get around us, not giving any courtesy to the others by finding a suitable place to talk. She gave me a sharp glance that my turn was over, and she would get Michele now. There was something so steamy she just had to ask Michele about. I forced myself out of the way but didn't leave. I still wanted to be around Michele, too.

"Sooooo, tell me everything about your date with Chris!"

Yes, I had gone out on a 'date' with Michele.... finally. Like I said, I'm an optimist, so even though I was up against Tony's friends, I worked up the courage to ask Michele out. Many times, actually. It verged on the point of creepiness and definitely reached a level of awkwardness. Every time I asked her out, she would kindly tell me she was too busy. She was taking a full load of classes, working at a preschool, and serving as a sponsor for the high schoolers at her church. And unlike me, Michele had friends and spent considerable time maintaining those relationships. By this time, I knew the answer was going to be no. It wasn't really a question, but more like giving her information that if she wanted, I would go to Christian night at Disneyland with her if she was available.

"Umm, that sounds fun. OK, yes, I'll go with you," she said.

"Right, I understand, no problem. I know you're bu — Wait, what?" My eyes, wide with disbelief, jumped up to meet hers.

"Sure, let's go," she giggled. "It sounds fun."

It took me far too long to realize I was staring at her with my jaw on the floor. When my brain finally reconnected with my body, I tried to play it cool.

"Yeah? Neat-o! I mean…that's great, er, I'm glad you can make it. Um…right…"

Facepalm. Really? Neat-o? Well, if that didn't drop me back down to my actual level of coolness, the next part of the conversation would. I didn't have a car; how would I get us to Disneyland?

"So, um, I hate to ask, but could we use your car?" I had to look away. Her shining green eyes were too cheerful for my embarrassment.

"Yeah, no problem! You can drive it."

Perhaps it was for the best that I didn't have a car. It gave her a reason to consider the date as just a hangout between friends. Maybe that made things just casual enough for her to feel at ease and be willing to spend time with me one-on-one.

Did we have a good time, you ask? Oh, yes, definitely. I'm telling you, it was the best. I got to spend hours with Michele all by myself. And I got to drive her 1965 cherry-red Ford Mustang.

Back to the doorway of Crowley Hall. My shameless optimism told me Michele was going to confess her love for me out loud. But even my naivete was telling me she couldn't just start telling Heidi about her feelings for me with me standing right beside her.

Michele glanced at me apologetically, still not responding to Heidi.

"Well, tell me everything about your date with Chris Marshall!" Heidi exclaimed.

My heart dropped out of my chest. This was just like all the times when I moved as a kid. I had to move on and drop those friendships cold turkey. It was out of my control. Now, I also felt that since I wasn't a good enough friend, she was moving on to another guy. A really cool guy.

Chris Marshall was one of those very impressive friends of Tony's. I had heard a rumor about her going out with him, but Michele was respectful towards me and didn't bring it up. She must have gone out with him last night. I took her to Disneyland two nights ago, and she hadn't seen Heidi yet to talk to her about it.

Clearly, Heidi had decided Michele was wasting her time with me, but Chris Marshall, now, he was a catch. A mature man who had it all together. He had a job and owned a car. In addition, he also served as a youth minister. He played beach volleyball. He had everything I didn't.

For a super awkward second, I pretended not to be listening so Michele would have some privacy to talk with her friend. But it didn't really matter what I did at that point—I was out; Chris Marshall was in.

Without saying goodbye, I pushed my way through the crowd rather hurriedly. Holding back tears of loss and jealousy, I got as far away as I could. Heidi was so eager to hear about the date that the last thing I saw was her hand turning Michele's face back toward her so she would finally tell her everything.

I walked until I found a bench out behind the tennis courts, where I sat down and let the tears flow. My broken heart told me Michele was gone and Chris Marshall won. He won the whole thing. He beat me in life altogether. I would never again have a chance at a genuine friendship or girlfriend.

After that day, whenever I ran into Michele on campus, I quickly excused myself, blaming my busy schedule. I stopped saving her a seat at chapel and sat up high away from everybody. Every class I shared with Heidi, Michele, and Minette was now awkward. Michele knew it. Good thing I knew Michele's schedule and routes to class. It was easy to plan my timing and route to avoid her, since I had meticulously figured out how to serendipitously run into her before.

I consoled myself in the lesson that I found a girl with every quality I would want in a wife whenever I finally grew up enough for all that. She checked all the boxes. What I feared now was losing Michele, not as a potential romantic partner but as a friend. And if that happened, I'd probably lose her sister, brother-in-law, and the rest of her family—people I really wanted to belong with. Was I going to have to do the whole friend-finding routine over again?

I got the same old feeling that I'd only ever have people in my life for a short time, that I just wasn't the lifelong friend type. It fed my belief that I had some defect that kept me from being someone people wanted around for the long term. People like Michele and Minette seemed to have lots of friends. Not like cliques at school. Not "fans." But friends from grade school, camp, and church. They had grandparents and cousins who were close to them. This confidence and identity made them more attractive. Attractive in a winsome manner. You wanted to be around them. Lots of people wanted to be around them. People who saw their integrity, character, and thoughtfulness. I really wanted an identity with people like that. I wanted to be someone who offered something interesting and valuable as a friend. My soccer team was a friendly bunch of guys, but for the first two years, I spent a lot of time on the bench. It's difficult for a substitute to contribute much to the starting players beyond things like offering them water or giving up one's seat when they're replaced. There was this hole of loneliness that felt good in a dark way. You can go off by yourself and not want anyone around and find satisfaction in the melancholy. It is also easier, because you don't have to do anything for anyone else or worry about them and their feelings.

One day, I had had enough of my self-pity party.

Why are you feeling so sorry for yourself? I thought. *You have a best friend, remember?*

Before my parents divorced, they fought terribly. One summer, when I was seven years old, to get me out of the house while they fought with each other, they sent me across the street to a children's Good News Club. I liked it there so much better. With a bunch of other kids and a nice blonde lady who introduced me to Jesus, that's where I met Him, my best friend for life. It didn't take long for Jesus to become my closest companion. Regardless of my family's situation, I'm not saying things were suddenly easy. I still had to move way more often than I wanted to, and I still felt the sting of losing friends every time I did. But rather than feeling beaten down by despair, I had someone permanent in my life to navigate all of it with.

In reminding myself of this, I decided the letdown would not defeat me with Michele. Instead, it was time to refocus on Jesus and why I came to Biola in the first place. So, I renewed my commitment to the things I could do something about: my role on the varsity soccer team, my night job, my studies, and financial aid so I could stay in school.

After a few months of reflection and refocus, I just couldn't ignore Michele any longer. She really was the best person I knew at Biola. Her relationship with God was a serious matter to her. She was an excellent student and fun to be around. I started jogging with Michele again when she wanted to work out. I had to be careful not to let my feelings for her get away from me. That hurt too much. But we were becoming sincere friends. I guess this deep friendship stuff takes a bit more time than I thought. We were really enjoying challenging each other as we were learning about missions and the Bible.

Around that time, I read a book by Dick Eastman called *The Hour That Changes the World*. It offered a structured program on praying for an entire hour every day. I was so inspired by the idea that I had to share it with Michele.

When I did, she asked if she could join me. She met me every day for a month at the Rose of Sharon prayer chapel, a place that was already special for both of us. We spent the entire hour praying for each other, Christian missions, our hearts to be pure, our futures, our studies, and much more. Our romance may have collapsed, but our friendship was becoming rich. The only way I know how to develop a friendship is by doing things together. I can hardly remember someone's name unless I do something with them. Jogging, studying, working out, playing games, traveling, camping. I could finally invest the time needed to potentially develop a solid relationship. Something I really longed for. Something I never had the chance to do before.

The second most-frequented department for me after the financial aid department was the career center. I had to work every day I was in college, including during school breaks and in the summer. The problem wasn't finding work; it was finding a place to live when I wasn't on campus.

My first summer, right after I graduated from High School, worked out well because I got a job at Woodlake Ranch Camp. During my senior year in High School, I had been helping my neighbor with his horses all that year. He had a ministry that took troubled teens out horseback riding. He hooked me up with this horse ranch camp that was part of Hume Lake Christian Camps. Bunking with real rodeo guys was cool. I got to clean up the horse poop and fix clogged toilets most of the time, and in the summer, the heat at Woodlake was extreme. The summer after my freshman year, I looked for other camp jobs that came with housing. At the Biola "Career Center," I told the placement people I would like something in the mountains where it would be cooler.

"We would like to offer you a position in maintenance," said Jim Slevcove, the owner of Yosemite Sierra Summer Camp (YSSC). I don't know if I ever received an official job offer. It was usually, "Can you start tomorrow, and we'll see how you do?"

I was elated! YSSC was on Bass Lake up in the Yosemite National Forest. It was a major improvement over the 120-degree heat at Woodlake Ranch Camp, and maintenance sounded better than shoveling horse manure. Bass Lake had water skiing and jet skiing, two things I had never done. I would have been happy just to jump in and swim around a bit. The Pine and Oak forests were such a wonderful reprieve from the dry and dead grasslands at Woodlake. Just below the pool was the creek that ran through the camp. The dining hall had a large balcony overlooking the sand volleyball court, where I mistakenly thought I'd earn some cool identity points.

My boss at YSSC was Ron Grant. Ron was more than a boss. He was the first mentor I had in my life. I quickly felt, for the first time in my life, that I was part of this team, the staff. The cooks, program team, counselors, and maintenance people were all a part of one team. I felt a sense of identity here. Ron had been an industrial arts teacher, so he taught me how to work with wood. Other than my dad, I don't think I ever had anyone interested in or around long enough to teach me something useful. My dad taught me a lot about mechanics. He was an airplane mechanic supervisor, and we always worked on his cars together. I know how to do most mechanical repairs on cars. Airplanes must have been engineered much better than cars, because he was always really mad at how awful cars were engineered. He would cuss up a storm and throw tools around the garage every time we worked on his cars. I don't think it was an overall pleasant experience for me.

Ron took me out to cut down trees for lumber. What a cool skill to learn. If you don't have someone to show you the nuances and dangers, you could get yourself killed. It may have been one of the first actual job skills I enjoyed learning. He had a friend who worked for the electrical company. They would mark trees that had to come down near power lines. Ron and I would take the boom truck and chainsaws and go drop the trees. We had to miss the power lines, or.... I think something bad would've happened. We would set up the portable sawmill and mill the trees into regular lumber. Then we'd haul the lumber, which was all rough cut, to the shop where I'd plane it down, dry it, and stack it for seasoning. After it was dry and seasoned, we used it to build new buildings at the camp. Ron had plenty of frustrations working with inexperienced college students, like me, and having hand-me-down equipment to work with. Hand me down boats, trucks, and tools. But even with his poor hand of staff members, he didn't have to cuss you out if he got frustrated. One time, I took an entire day to plane down a bunk of lumber. The entire wood shop was waist-high in wood shavings. I was trying to see how deep I could get the shavings, like some sort of Santa's workshop. Ron spent the entire day at the lake dealing with water ski boat problems. I was so proud to have all the lumber surfaced and stacked up nice and neat. Ron came back late that day, tired of dealing with boat problems. He didn't want that lumber surfaced after all. He wanted it rough for another purpose. Using his three-fingered hand, he wiped his balding brow and sighed.

"Well, we'll use that lumber for something else, I guess, and get us another tree or two to mill for the rough lumber I need for the new cabin."

That was the first time I remember not hearing a tirade of cuss words when something went wrong. I liked that response so much better. Lesson learned.

Working and living at camp meant doing lots of activities with your co-workers. We'd water ski together, hike, do zip lines, and play volleyball. I got to have dinner at Ron's house with his wife, Margie, and their two sons. Other camp staff didn't get to have dinner at the boss's house. But I still didn't feel as cool as camp counselors and the 'program' staff. I didn't feel cool like Tony and Chris Marshall were. They were popular and knew how to engage and make lots of friends. I don't think I knew what to do with myself in a group of people. It was more natural for me to just fix or clean things by myself. I felt like an outsider watching people connect and enjoy themselves.

After I told Michele what I was doing for that summer, she announced she had just gotten a job at a camp, too. She was heading to work at Camp Soldotna in Alaska. As a camp counselor, of course. It was the first time she had left home and gone away. I couldn't believe she did it. I was so proud of her. What a coincidence that we both decided to work at a summer camp. I was a little confused because she didn't need a place to live for the summer. She could have lived at home. Minette was going to live at home. This was my only option, so I could have housing until school began again.

After a great summer working at camps, both Michele and I changed our major. Believe it or not, Biola had a major in the recreation department called Camp Administration. Neither of us wanted to go through the process of raising support for our careers as missionaries. I guess we didn't realize that the salary at a camp was the lowest-paying profession we could have chosen. Hey, we wouldn't have to raise support, though, right? It was a step up; I guess. My first semester in that major was on campus, but for the second semester, I signed up for a semester away, which was at YSSC, up at Bass Lake,

CA. It felt so natural to go back there to work and learn. I would work with Ron again, and I felt I was actually learning from him and the work we did at the camp as much as or more than the classes we were doing remotely.

Michele and Chris Marshall were still dating, and Minette told me an engagement was coming. I accepted this. I didn't know how Michele and I would remain as friends if she got engaged. It was feeling very familiar to have friends move on without me. I was mourning the reality that Michele was slipping away. And unlike Bass Lake in the summer, the wilderness there in the winter was a bleak reminder of the cold assault on my heart.

I stayed in a humble mobile-home bunkhouse where my bed was a cot with one of those thin, stripped, jail mattresses. The poor heating in the mobile home meant I stayed under the covers as long as possible every morning, especially on days off.

Leafless Black Oak trees stood naked and motionless outside my bedroom window in the frigid air. There was no wind to move them, to give them any hint of life. I would stare at those dark, dormant branches silhouetted against the white, foggy sky. Then I would close my eyes, and the contrasting image would appear vividly on my mind's screen. After all these years, I can still picture those trees in their beautiful but mournful stillness.

A single Stellar Jay visited regularly and squawked from his perch on the branches. Some days, it felt like he was my only companion, the only one who could understand my loneliness. Even with his blue feathers, the jay's vibrant color only looked dark against the overcast, backlit sky. The distinctive tuft on top of his head was the clue that it was the same bird visiting each time, talking to me in my gloom.

With Michele lost, I wanted my identity to be tied to the mountains, but living humbly in the Yosemite wilderness is quiet and lonesome. Tourists don't visit in the winter. The lake has frozen over. Most of the houses are closed up for the season. I understood mountain folk live in isolation. Mountain men are lonely people. My need to belong and have someone was much stronger than my desire to rough it up in the mountains. All the good stuff is in the valleys, lakes, and rivers. There's nothing at the top, above the trees. The rocks are all broken and scattered in piles of shale. A brilliant but brutal sun will burn you in minutes. The wind howls, even on a summer day, and if there are clouds, you'd better get off the peak. If you want to taste the vibrancy of life, you can't summit the peak every day; you have to make your way to the valley. That semester dragged on longer than I expected. It was difficult for me to see, but winter doesn't last forever. Summer was coming.

❦ ❦ ❧ ❧

Michele began writing letters to me regularly during that lonely semester. I never got letters from friends before. My mother or father wrote letters to me occasionally when I was living with the other parent. My grandmother didn't write to me, but when I wrote to her, she would send my letters back to me, red-lined with spelling and grammar corrections. I really, really enjoyed reading Michele's letters. It stunned me that someone would write to me, or even know I was in the wilderness. I was even more stunned that it was Michele. I was holding on to the hurt I was still feeling from our almost-relationship and didn't know how to reply. It was easier to stare out my window, stay under my covers, and just think about what to say. Besides, she was all wrapped up with that Chris Marshall, anyway.

It didn't take long for me to break out of my funk and respond to her letters. After all, she was the only one writing to her reclusive friend up in the shrouded, bleak forest in the winter. Michele was a natural cheerleader, and she made me feel like an entire squad of people was rooting for me back home. It probably wasn't an entire squad, but her cheering, even on paper, was plenty loud enough to feel like it was. This character trait of Michele's was a surprise for me. In my short list of traits to look for in a spouse, I hadn't put this one down yet. I love pleasant surprises!

As summer approached, I was thrilled to get a job and keep my bunk spot at YSSC for a couple more months. The trees grew back there, lush, vibrant green leaves. My friendly Stellar Jay rounded up lots of his various friends and filled the woods with lots of new cheerful sounds. That lonely semester was over, Michele was writing me letters, and a bunch of really fun people were coming back to the lake for summer.

In one of Michele's letters, she told me she bought a plane ticket to fly up to Fresno to visit me at camp. Yes, just to visit me. I never had a friend come to visit me! During this visit, she let me know that chump Chris Marshall was toast. She didn't pledge her undying love for me or anything, but she came to visit me. I was on cloud nine. Her visit was over too fast, and dressed in her cute, dark-blue sailor suit and hat, she flew home. So long, Stellar Jay! I hope the world does you right, my friend.

Mrs. Roach was the financial aid director at Biola University. She was a very well-dressed 50-something lady with trendy glasses almost beyond her era, with a silver chain on them. She had the grandma perm, but still brown. You could tell she wasn't really 'old' and wanted to stay a part of the college scene still. She and I spent a lot of time together over the last two years. I think I may have been her hardest case. She cast magic spells to keep me in college. She didn't have a big green curtain like the Wizard of Oz, but she really did some mysterious things each time I left her office, thinking, next time, next time, she'll drop the hammer on me. She would have to deliver the grim news that it just would not work this time. I wouldn't be able to get a college degree, I'd have to go back to letter writing with Michele, and I'd have to leave my dorm room. I was still at the mercy of the Dread Pirate Roberts.

"Good night, Westley. Good work. Sleep well. I'll probably kill you in the morning."

I had a down payment on the first semester of my junior year locked up, so they let me start classes and have a dorm room. I was still not considering my chances with Michele very high, but our friendship was strong and growing deeper. After all, she flew up to visit me at camp. Michele had a couple more suitors right away that semester. One was an Italian Master's Degree student, Marcelo. Why couldn't one of these guys be a punk freshman nerd or tuba player in the school band? I had nothing to offer Michele. These guys kept showing up. As a backup plan, I applied to the U.S. Naval Academy in Annapolis, MD. I really didn't think Mrs. Roach could string this out much longer. After studying, I retook the SAT. I interviewed with my congressman and got his official recommendation. I made the initial cut and finally felt like I would not have to find housing and food next semester. The competition for Michele was only getting tougher. This would eliminate my fear of losing her to the next awesome guy. And the Navy would immensely please both my father and stepfather.

One rainy winter evening that semester, Michele and Minette came to see me at the pizza restaurant where I was working and gave me a ride home. I still didn't have a car. It wasn't even an idea in my head to buy a car. I could not even afford to purchase another used 10-speed. Minimum wage jobs were the only jobs I ever found back then, and that money was for food only. The manager at the pizza restaurant didn't allow employees to take uneaten pizza out of the trash. My coworkers knew how hungry I always was, so they turned the other way while I ate pizza out of the trash.

Sitting in the back of their cherry-red Mustang, I said, "I have something interesting I'd like to share with you two. 'Paul, an apostle of Christ Jesus by the will of God, and Timothy, our brother. To the saints and faithful brothers in Christ at Colossae: Grace to you and peace from God our Father.'"

I then recited from memory the entire book of Colossians. It wasn't a very long drive back to campus, and when they parked, they sat with their mouths open in a half smile, while I finished.

We didn't have any entertainment at YSSC. No TV or movies, and this was well before cell phones and personal computers. Someone lent me a book about John Muir, and it was great. I didn't get another book from anyone, and I didn't have enough money to buy one for myself. Thankfully, I had a book I brought with me, one that I always kept nearby and read again and again: the Bible. I filled my time memorizing Scripture. King David's idea of hiding God's Word in his heart captured me. I wanted it in my heart, and I figured memorizing it was a good way to get it there.

This was the beginning of several years of memorizing Scripture. First, I memorized James and then Colossians. After a few years, I memorized most of the Epistles, half of Proverbs, and several significant passages, like the Sermon on the Mount.

Michele says that day was the turning point in our relationship with her. I didn't pick up on that, and I didn't do it to impress her (OK, maybe just a tad). I genuinely wanted to share the Word with my friends and found joy in committing it to memory. From my perspective, though, nothing had changed. Michele and I were busy.

Leading up to Valentine's Day in 1983, my roommate, Gordon, tried to convince me to buy Michele some flowers. For days, he tried to persuade me. I explained that my friendship with Michele would never be the same if I misjudged things.

"She likes you, Chris, I can tell," he said.

"This is what you've wanted for so long, and now I think you have a shot. Are you seriously not going to take it?" he asked.

"What if she still just sees me as a friend?" I replied. "Our friendship will never be the same. I'm not sure it's worth the risk."

"How about getting her something innocent, not like red roses and candy hearts, but something cheerful and friendly?"

"Maybe that'd be OK, but I don't have any money to buy flowers. It's just not gonna work."

"Tell you what, I'll drive you to a flower shop and pay for the bouquet. I can't just sit back and watch you miss your chance."

This felt like the biggest risk I had ever taken in my life so far. Michele respected me, and I didn't want to lose that. After all, I was nothing compared to the Italian master's student that her parents probably just met.

Michele deserved those flowers. I never had such an amazing friend as Michele. She made time for me. She was the only person who came and cheered for me at my soccer games. She smiled at me. She hugged me. I felt like her best friend.

With that, I agreed to Gordon's plan.

I reluctantly crawled out of Gordon's car and dragged myself into the flower shop. He picked out a simple bouquet of white roses. Harmless, right? He dropped me off in the middle of campus. With flowers in hand, I walked all around the Biola campus to find Michele. The bouquet felt as big as a sofa I was carrying around aimlessly by myself, blocking my view as I walked. People seeing me must have thought I was looking for the queen of England, carrying around such extravagance. Some smirking fellow student said he saw Michele playing football with a bunch of junior high boys out on the soccer field. I don't remember why in the world she did that. With my stomach in knots and my heart beating uncontrollably in my chest, I walked out onto the field and stood there waiting for her to notice me. Close enough for someone playing football to acknowledge my presence or ask me to move out of the way. I was even worried the junior high boys would laugh at me. The moment of seeing her sorrowful expression of mistaken intentions was all that was on my mind. I hadn't allowed myself to visualize or fantasize if this went well. I was only preparing for the fallout and how to handle that awkwardness. You know the one where she walks over, slowly, wearing a regretful frown. Then graciously accepting the flowers and giving me the "two pats on the back, friend hug." All carefully given to bring this relationship to a quiet death. Then, an apology for being the one who caused this mistake to happen. Then alone again.

When one boy kindly put an end to my emotional turmoil and motioned for her to see me, she looked right at me and froze for an instant. Upon her realization of the situation, she came bounding over to me like a galloping horse to receive her flowers. Her arms were windmilling around as she galloped across the grass. Shocked and totally surprised, I slowly allowed myself to smile a little and then laugh at her antics. Michele was bouncing up and down with excitement, and around me, before letting me hand her the roses. Then she jumped into my unprepared arms and threw her arms around my neck. My heart was just dunked down into the deep pool of acceptance and having someone to belong to. So exhilarating. After the initial fulfilling rush, there was fear of losing what had just happened. Or being wrong about the whole thing, or screwing it up somehow, or getting ruined by something I had no control over. You know, how every Hallmark Christmas movie has the big "issue" that threatens the blooming romance. I suddenly felt so unqualified and undeserving. She was making a huge mistake. No money, no car. I didn't belong to any cool group. I barely knew Tony. I didn't even have a proper job yet.

For now, though, Gordon was right. Michele was ready for a relationship with me.

I saw for a moment, anyway; I didn't need an impressive list of accomplishments, a big bank account, a bunch of cool friends, or anything like that. It seems I just needed to be myself. Just regular, everyday me. My mind was racing, trying to make sense of this turning point. I guess people around me liked me being a friend to them and not walking away if something didn't go the way I wanted. That part of life was largely a mystery to me. I knew I belonged to God. I never felt the need to walk away from Him. But I didn't really have anything to do with that one. It felt like He chose me. Belonging to God seemed effortless and obvious. But now I needed to love those around me. It seems that if you want to have a friend, you need to be a friend. It also pays to have your friend buy you flowers that you can give to your crush.

There wasn't really any question; in my mind, Michele and I were going to spend a lot of time together. I got an official letter from the United States Naval Academy right after that. It said they regret to inform me, blah, blah, blah. I wasn't going anywhere now. I started going to Michele's church, spending Sundays after church at her parents' house, and spending every moment I could with her. The summer before our senior year, I worked again at YSSC, and this time, Michele got a job in the kitchen with Ron's wife, Margie. Margie and Michele prepared food for over one hundred people every meal. This was Michele's first time working in food service. Margie quickly became very impressed and fond of Michele. Ron and Margie both became wonderful friends and gave us lots of advice as a couple. We got to spend our first summer together, working at a camp on a lake in the mountains. It really was a dream come true, and once again, I had a place to live. And this time, I had my best friend, ever, to share it with.

I was finally able to finish my senior year at Biola University. Because I owed money, they withheld my diploma. I don't know if I ever received the actual diploma. They let me walk at graduation, though. This was very important because Michele's parents attended, and it showed well that I got to walk through the ceremony anyway. It took several years, but I paid off all I owed to Biola. Of all I got out of college, Michele was the obvious value. So, I looked at the money and debt I paid as a kind of dowry. It seemed more accurate and made paying off the loans easy.

After graduation, we worked together for a second summer at YSSC. Back at YSSC, my association with Michele elevated my identity among other staff members. I was delighted to see my coworkers from the previous summers fall in love with her. I'd always felt I was fooling people about whether I was a good person, but with Michele vouching for me, it worked.

That summer, the owner of the camp, Jim Slevcove, called us to his private residence at camp.

"I'd like to have you two and Becca and Tom organize and run the first-ever three-week wilderness camp for our High School seniors."

Becca was our favorite professor at Biola. She was super smart. She'd written a couple of books, had her PhD, and had recorded a few music albums. We were astonished at being asked to work with her and Tom. I always knew Michele was her favorite student at Biola. For our essays, I would explain the subject carefully to Michele after class because she wasn't usually clear on it all. On the assignment, she would get an A+, and I would get a B. Becca always had red comments on my essays like my grandma's returned letters, but on Michele's, it was all compliments. To my surprise, they asked me, despite the years of experience of other staff members at camp. They'd obviously ask Michele, but why did they ask me? Ron asked me to go up several weeks early with him to mill some lumber and build the cabins and kitchen for the new campsite. I finally felt valuable. I still think only because I was with Michele, though.

The High schoolers left us after a month in the backcountry of Yosemite, to clean up and winterize everything as summer cools off at that elevation sooner than the camp down at the lakeshore.

When we returned to the Lake, Mr. Slevcove called us back to his private residence at camp.

"As a show of my appreciation for spending your summer roughing it up in the high country and starting a very successful new program for me, here is my credit card. There is a Michelin-rated Viennese, five-course restaurant I'd like you two to go to, on me."

Thankfully, I had a car by now. I could drive us there. Granted, it didn't start without crawling under it to touch over the starter. But that worked every time and only took a moment. They treated us like royalty. It was a spectacular meal, and every moment was the most extravagant experience I'd ever had. It was the complete opposite of eating while sitting on our favorite logs or rocks, as we'd done all summer. Or eating pizza out of the trash at work while in college.

When summer ended, YSSC offered us full-time jobs. Michele would work in the kitchen with Margie full-time, and I would work with Ron full-time. We wanted to stay there so much! I spent all my college summers there and made so many memories. I learned woodworking and carpentry from Ron and found a love for Scripture during my lonely times. Michele enjoyed her time in the kitchen with Margie, and we found a great organization we belonged to.

But I also had an opportunity at Angeles Crest Christian Camp. It was a better job position with more responsibility. This was the camp Michele and Minette went to as high schoolers. It was also the camp her church supported and where she became a Christian. Angeles Crest was very special to Michele and her sisters. It was also just one and a half hours away from Michele's parents.

It was so hard to choose which opportunity to take. We really loved our community at YSSC, and Ron and Margie. Angeles Crest was a bigger camp and a better career path for me. Ultimately, I chose the job at Angeles Crest Christian Camp. It was a little better for my "career." Choosing the Angeles Crest job, I reasoned, would let us plan our wedding quickly and keep Michele and her family close. I would have to break into the cool group of Tony and Chris Marshal finally. I wondered if I was good enough to be accepted into their group.

I moved to Angeles Crest in the fall of 1984 and began working on the facilities with the existing camp manager. I was a college graduate and had a full-time job and a place to live — well, a bunkhouse, anyway. But it didn't expire every semester! I had all the food I wanted. I could walk into the large commercial kitchen and help myself to anything. There were shelves of flour, cake mixes, peanut butter, and pancake mix. There was a fridge, where you open the large stainless-steel door, and walk into it. Cheese, leftover lasagna, gallons of milk, and cases of bacon and eggs stacked the shelves inside. Food, glorious food!

But I was so lonely for Michele when I was up in the mountains working. She moved back home for the time being. I started that fall right after the summer at YSSC, which is the off-season when campers were seldom there. It was an hour and a half drive to get to her house, and it was so hard to be away from her all week and most weekends. I dreamed of the day we could be married.

It was time to have the big talk with Michele's father, affectionately known as King Louis, and her mother, Linda.

I was becoming pretty familiar with King Louis and Linda. I spent nearly all of my days off at their house. Heck, Melissa, their older daughter, even invited me to her wedding. Plus, I fixed Michele's cherry red '65 Mustang for her and washed it every chance I got. I fixed Michele's grandma's car, too. I was really becoming part of the family, I felt.

So, with the confidence that only a twenty-something would have, I scheduled a meeting with King Louis and Linda. There was no way they could disapprove. I had a career, a car, and food. Angeles Crest was telling me I was going to take over for the previous camp manager, which was a major promotion. I was determined. Marrying Michele was really going to happen!

The participants mutually chose the breakfast nook at Michele's parents' house as the meeting venue. This was where King Louis spent his daily time catching up on the news and making his big business decisions every morning. This was his territory. Here, I thought he'd feel confident and comfortable talking to me. I didn't want to create any distress or anxiety. I was going to meet him on his turf. Rejection didn't scare me. I had it all figured out, and there couldn't be anything they'd object to. Michele and I sat at one end of the large table while King Louis was finishing his newspaper at the other end.

As I struggled to turn the idle conversation to my serious topic, Linda came floating in from the other room and landed in her chair next to Louis. I was glad Linda was interested in our man-to-man talk. Frankly, if she hadn't been there, I don't know if I could have brought up the subject, so I was kind of glad she slipped in as I was stretching out the small talk too long.

"I think it's too soon," she said.

"Um, too soon? For what?" I stammered.

"For getting married," Linda answered.

I hadn't even asked the question. Louis hadn't even heard the question. He hadn't fully folded and laid down his newspaper yet. We didn't actually welcome Linda to talk; we welcomed her to listen. What was going on here? Can't I even present my case, for goodness' sake? I'm sure my face contorted with confusion like the combination of sucking a lime and being shocked by a cattle prod. Linda's word was gospel when spoken. Was that it? Was this an immediate conclusion to my big plans? Not at all the outcome I'd planned on. As sure as I was of failure when presenting Michele with her white roses a few years earlier, I had all the success of our blissful plans of marriage fully visualized this time. I had not considered, in the slightest, this development.

"It'd be better if both of you had a little more security in your jobs and finances first," she continued.

I looked hopefully back and forth between Michele and King Louis. Surely one of them would speak up. It would have to be all three of us now to even have a shot at overruling Linda. Linda didn't get overruled. First, because she truly was wise, and secondly… it had never happened.

Nope.

Michele was completely accepting of what her mother told us. And after staying silent for most of the meeting, King Louis finally agreed with Linda. Meeting adjourned.

I left their house in a daze. What just happened? It made little sense. I was a grown man now and could work and stuff. And I had a car! And lots of food. Yeah, I had as much food as anybody could want. How can that not be good enough?

As I was kicking at the guy with the cattle prod and spitting out the lemon rind, I recognized how immature I was being. Obviously, Linda did have a say in her daughter's future. Any hope of belonging to this family would involve them having a say in things that affected everyone in the family. This was a new feeling for me.

Harmony wasn't typical in my childhood household. My experience with conflict was more aligned with frustration, selfishness, and impatience. I didn't know what healthy collaboration looked like. This is where, in my childhood, I would move away and look for new friends. I wouldn't have to deal with this. But I was not going anywhere away from Michele. I was going to do whatever it took, no matter how long it took, to stay with this girl. But how did I not see this?

The longest drive up the mountain took place that evening. My mind was reeling. I had to visualize a whole new life. Me becoming a hermit living up in the forest, probably. We ran across a few of these while at camp. They were usually military veterans with a level of mental illness who couldn't get along well with other people. Not full-blown homeless drug addicts, they just coped better alone up in the mountains. They were guys like Dennis, who, for various reasons, didn't get to marry the love of his dreams, never had enough food, couldn't hold a job, or get along with people around him. Somewhere near Chilao Flats, just a few miles from Angeles Crest Christian Camp, it hit me. Wait! Linda hadn't said no outright; she just said it was "too soon." The one-in-a-million chance I started with five years ago had massively improved. I was down to maybe one in two chances now. "Too soon." That's all she said. If I could hold out and not lose my car or lose my job, or make a total fool of myself, I might make it. I almost did the latter, joining a family camping trip to the Colorado River. Melissa was catching the sleeping bags I was unloading out of their truck. Wouldn't it be funny if I threw it at her head before she was ready? My chances slipped to 1 in 4 in an instant.

The young man who had to make his own way in life now saw through a cracked door into a beautiful opportunity to be a part of a new family. A family with my best friend. A family with no loneliness.

CHAPTER 3:

When Miracles Happen

"Hi Minette, can you call me back on the camp phone?" I asked through the line.

Up in the Angeles National Forest, the camp pay phone was the most advanced technology we had. We used it to call ambulances, request tow trucks to haul broken-down church buses down the mountain, and the like, but my favorite use was talking to my girlfriend every night in the pitch black.

There was nothing luxurious about using this pay phone. It was kind of like a cell phone that has terrible connectivity. You had to stand in one place while you called, and your minutes were extremely limited unless you kept feeding it quarters. It took a lot of quarters to talk about everything in the world with your favorite person, and those quarters were hard to come by. But love drives you to make a way.

The trick was that if a non-pay-phone party called the pay phone, you could talk as long as you wanted for free. So, I'd call Michele and let her know to call me back. I did this with almost everyone I needed to talk to. This time, I needed to talk to Michele's sister, Minette.

In the fall and winter months after YSSC, I spent all my free time at Michele's house. I didn't celebrate holidays with my family, even though they were softening up on the never come back thing from a few years ago. Holidays with Linda, Louis, and their daughter, Michele, were wonderful. They had a big formal dining room in their house. The house sat on seven acres of thickly treed Southern California foothill property with horses and pastures. I had never known abundance like this before. The house, the property, the laughter filling every corner—it was all so foreign to me. At first, I felt a sense of being an outsider, someone trying to fit into a world I wasn't sure I belonged in. But with each passing day, I grew more comfortable, even hopeful that I could one day earn my place in this family.

The Thanksgiving table was the biggest I'd ever experienced. It was bursting with food. Louis said little, but the ladies all filled the room with all the conversation we could handle. Michele liked to ask if everyone could go around and share what they were thankful for that year. It's what I dreamed Thanksgiving could be like. But Christmas was Linda's favorite. Louis strung multi-colored Christmas lights all around the roof outside. The large family room had a very high ceiling, yet Linda always found a tree that needed a little top trimming to fit in the room. Linda placed potted poinsettias inside and outside each entry door. Garlands hung from the railings to the great room. Christmas greens lie on both fireplace mantels. Christmas candies were in jars on the kitchen counters, with no rules. The big event was when Louis would put the red nose on his mounted caribou above the enormous brick fireplace in the great room and say, "Ho, Ho, Ho," officially starting the Christmas celebrations. My first Christmas at their house introduced me to a new level of gift-giving. I had never known someone with the actual "gift" of giving. Linda had this gift in abundance, and she passed it on liberally to her daughters. Never in all my 22 years had I experienced such an abundance of gifts. I wasn't a part of this family yet, but it didn't feel like I wasn't.

"Hi Chris, what's going on? What do you need?" Minette asked when she called me back.

It was easy to talk to her and get help with everything I needed as a boyfriend to her twin sister. I never had to struggle to decide on a birthday present, a Christmas present, or Valentine's Day ideas. But this time, I needed help with something a little bigger.

The camp's winter college weekend was coming up. Michele was coming up to my mountains. I had been looking forward to this for months.

"I'm so excited for you, Michele, Melissa, and your friends coming up next weekend for the Winter College camp," I started. "And I bought a ring—"

Let me introduce you to the infamous twins' expression of surprise and delight. It's a magnificent and frightening scream in the high C range. Not a quick, shocked scream cut short by a normal sense of modesty and decency. No, no. Somehow, the two of them could instantly expend a full charge of energy and breath so that the scream could reach its full measure of effect.

After you looked around to make sure a train would not run you over, you would cautiously smile at the hilarity of the moment. After those around realized no one was getting violently kidnapped, they too would turn to see what spectacle this could be.

The stamina of the perpetrator was always surprising. The scream went on longer than anyone thought it could have. In this case, if I hadn't had Minette call me back on the payphone, it would have cost me almost a dollar in quarters till her scream ended.

"Finally, our dreams are coming true," I said, my voice unsteady with emotion.

"Yes, you finally are having your dreams come true, brother," she responded warmly.

Brother. I sure did like the sound of that.

"Can you help me think of how to surprise Michele and make her feel like the most precious girl in the world?" I asked. "The only thing I can think of is hiding the ring in her suitcase, so when she opens it in her cabin with all her girlfriends and her two sisters, she will have a tremendous surprise to share with all of them."

"Oh, what a fun idea! I've been taking a calligraphy class. Can I make a pretty sign that says, 'Our dreams are coming true'? Then I'll slip the ring on a twine bow wrapped around the framed sign and put it on top of her clothing, so it won't get lost in her suitcase."

"Perfect, Minette! Once again, you've come to my rescue to think of something only you know would touch Michele's heart."

I lived up in the mountains alone and wore torn and stained flannel shirts. I had a long way to go to learn what being romantic meant. But I had Minette! A magic genie who knew Michele better than anyone else in the entire world. I just needed quarters.

"Can you keep helping me so maybe someday I'll learn how to do what you do?" I requested.

"I have a feeling you'll do just fine on your own," she replied.

Minette's confidence in me meant a lot. In fact, I appreciated the wisdom of the Marcellin family. Linda had been correct; waiting to get married was the right choice. Not only did waiting allow everyone in the family to get more comfortable with me and me with them, but it also gave me four solid months of not looking for food scraps or being homeless. My job at Angeles Crest was working out, and I was about to be promoted to On-Site Camp Director.

This time, I didn't plan a big meeting with either of them. Throughout the holidays and after, I wanted to ask them permission to marry Michele again, but held back for fear of another rejection.

I was becoming more and more cautious because this family was really growing on me, and I didn't want to ruin anything. One day, I humbly brought up the topic of a wedding.

"Finally, I thought you'd never get around to it!" exclaimed Linda.

I like this lady, I thought. I struggled a little with Linda's subsequent advice to wait, still a little longer, and schedule the wedding for June. But I was seeing a pattern of wise choices this lady was helping me with. How was I to know Louis had to double up on all his spring flower plantings in all his gardens around the property for the spectacular reception that was to take place on their California estate when they all bloomed?

Even though I was making progress becoming a part of Michele's family, I couldn't risk buying a ring until I got that nod from Linda and Louis. That went better than the first time. The engagement ring was the most expensive thing I had ever bought. But the money was a drop in the bucket compared to what Michele deserved, and I wondered if a diamond could ever truly represent the depth of my feelings for her. But in my heart, I knew it wasn't about the size of the ring—it was about the promise I was making to her. That promise was worth every penny, no matter how small the diamond was. I needed her to know her future husband prized her above all others in this life, that I cherished the precious person God created her to be. I spent every penny I had on her ring, and a little more.

All the girls in Michele's cabin knew of the surprise Minette and I had created. They all awkwardly loitered inside their cabin, waiting for Michele to open her suitcase for the first time. I wanted to stand outside and hear the infamous scream through the cabin walls, but I forced myself to pretend to be busy down at the dining hall directing parking for all the college kids who arrived that evening. After what felt like an eternity, I saw her racing down the hill from the girls' side of camp. It was the same gleeful bounding she had done on the football field when I brought her that first bouquet of white roses. Her arms were again windmilling, and her head was tilting from side to side. As she ran, giddy with excitement, she kicked her heels up and out to the side. I watched with pure delight as Michele let all her joy gush out. This reaction was precisely what I was hoping for. Our dreams were coming true.

By June, Michele and I were married and settled into living up at camp. How many people have ever dreamed of living up in the National Forest, in their own cozy little cabin as newlyweds? We were full of expectations for our work, our relationship, and our life in the mountains. Right away, summer camp was going full bore. Hundreds of young people arrived, over-excited, to be swimming at the camp pool, playing sand volleyball, hiking, learning about Jesus, and being around all their friends.

I had never been a camper at Angeles Crest, and now I was the camp director. I think they selected me to be the camp director because I was marrying Michele. She had the experience at Angeles Crest, and she just somehow knew how to excel in virtually everything she did. Michele ran all the food service at the camp. She oversaw a large commercial kitchen, preparing healthy, balanced meals for hundreds of people every day. Because Michele had worked for two summers in the kitchen at YSSC, she had good experience cooking and being part of a well-oiled machine. Just like she did everywhere, Michele worked harder at that job than was required. She wanted the work environment to be enjoyable even while everyone was sweating it out in a hot kitchen. She would make little treats for the staff or put a little vase of wildflowers at each table in the dining hall. Her coffee cake became legendary.

In week two of our first summer, a popular youth pastor and high school camp counselor, Keith, surprised a camper at their breakfast table by flicking a little bit of bacon at their face. The camper couldn't leave the gauntlet unchallenged. He doubled down and tossed a spoonful of scrambled eggs back at Keith. In about 3.2 seconds, all 300 high school kids were in on it. Food—good food—was flying all over the dining hall. Biscuits, pancakes, coffee cake, bacon, scrambled eggs, and butter. Nobody was considering how they were going to make it till lunch without eating their breakfast.

At Angeles Crest, Michele had a staff of four and a team of volunteers. She had her own domain to pour into, and it was a lot of work. Her cooking responsibilities more than doubled compared to her time at YSSC. She would start work each day at 4:30 a.m., and though she had breaks between meals, she didn't end until 8 p.m. when all the dishes were washed and the prep for the next day's breakfast was completed.

She built relationships with everyone on her staff, including one very special man, Mauro. Mauro was in his fifties and was kind of like a grandpa to all the staff. He respected Michele's work ethic right away because it was the only one that surpassed his own. As an immigrant from Guatemala, Mauro spoke little English, but he and Michele learned to communicate just fine because both of them recognized in each other an exceptional character and a deep faith.

As Michele, Mauro, and I were standing in the kitchen, looking out the pass-through window, we watched this food fight get wilder by the second. I hung back, shocked by what I was seeing. Two shy girls and the program director's wife barely escaped before getting hurt. Yes, people were getting hurt. The camp nurse was directing people out the door to her cabin.

"Hermano Chris, you tell them stop!" Mauro said, coming up to me and shaking his head. "This disrespectful and waste."

I looked at him, dumbfounded. What was I supposed to do? Yell at everyone over the microphone? What if they didn't listen to me? I mean, I was just a young guy, barely older than the campers. But that excuse would not fly with Mauro. He and Michele and their kitchen crew had just prepared all this good food, and now campers were just throwing it around like trash.

"They know you the leader," Mauro told me. "You don't know you the leader, but they know. Speak, they listen."

I felt a wave of panic rise in my chest. I was just a kid trying to act like an adult. What if I failed? What if they didn't respect me? Maybe they wouldn't like me anymore if I intervened. Maybe they wouldn't let me join in the sand volleyball game later. I just wanted to be cool and accepted.

But I knew how much Michele and her kitchen crew had just put into making all that food. The wasted food hurt Michele and her kitchen crew. For their sakes, I had to do something, so I started walking toward the microphone. With each step, I realized a leader is the one who takes action, even if he's scared.

As I picked up the mic, I paused, wondering if this would work. I glanced back at Mauro. With arms crossed over his chest, I could tell he was very offended by all of this. He expected me to step up. More importantly, Michele was standing nearby, humbly waiting for me to accept my responsibility. I couldn't let them down.

So, for the first time in a 40-year history, the camp director took the microphone and addressed the campers in the middle of a food fight. He cooly asked everyone to please stop wasting all the food prepared by the amazing kitchen staff. He got cheers when he reminded everyone of how good the coffee cake was. And he somehow got everyone to cheerfully clean up the dining hall, so the awesome camp staff didn't have to.

He put a smile on Mauro's face, who knew he had just helped create a new leader. Even better, the camp director's wife beamed with pride and gratitude. And to the camp director's surprise, he became one of the favorite doubles partners in sand volleyball for years to come.

Michele and I lived in the Camp Director's house. To get to our house at Angeles Crest, you turn off the 210 freeway in La Canada, onto the Angeles Crest Highway. You immediately enter the Angeles National Forest. This two-lane highway is very windy and slow. First, you see deep ravines full of oak brush and dry creeks. About halfway up, the Oaks change to Coulter Pines, and then to Ponderosa Pines and Big Cone Spruce. It always felt great when you made that turn off to leave the Los Angeles city basin behind. When you live in the city and drive on asphalt or concrete all your life, it is pretty exciting when you go "off-road" onto a dirt road. When you entered the gates of camp, you went off-road. Everyone looked out the window as they entered camp, excited to finally arrive. The first building you passed as you came into camp was the Director's cabin. It's the one every counselor and youth pastor turned toward as they finally completed their long drive up the mountain and remarked, "Those people are so lucky to live here!"

After a busy summer season, things at camp quieted down. We loved all the activities of summer and all the people we got to work with, but the quiet fall and winter months made the camp feel like our own. Michele and I loved to read, write letters, and play games by the fireplace. We didn't have a television or a sofa, and folding lawn chairs were our living room furniture for that first year. We would bundle up and go out on hikes throughout the mountains around our home. Sometimes we'd go to the basement of the Chapel, where the rec room was, and play ping-pong for as long as we wanted. We craved every snowstorm and wanted it to dump four feet of fresh snow every time we saw clouds.

In February 1986, during one quiet evening at home. Michele pulled on my shoulder and turned me around. She scooted up to me a little closer than usual, right up under my chin, then tilted her head up and said, "Let's have kids."

It didn't register. My ears must have been trying to protect my brain. In fact, I have no clue how much time passed, but when she realized I had become catatonic, Michele tried to clarify.

"We are living our dream! This marriage is just what I dreamed of, so let's have kids!"

"What? Kids? I'm a kid. Why are you thinking of that already? Are you serious? I don't know how to do kids. Could we possibly be ready for kids? I don't think so. You think we can do this?

As questions swirled in my mind, I turned to look out at the snowstorm. I was the one who had the vision for our marriage and life at camp. How could I have missed this whole idea of kids? How was I completely unaware of Michele's desire to start a family? This was the first time of many to come, where I hadn't the foggiest notion of how this would go. In the final record of best decisions made in my life, the ones where I deferred to Michele's intuition will all occupy the top rankings. With that, I pulled Michele close, smiled at her, held her hand, and poof, she was pregnant.

When we had our first child, Keagan, Michele would work on her feet in a hot kitchen, carrying him in a backpack for much of the day. The same for our second, Kailey, and the same for our third, Sawyer. To this day, I'm still amazed at how hard she worked in that kitchen.

But even with all her hard work, things didn't always go right. I recall a time when preparations for breakfast failed miserably, at least by Michele's standards. The bacon was burned, and she couldn't prepare a second batch on time. Also, the scrambled eggs were a "tich" green. Plus, someone had measured ingredients incorrectly for the coffee cake recipe, and Michele didn't think there would be enough. As she huddled in the back room, crying as she nursed Sawyer, she thought the entire meal was going to be a disaster.

With moments to go before the campers filed into the dining hall, the kitchen staff still did not have food on the serving counter.

The program director took the microphone and quieted everyone down to say grace for the meal. Still, the kitchen staff was frantically pulling the second batch of bacon out of the oven and scooping the new batch of scrambled eggs into the serving trays. But just as the prayer finished, the serving counter door lifted, and one tray at a time began sliding into place.

As I often did, I walked around the dining hall as the campers sat down to eat, making sure everyone was enjoying the food, refilling items they needed, and talking to counselors. That breakfast, everyone was happy and quiet while devouring the food. We always said if it's quiet during a meal, it means they love it.

I knew Michele was wiped out, and she had only finished breakfast for the day; she still had lunch and dinner to go. Sawyer was getting heavy in his backpack, and she was regularly checking on the babysitter with Keagan and Kailey down at the house. To cheer her up, I went back into the kitchen and told her that everyone was loving her breakfast. I told her no one out in the dining hall knew what went on in the kitchen for this meal.

We used that picture for many things in our lives going forward. When something was going wrong or stressing us out, as long as our family was working hard on accomplishing our mission of loving God and loving those around us, we'd say, "No one really knows or cares about what's going on in the kitchen. They're just happy to be here eating the delicious food."

A few weeks after that stressful breakfast, I took Kailey down the mountain to get supplies. She was my travel buddy that day, a day with Dad. She was 3 years old, and I loved having days together with my kids. That day, the pay phone at camp rang.

"Hello, Angeles Crest Christian Camp, Kevin speaking."

"This is the Los Angeles County Sheriff's office, and we need to get a message to the wife of Christopher Smith."

Kevin was our head cook now. Because Michele was caring for our three kids, she had cut back to only overseeing the food service department rather than being involved in all the meal preparation. Kevin was busy preparing lunch for the 250 junior high campers attending summer camp that week, but he dutifully took the call on the payphone outside the kitchen. Since it was the only way to contact the outside world, all staff members were trained to answer calls and relay messages carefully. That receiver laid off the hook more than it was on it while people like Kevin ran around the 14-acre campus looking for the person requested by the caller.

Kevin reported directly to Michele, so he knew exactly where she was at that moment. She was down at our house with two of our three children, Keagan and Sawyer. She was homeschooling Keagan, who was learning to read.

Kevin laid the receiver down and sprinted down the dirt road about 200 yards to our cabin. He found Michele having a pleasant chat with Steve on our porch. Steve was the pastor who married us, and he had also been Michele's youth pastor when she was in high school. Steve was there at camp this week with his youth group from Long Beach First Christian Church.

Recognizing the call was probably serious since it was from the L.A. County Sheriff, Michele and Steve jogged back up the hill right away. Kevin kindly stayed with Keagan and Sawyer.

"Hello, this is the wife of Christopher Smith," Michele said over the phone.

"Hello ma'am, may I have your name?" asked the caller.

"Michele, Michele Smith."

"Thank you. Mrs. Smith, your husband and daughter have been airlifted to Huntington Memorial Hospital in Pasadena. Can you get over to that hospital?"

Even though most people envied our life living at camp, many of them thought living in the mountains would be too rugged for them, even scary. But the natural world up there is quite peaceful and beautiful. Things like wildlife or rugged terrain are to be respected, not feared. The severe weather that occurs in the mountains can be life-threatening but so can breaking down in the middle of a freeway in the city. You must obey nature's laws, but you can learn them, and once you do, you can live in beautiful harmony with all the wonderful and frightening elements of the wilderness.

One of those laws is being extremely cautious when driving on winding mountain roads. It's a law I broke this one time—not intentionally, of course—and I deeply and instantly regretted it.

In the Angeles National Forest, Highway 2 is a very scenic road that travels west to east through the mountain range. It quickly ascends out of La Cañada and soon runs along the ridgeline of the entire forest before ending in the Cajon Pass about seventy miles to the east. From your car, you continuously have an expansive view of the rugged beauty of the mountains. But many motorists are frightened to drive along Highway 2, and understandably so. The edge of the road sits precariously near the top of steep cliffs. The shoulders of the roadside are minimal, and sometimes, the white line isn't even there. There are multiple deadly car accidents every year on that highway.

"What happened?!" Michele asked the caller with fear rising in her voice.

"Your husband and daughter were involved in an auto accident on the Angeles Crest Highway," the caller replied calmly.

"Can I ask what happened?"

"I can't give you specifics, only that a helicopter took them to Huntington Memorial Hospital. Can you get over there?"

"Yes, I can. I'll go right away."

Michele was perplexed because the person on the phone didn't sound too awfully alarmed. She was pretty matter-of-fact. She wasn't consoling Michele or preparing her for something tragic. In Michele's mind, this meant the situation wasn't too bad. If it was bad, the lady on the phone would have been sobbing uncontrollably and saying things like, "Your husband and daughter have been in a horrific accident. We miraculously found them alive and swiftly moved the entire sheriff's department to get them to the nearest major trauma center. They are clinging to life right now, and it's all in God's hands from here."

But that's not what she heard, so she figured the sheriff's office showed excessive caution for a minor fender bender, or maybe the other car sustained significant damage, and Chris and Kailey were needlessly caught up in the airlift.

Steve took it more seriously. He volunteered to drive Michele down the mountain right away. He prayed with her during the drive because he knew they would pass the accident and worried that Kailey and I might be hurt.

Michele was pretty calm, Steve said, until they came upon the scene. The road was closed for a time as they brought in not one, but two tow trucks. They had to take the extra 500-foot cable from the second truck and splice it to the first one so they could reach the bottom of the 1,000-foot cliff where my truck sat in a crumpled heap.

The tow-truck drivers hauled my truck up the cliff and opened the highway back up to let Steve and Michele slowly pass by the scene. Michele was confused. There must have been a different accident on the same day, she thought. She didn't recognize my truck. The entire truck was smashed. The entire top of the cab was nonexistent. It was almost like a car in the wrecking yard after it's been crushed up for recycling.

Steve recognized it immediately. He stopped the car, leaned over to put his arms on Michele's shoulders, and told her it was my truck.

"It just can't be Chris' truck; it's way too small!" Michele shouted as they got out and looked closer at the wreckage.

"It just can't be Chris' truck. It's way too small!" she repeated in disbelief.

Then, after a brief pause, reality started sinking in.

"NO, NO, NO, NO, it just can't be his truck!" she wailed. "Nobody could survive that! NOOOOO, Kailey! Where is my daughter? Did anybody see her?"

It was just a normal day, and now Michele's entire world was exploding. Her husband and daughter, possibly gone. She was in a state of shock. Steve had to pull himself together enough to keep driving her down the mountain to the hospital.

As Steve and Michele burst into the emergency room, they found me lying on a gurney, on my way back from X-ray. She couldn't believe I was alive. I could tell by the way she was looking at me that she was trying to comprehend what she was looking at.

My head looked like someone had beaten it with a baseball bat repeatedly. The whites of my eyes were completely dark red. My left arm suffered severe bruises and cuts. I was having trouble breathing as I had broken some ribs, and there was bruising on my chest from the seatbelt.

"What happened?!" she asked me with desperation in her eyes.

"Just go check on Kailey," I eked out. "They've separated us for evaluation, and I don't know what's going on with her."

We were both strapped down in stretchers in the helicopter as we left the crash scene. Both of us had neck collars on, so we couldn't see each other, and we couldn't hear each other over the noise of the open helicopter. Kailey appeared to be moving as we boarded the aircraft, but I didn't have a way to talk to her or find out if she was OK.

In the accident, as the truck tumbled over and over, I attempted to reach over to her, but the force of the spin became more and more violent as it tried to catapult me out of the driver's window. I could feel the roof smashing down on my head each time the truck rolled, and I had no control over how my body was being tossed around. My seat belt kept me from being ejected and injured far worse.

When the truck finally came to rest at the bottom of the cliff, the first thing I did was look over at Kailey's car seat. The seatbelt was still secured in the car, and all its straps were still completely buckled.

But Kailey wasn't in the seat.

A heavy wave of dread hit me like a freight train. Where was my daughter? She must have been ejected, but how? Every strap and belt were intact and buckled!

I had to find her, but I was hanging upside down, being held by my seatbelt. And I knew I had been injured. I was having trouble breathing, and my head was throbbing with so much pain that I could barely see. I ran my fingers through my hair to feel my head, and when I pulled my hand away to look, blood covered it. My skull felt like it was probably crushed. How was I conscious?

Then I checked each of my arms, looking them over and moving them and my fingers. Blood was everywhere, but my arms didn't seem broken. Next, I ran my hands down each leg, thinking I may be in shock and wasn't noticing a shattered femur or foot. No, everything seemed intact.

Immediately, my mind bounced back to Kailey. Where was Kailey?

With panic coursing through my body like a power surge, I somehow unbuckled my seatbelt, climbed through an opening, and left the vehicle. Then I started going in and out of consciousness. I knelt down like a football player taking a knee and said a quick prayer while trying not to pass out. Then, with all the strength I could muster, I screamed, "KAILEY!!!"

When no one responded, I called out another time, almost blacking out. In fact, maybe I lost consciousness. I don't really know, but the next thing I remember, I was standing up and noticed a couple of people trying to climb down the hillside to get to me. As I yelled again for Kailey with a weakened voice, turning to crying, they called down, "Your daughter is OK. She's up here and she's fine." My first reaction was complete bewilderment. How did she not go down the mountainside with me?

I had created a horrifying image in my mind of my 3-year-old daughter smashed up and bloodied, and it was all I could think of.

Adrenaline punched through my chest, and I had to see for myself that Kailey was unharmed. As if I had no injuries at all, I started crawling frantically on all fours to get back up the hillside. As I neared the top, I met up with the men who had been trying to get to me. They weren't able to make it very far down because of the steepness.

"We've called the sheriff, and they've sent the Life Flight helicopter already," one man told me.

It's incredible that you're alive! We were following you and saw you hit that pothole and go over the edge! We just can't believe you're alive," said the other.

I was grateful for their help, but all I could think about was Kailey.

"How is my daughter? What happened to her? Is she hurt at all?" I asked, as I helped them back up the slope.

"We saw a little girl in a bush just over the edge of the highway, and this shocked us." She didn't appear to be hurt and wasn't even crying," they told me.

Once I crested the hill, I spotted Kailey sitting on a rock on the side of the road. We locked eyes, and she smiled at me. I could no longer contain my emotions. Rushing over, I sat down next to her, pulled her close, and coughed up blood in between sobs. I have never felt such relief as I did at that moment. It was like all the fear in my body that had been threatening to explode me into bits suddenly vanished. I didn't care about anything else except that she seemed OK.

As I was holding her in my arms, I looked over her head and noticed the rear window of the truck lying on the side of the road. The glass was completely intact! Before I could process that or even talk with Kailey, the helicopter landed right next to us, and paramedics strapped us to the stretchers.

Seeing Michele and Steve at the hospital was an immediate relief, mostly because I still didn't know how Kailey was doing. Now, they could find out. When I asked Michele to check on Kailey, she didn't hesitate. She left my side and rushed to find her.

"Oh, sweetie, what happened?" she asked.

"They cut off my polka dot dwess, Mommy," Kailey replied.

Michele was stunned and mystified. Kailey's only worry was her polka dot dress. The ER medical team cut it off as they carefully went through a thorough evaluation of her. They found no injuries on Kailey except for some bruising on both sides of her neck where the car seat straps rubbed on her. How could this be after such a horrific crash?

"Are you OK, sweetie?"

"Yes, I'm fine, Mommy. The two nice men took care of me."

"What do you mean?"

"I was sleeping in Daddy's twuck, then these two men woke me up and pulled me out of the back of the twuck and set me on a bush, and I watched Daddy wolling down the mountain."

"What two men?"

"The two angels who pulled me out of the twuck and set me on a bush while I watched Daddy wolling and wolling."

"What did the Angels look like?"

"They were very tall and had on tan suits. They had to hurry so they could go help Daddy."

It seems we all have events in our lives that seem so random and unexpected. These can feel undeserved or unfair. When it's tragic, it seems like we spend a lot of time asking, "Why me, God?" or maybe just, "Why?"

Tragedy feels unfair. A miracle feels undeserved. Both are unexpected. When this miracle happened, we were stunned. We felt someone else was in control. It was humbling. We didn't want to ask why. These two types of events seem related. But we react differently to them. It feels like we learn some of the same transcendent lessons of life in both.

There are probably parents out there who wish the car accident that killed their child had been stopped by an angel, but it wasn't. I don't know why we received His protection while others haven't. Little did I know another terrible accident lay ahead, a tragic one.

CHAPTER 4:

Camp Life

Michele made our little cabin in the woods her own with any decorations she could find. Many of those were as simple as a Coulter Pinecone or a bouquet of dried wildflowers. I also enjoyed making much of our furniture in the evenings at the camp wood shop.

But there came a point when we wanted something fancier than I could make, so we started setting aside some money. Once we had finally saved enough, we went out to a real furniture store and came home with a brand-new sofa.

Michele was so excited to tell Minette that she went straight out to the payphone.

"Minette, you won't believe it. We bought a brand-new sofa!"

"Call me back so I can tell you about it," she said.

Within seconds of Michele hanging up, the phone rang.

"I bought a brand-new sofa too!" Minette blurted out right when Michele picked up.

"What? We both have new sofas..." Michele replied with a sigh.

Sometimes this twin thing was kind of anticlimactic. But she still tried to make the call interesting.

"I looked at all the sofas they had and finally selected a blue and white checkered pattern, kind of lighter blue and white with a stain-resistant fabric," Michele explained.

"Wait, the one I bought is blue and white checkered pattern too," Minette replied.

"Hang on, did we buy the exact same sofa?!"

"I think so!"

It's just like last Easter when we both bought the same dress for church and showed up as matching twins. At 25 years old!"

"Or two birthdays ago, when we gave each other the same birthday card."

They then spent the next few minutes laughing about the many times they'd done the same thing at the same time. The twin dynamic between Michele and Minette was truly strange and amusing. Michele and I still made some unique choices for our family, anyway.

One was to homeschool our kids. This idea was novel to us and not nearly as popular as it is now, but it made sense for our situation. The closest school was an hour's drive away, and although there was a school bus, we could not justify 5-year-old Keagan spending an hour riding the bus twice a day on a treacherous mountain road to go to half a day of kindergarten.

In typical Michele-like fashion, she rolled up her sleeves, gathered information, and figured out what we needed to do. We started by attending the CHASA Homeschooling convention at the Disneyland hotel that year. This was in 1990, so I thought we would be the only strait-laced, "normal" people at a convention full of hippies in Birkenstocks or Amish ladies with braids. And I was mostly right. There were 5,000 people at that convention, and only a few were like us.

But regardless of our differences, we were all looking for what was best for our kids. As Michele and I sat in that convention, surrounded by other parents who had made the same choice, I realized that this wasn't just a practical decision; it was a way of shaping our children's lives and preparing them to think for themselves. I felt like we were among the small remnant of parents in Southern California who were faithfully raising their children up in the ways of the Lord amid a degrading American culture.

Armed with the tools from the convention, Michele was eager to lead the charge when we returned home. It didn't take long to see the depth of Michele's commitment to this path, and it made me proud to be walking beside her on this journey. Not surprisingly, she proved to be a gifted teacher. She loved coming up with lesson plans, finding good books for the kids at their reading level, and keeping ahead of them with activities.

Though Michele's responsibilities as a teacher required her to step out of working in the kitchen as a cook, she continued to plan menus, supervise the staff, and teach food service directors from other Christian Camps. She stayed very busy juggling her roles, and she always did so cheerfully and with boundless energy.

Amid homeschooling Keagan, Kailey wanting to be a big kid and start school, and Sawyer as a toddler, Michele became pregnant again. When it came time for Michele to deliver our fourth child, we went down to Huntington Memorial Hospital in Pasadena. After the long drive down the mountain, I figured Michele would be pretty far along in her labor. She wasn't. Thankfully, the doctors agreed not to send us home since we lived so far away, but we were going to have to wait.

Being the experienced (and a tad overconfident) father of three now, I wasn't too concerned about the whole thing. In fact, I was a bit surprised I wasn't feeling as anxious as I had been with the other three. Since this was the fourth pregnancy, it all felt like a very familiar thing—taking a pregnancy test, telling family and friends, and letting them know we were going to have another baby girl. Then there was the morning sickness every day of Michele's pregnancy, going to the hospital for delivery, meeting the new baby, and so on. What's the big deal?

Once in the delivery room, I said a nice little prayer with Michele to be brave and for our new child to be healthy, and I sat back with a magazine to pass the time.

"You'll be fine, sweetie, same old thing, huh? Just another baby," I quipped as I tried to fight off boredom by grabbing another magazine.

Michele wasn't particularly comforted and didn't reply.

As contractions picked up a little, we called Linda and Louis to come over to the hospital. We also called Michele's youth pastor, Steve, and his wife, Cindy, who was a neonatal nurse at a different hospital. When they arrived, Cindy strolled into the room and felt Michele's stomach.

"Wow, you're quite large. Has a doctor checked you for twins?" she asked.

"Oh yes, we have had several ultrasounds, and it's just one baby," I replied confidently before Michele could even open her mouth. "They all revealed only one baby. No twins."

Cindy remained skeptical, but I was confident and calm. I was a seasoned husband and father, and I knew it was going to be a normal, healthy birth, just like the others. Sure enough, Michele gave birth to a beautiful girl shortly after Cindy left the room. It had all gone just as planned. Michele was strong and good at it.

What a special moment to hold my newest daughter, Sydney. My relaxed familiarity with the process in no way diminished the joy of receiving God's newest blessing for our family. We had her name picked out well in advance. Michele was obsessive when it came to naming our children. Each one was so meticulously selected. She spent months researching the meaning of different names. She found

Bible verses that added insight into each child's name. To consider special names from earlier times in history, she read entire books. She made name signs and brought them to the hospital for each baby to have from their very first day of life.

Pleased with how everything went, the doctor was ready to move on. He congratulated us and said that after an overnight rest, we'd be heading home with our newest little bundle of joy. But as he turned to leave the room, Michele grabbed his arm.

"It's not feeling right down there, doctor," she groaned.

"You'll be fine, dear. You just had a baby, and you will be a little sore for several days," he replied a little condescendingly. He was the Chief of Staff at this very large hospital. Our regular OB-GYN was out on vacation, so he was just filling in. He didn't have time for theatrics.

Before he could turn away again, she reached up, grabbed his lapel, and yanked him down until his face was within two inches of her own.

"It's not fine! Check me again!" she yelled. "I'm telling you, something isn't right."

With an exasperated sigh, he agreed. He casually pulled his rolling stool from the back corner of the room and sat down at Michele's feet.

"OK, let's take another look-see here if that will make you feel—"

His eyes popped out in shock.

"Oh, shit! There is another head coming out! Who missed this, dammit?"

The entire room froze, not knowing what to say or do.

"Well, don't just stand there! Get another set of everything for a second baby. Quickly," he barked sharply at the nurses.

There were other expletives to follow, but our ears were already burning, and we were too shocked to care.

The nurses began running back and forth, some screaming a little. Lights started flashing, and the loudspeaker was saying something about our situation.

Down the hall in the waiting room, Cindy stood up and said calmly, "Yep, I knew it."

She and Steve were sitting with Linda and Louis.

"This is just like what happened to me when we had Michele and Minette," Linda added. "They were surprise twins too! Everyone was rushing around just like this."

We had twins! But how? No one said twins. We had copies of the ultrasounds, and none of them showed twins. Even when Michele questioned her doctors about why she was more tired this time and gaining more weight, they all dismissed her questions.

"Nope, just one healthy girl," they said each time.

I felt like a total moron. I had just said that this whole thing would be predictable. No surprises. How did I get it so wrong? The idea of twins never crossed my mind.

As soon as humanly possible, family and friends started pouring into the delivery room, filling it with excitement. The commotion of handshakes, pats on the back, and congratulations instantly swept me up. But as everyone turned their focus to Michele and the babies, I realized something.

"Um, Michele? We have a bit of a problem," I said. "We have an extra baby! What are we going to name her?"

Unlike with all our other kids, Michele didn't have months to come up with a name for the second baby. What would we put on her birth certificate?

"Her name will be Kassidy," she said right away.

It was so definitive. Had Michele suddenly become a prophetess? How else could she know that was the right name?

"How did you come up with that so quickly?" I asked in disbelief.

"Well, Kassidy was the second favorite on my list. No big deal."

Even though this naming thing had consumed her for months, now it was no big deal. In fact, she even had a backup ready.

"OK, Kassidy it is," I replied, thankful I didn't have to go through the months of "what about this one?"

As I stood there, thinking about the logistics of going from a family of three to a family of five overnight, I wasn't sure we were ready. But amid the chaos, the excitement for the adventure of it all was telling me we would make it work. The love we had for each other was more than enough to carry us through. We would adjust, adapt, and grow—together. We didn't have two car seats for both babies, and the hospital would not let us walk out of there with twins until we did. Also, our small house wasn't just going to be crowded; it would be bursting at the seams. The kids' bedrooms were already small, and now we were going to have to put three kids in one room and two in another.

We had to learn how to work around each other and be cozy, which was just how Michele wanted it. She thought everyone would love being all over each other. Our little cabin was bursting at the seams, but there was an undeniable sense of adventure in the chaos. We were starting something new—growing our family in ways we never imagined. Yes, the challenges were many, but in those moments, I saw the future filled with laughter, love, and learning to adjust together. We would make it work, and that hope carried us through the growing pains.

Michele and I were feeling some fear and anxiety about raising a large family. Only 8 years ago, I had just been introduced to the brand-new idea of even being a parent. Thankfully, God placed in our lives some beautiful examples of parents doing it well.

One day, I got a strange phone call.

"Hello, my name is Jackie Hodge. We're planning to move up to the Bandito group campsite next to your camp for the summer. We wondered if you had space to keep our herd of goats?"

"No, I'm sorry," I replied rather coldly and ended the call shortly after.

Who was this weirdo I had just talked to? What kind of request is that? I quickly shrugged it off and went about my day.

A few weeks later, that weird lady came to our house with her husband, Rick, and seven kids to introduce themselves to us as our new neighbors. They were going to live in their fifth-wheel camper and serve as camp hosts at the Bandito campsite down the road.

"That sounds great. It's nice to meet you," I said insincerely.

I was pretty skeptical of these people and their situation. Seven kids and two adults living in a trailer? Are you crazy?

Over the years, we saw hosts come and go. About half were retirees who wanted to spend the entire summer camping and helping others enjoy the outdoors. The other half was strange. They seemed to be trying to escape something in the city. Either they were tired of the stresses of the city, or they were unstable and a bit shifty.

I assumed the Hodge family was the latter, but to my shame, they weren't at all. They were in distress, yes, but they were very hard-working people. Recently, they made a big move to leave the corporate world and start their own family feed store out in the country, away from the big city. After only a short time, they had a sequence of terrible misfortunes. First, they had been swindled in the real estate deal to buy the business and the home that was included. Jackie, the wife, had a brain aneurysm and almost died. This all happened while being uninsured. They had huge medical bills and just lost all their life's savings.

They decided to go live in a trailer until they paid back the medical bills and the remaining mortgages on the properties they lost. They were very principled and didn't believe it was right to declare bankruptcy. Jackie's husband, Rick, could get his old job back, but they could no longer afford to live in the city or even pay for a camper spot. Rick would drive down the mountain each day to work. All the family pitched in to maintain the campground, and almost all the money they made went to pay debts.

The Hodges' work ethic and integrity impressed us, but what really caught our attention was the great example they were of a large family. For one thing, all the kids were very well-behaved. Also, they had been homeschooling them for a while. They were the first family we knew personally that homeschooled, and it was so helpful to hear about their experiences and insights. Jackie was an amazing homemaker, and Michele soaked up everything she could from Jackie.

That first winter, one of the local ski area owners asked the Hodges to manage the ski area for them. Rick and Jackie jumped on the opportunity right away because there was housing they could live in. Calling the housing modest would be a generous compliment, but they were grateful to have some warm space for the winter. They also got to learn to ski and ski for free when they weren't working.

The whole family learned how to flip burgers, teach ski lessons, run ski lifts, and sell lift tickets—all while Rick was driving down the mountain each day to his job. The Hodge kids helped me teach Keagan and Kailey how to ski and have fun in the snow. Plus, the ski area had a ski team, and I joined it with all the Hodge kids.

The biggest contribution the Hodge family made to our lives, though, was the mentorship Rick and Jackie provided. For a couple of years, we would drop off our kids with theirs each week. Their older kids were teenagers and were great babysitters. Then Rick and Jackie and the two of us would drive all the way down the mountain to have dinner and attend a Bible study on parenting at their church in Hollywood. Their pursuit of God as a family and as individuals helped us grow in the Lord as husband and wife and as parents during those early years. Of all the friends we had in life, only a tiny group of them were the type of people you could drop in on anytime, or stay as long as you wanted. They could do the same to us. The Hodges were those friends.

❦ ❦ ❦ ❦

Some other lifelong friendships we had were with the camp staff at Angeles Crest. Many were college students who came back for several summers. They came to camp initially because living in the mountains is exciting, and it was beautiful there. But they kept coming back because of the relationships they built. Some even found their spouses at camp.

As staff, we not only worked together, but also lived together. Being around your coworkers 24/7 differs from other jobs. You can't really have a work life separate from your personal life. At a Christian camp, you can't really fake your faith. You will self-select out and leave camp or change and get stronger in living an authentic life. Our lives were very transparent. I think the summer staff really enjoyed being around people who worked alongside them, and then still wanted to do something fun together or have them over to our house.

Michele and I realized in our first summer as Directors that we weren't working in camp ministry to help kids find Jesus. That (very important) job belonged to our staff. Our ministry was to our staff. We had a responsibility to live as an example by maintaining a healthy marriage, by being exemplary parents, by working hard every day, by studying the Word together, and by encouraging staff members and cheering them on. That's how we discipled them. Working at a summer camp sounds like a gravy job, but everyone still gets tired.

Our kitchen staff worked long hours in a hot kitchen. The camp nurse was on call 24/7. Counselors would rarely have a minute to themselves. They often had campers with serious problems and only had a week to help them out. Summer camp staff start the summer off with adrenaline pumping, meeting new people, experiencing rock climbing for the first time, with activities from breakfast till late at night. After four or five weeks, rock climbing isn't as novel, and giving the same instructions to campers gets old. A nice, quiet evening with nothing to do sounds like a dream. But they still had the second half of the summer ahead of them. So, although it all sounded fun, our summer staff went through the summer season working really hard. Going through tough times with other people causes you to grow close, kind of like soldiers fighting side by side. They create bonds for a lifetime and would give their life for their fellow soldier.

Our own faith reached new levels. My faith grew, especially when I began leading Bible studies for the staff. Often, Mauro would chime in with his wisdom in Spanish. He and his two sons, Byron and Elvis, were teaching me Spanish, and I would try to translate Mauro's commentary to the staff each week. Mauro would sing a few Spanish worship songs for everybody to learn, too. Mauro, Byron, and Elvis may not have been totally legal immigrants, but they were undeniably the kind of people who deserved to work legally in the U.S. They outworked almost everybody every day. They taught us respect and were amazing coworkers.

Michele and I had been very deliberate about living in an environment where we were self-sufficient. We loved the feeling of creating our own life. We also absolutely cherished the mountain lifestyle. Trail running and family hikes were frequent activities we both loved. There were several trails right out of the gate of Angeles Crest Christian Camp.

CAMP LIFE

When the kids were little, I trained our Alaskan Malamute, Kenai, to pull a cart, and she would pull them in the cart as we hiked or mountain biked. One time, Michele and I went on a long mountain bike ride at night during a full moon. Keagan and Kailey slept in the cart as Kenai pulled both of them the whole way.

We would frequently hike to what we referred to as Flintstone Rock and scramble up to watch the sunset. As Keagan, Kailey, and Sawyer got big enough, they would proudly climb it themselves and feel like real rock climbers.

One time, Keagan and I were on a long hike and came across a bear skull with an arrow in it. We knew it was the one our director at the neighboring camp had shot two years prior, so we took it back to him.

As if the hiking adventures weren't enough, we also had a ropes course in our front yard, and I would go work out on it daily. When Keagan got old enough, he did too. I also started mountain bike racing while living at camp. This gave me an advantage—living at elevation and being able to train right out my front door on single track.

One of our staff, Kevin, got into birding. He would help a Forest Service researcher by counting the spotted owl population in the Angeles National Forest. We would often go out at night with him. We would drive and then hike up to the top of a watershed canyon that had the right trees for spotted owls and play a tape recording of their call. If they called back, we knew there was a pair living in that valley. We got recordings of other owl calls and started finding them, too.

Eventually, we could do the calls ourselves and didn't need the tape recorder. It was so fun to "talk" to the animals, even though the owls probably didn't view it as casual conversation. Their responses were likely an effort to defend their territory.

One of the kids' favorite spots was "Cave Tree." It was a big Coulter pine tree with long sweeping branches that they liked to use as a fort. In fact, we had unique trees throughout the surrounding forest that everyone in our family knew by name. We even established landmarks with friends like Kevin, for which only we knew the locations and the names we had given them.

In the middle of millions of acres of national forest, we had specific places that our close friends and neighbors could identify in a conversation. We knew our little slice of mountain paradise like the back of our hands. These mountains are where we rode horses. We tracked bears in fresh snowfall (we loved it when it snowed) to find their caves. We ran into bears often while hiking on trails. But we also hired hound dogs to chase bears away because they could be a real nuisance.

The biggest danger was rattlesnakes. At camp, we often killed them to keep the property safe for the hundreds of kids running around. One summer, we killed forty-eight of them.

We made Angeles Crest our home by fully embracing our life there. We were happy with our little community of neighbors and friends. These were Forest Service employees, the CalTrans families, the owners of the ski areas, a couple of other camp directors in the area, and the Hodge family. We had Easter egg hunts, Halloween parties, volleyball matches, and potlucks together. We felt like pioneer families making a life of our own with a few other brave souls out in the wilderness.

By the time Michele quit working in the kitchen, we had added outdoor education during the spring and the fall when church groups didn't come and increased our weekend retreats to fill almost every weekend of the year. These were the largest attendance years the camp ever had. As a result, they doubled our pay and promised to enlarge our house.

Living and working at Angeles Crest Christian Camp, deep in the National Forest north of the crowded Los Angeles City basin, was something we knew was a blessing and privilege. We never took it for granted when people would arrive at camp, knock on our door, and say, "You're so lucky to live in such a beautiful place." We never lost the wonder or took our lifestyle for granted.

But after nearly nine years, in 1994, we felt we had done what we had come to the camp to do. We doubled the number of people coming each year. We completed getting the camp accredited, and our staff was outstanding. Our income was still very low, and the prospects for building any kind of financial buffer or cushion did not exist. We needed to find a way to grow financially. Our little cabin in the woods was very cozy, but our kids were no longer babies. They were growing up. Keagan was eight, Kailey was six, Sawyer was four, and the twins were two years old. Our house was feeling tiny. We decided to quit while we were having fun and discover the next adventure God had for us, so we made plans to move down to the Big City.

Michele's chronic car sickness improved only slightly over the years of windy mountain driving. She was down to stopping to throw up only one out of three trips up or down. When she was pregnant, it was every trip. So, the improvement stats only applied to non-pregnant times. Moving to the city would give Michele a dramatic decline in vomiting, a big plus. We would not miss the windy mountain drive, but now I had to figure out what I'd do for a living. Camp work had been all we knew. For me, the natural fit was to continue as the "handyman" I had become at camp, so I got my general contractor's license and started my own little business.

We certainly experienced culture shock moving down to such a large metropolis, but city life has its perks. You have an endless selection of restaurants, grocery stores, clothing stores, and entertainment venues. You have auto repair shops right around the corner, meaning you can pay people to fix your car instead of having to fix it yourself. If you need a gallon of milk, it's not an hour drive down the mountain. Now we just had to make some money so we could pay for that stuff.

But more than anything else, the biggest draw to the city was family. We could see them every day! Staying late Sunday would avoid a 90-minute drive up the mountain with little kids passed out in the car, their heads sloshing back and forth on the windy roads. We could have family over for dinner at our house. Cousins could have playdates. We could go on family field trips together for school. That first Christmas, Linda gave our family a season pass to Disneyland. We couldn't go on certain crowded days, but who would go on those days anyway? We went all the time. Michele and I would go on weeknight dates to Disneyland. We'd see a show and eat dinner at the Pirates of the Caribbean restaurant. OK, the city wasn't all bad. And being around family was a blast!

CHAPTER 5:

The Blessedness of Family

Keagan and Kailey bolted out of the burgundy Mazda minivan we had.

"Go say hi to Grandma and Grandpa first," Michele and I yelled in unison as we unbuckled four more little ones.

"Hi Gwamma," Kailey shouted, not looking, as Linda opened the sliding patio door to greet her. But Kailey was already running past her, down to the brick steps on the terraced landscape.

Keagan was ahead of her and had conveniently missed the opportunity to greet his grandparents. His focus was on getting across the horse pasture and through the gate as quickly as possible so he could find his cousins at their house. The only thing slowing him down was Kailey; he was impatiently waiting for his little sister because he knew she couldn't open the gate on her own.

"Where's Meagan?" he shouted as he burst into his cousin's house, not stopping on his way up to Meagan's bedroom on the second floor.

"Keagan, be quiet, Jordan is sleeping," barked Auntie Lissa, trying to gain control of her once tranquil house as our kids invaded like Viking berserkers.

"She's at Grandma and Grandpa's, swimming with Uncle Joel. Now get out!"

With no remorse for the intrusion, Keagan caught Kailey on her way in the door and turned her around to go back to Grandma and Grandpa's house. No need to shut the door. Auntie Lissa was only mildly perturbed, so she would take care of it. The excitement of seeing their cousins had now doubled, as it would be a fun treasure hunt to find them.

Cousin Meagan was the oldest cousin. No one could have filled the role better. Meagan was the leader of the cousins. She had large, warm blue eyes and a head of curly blond hair. Her face always wanted to smile. The smile gesture was her natural resting expression. Her "resting face" was not RBF (resting bi#ch face) but RSF (resting smile face). She was the complete and utter opposite of a tyrant. The other little cousins were always included and made sure to have fun, thanks to her. She was the purveyor of imagination and play. Mostly outside. At any given time, you could look outside and see Meagan, the pied piper, leading a string of toddlers around the yard on some kind of magical quest.

Although Keagan was the third-oldest cousin, he often tried to wrest leadership from Meagan. Meagan wasn't threatened, but she had her hands full picking up the other younger cousins Keagan knocked down while asserting his dominance. Keagan eventually settled on a more lateral role with Meagan because even he saw her leadership as indisputable. Clancy, Minette's son, was the second-oldest cousin, but he enjoyed following and being a part of whatever Meagan wanted to do.

The next subgroup of cousins was Kailey, Molly, and Reilly—again, one child from each family. These three girls were like sisters more than cousins. They were thrilled to be junior mommies to the rest of the cousins.

But these subgroups of cousins were not exclusive. Everyone wanted to do things together, which is remarkable, considering we eventually added nine more cousins to the group. I think Grandma and Grandpa were a big part of driving that unity. Linda figured out how to connect with each child and bring them all together, and Christmas was the time of year she did it best. If you recall, Christmas was her favorite holiday.

Christmas Eve was the annual sleepover at Grandma and Grandpa's house. Good luck walking to the bathroom at night—everyone was sleeping on the great room floor around the Christmas tree. That's twenty-one people! The Great Room had the dining room at one end, near the kitchen, and the TV/family room at the other end. In between was a large area to accommodate the Christmas Tree. Yes, they designed the house around the Christmas tree and all the presents that would one day go under it.

Before the sleepover was the Christmas show, we shoved the dining room table into the corner and pushed back the sofas in the TV area. We then set up chairs in rows for the audience—Louis and Linda, all the parents, and any cousins not performing.

First, the toddler-age kids would parade down the open hallway and onto the make-shift stage. They were dressed up as reindeer or elves, or perhaps a sunflower from the poem they memorized.

One year, Sully was this iconic sunflower. He must have been three years old at most when he stood before his entire family and recited:

> *I'm a little sunbeam.*
> *Darting through the room,*
> *Lighting up the darkness*
> *Scattering the gloom.*
> *Make me be a sunbeam,*
> *Everywhere I go,*
> *Making glad and happy,*
> *Everyone I know.*

Several times, the stage remained empty as a mom or two were adjusting an outfit or trying to convince a little one not to be scared to go out and perform.

One Christmas, Michele, I, and our kids memorized a traditional French Christmas carol, "Il est né, le divin Enfant," and sang it to everyone. We did this as a tribute to the French heritage of Louis' family. He was born to two French immigrants who came over to America just before World War II when they were still teenagers. They met just outside of Los Angeles in a community of French and Basque immigrants.

Louis' father was a sheep butcher by trade and loved the outdoors. He would take Louis to the hill country east of Los Angeles to hunt pheasants, quail, and rabbits. This was the same land where Louis ended up building his house and planting his tree sanctuary. Louis remained an avid sportsman himself and had mounts of big game all around the house. One such mount was the caribou from Alaska that became Rudolph every Christmas. After the nose ceremony, we would all sit down and watch Rudolph the Red-Nosed Reindeer, just as we had done back when Michele and I were dating. It was a joy for me to see my kids experience the same traditions that endeared me to Michele's family all those years ago.

When Christmas morning arrived, we always started the day with doughnuts for breakfast. Then, we would exchange gifts. We would go around the huge circle, watching each person open their gifts one at a time. Soon, wrapping paper, ribbons, and tissue were strewn everywhere as kids played with new toys and adults tried on new clothes or plugged in new gadgets.

The gifts we gave each other were from the heart, but they were modest. Michele and I didn't have money to buy fancy presents, and neither did Minette and Tony. Melissa and Joel also had little means for buying nice things as gifts. I made extremely little as a new general contractor. Joel also had a humble paycheck from working in the warehouse for his family's dry cleaning supply business. As a youth pastor, Tony made the most of the three sons-in-law, but it still wasn't that much. All three of the wives were homeschooling and didn't have paying jobs.

The gifts Michele and I gave usually involved some kind of woodworking. Many nights were spent making Christmas gifts in my cold wood shop up at Angeles Crest Christian Camp.

When I came up with an idea for a gift, I would make the same thing for each family. One year, I made cherry wood bassinets for the newborn cousins. Another year, I made rocking horses.

Melissa loved making jewelry and made beautiful earrings and necklaces for her sisters and mother. Minette was exceptional at finding great collector books and devotionals for each family. These treasures and handmade gifts were plenty for each of us, but everyone knew the grand finale would be the gifts from Linda and Louis.

Linda and Louis were the wealthiest people I ever met. Yet they came from the humblest beginnings of anybody I ever knew. They lived frugally and were always shopping for bargains. They were more like Depression-era people. But for their kids and grandkids, they gave more presents than I had ever seen before. They came from a place of generosity that matched the abundant love they had for their family.

At first, we parents protested the number of presents, especially when it came to toys for our kids. Too many toys, particularly electronics and mass-produced plastics, felt to us like overindulgent materialism. In our parental idealism, we believed we were protecting our kids from becoming spoiled and greedy.

But as grandparents are known to do, Linda and Louis casually brushed off our concerns and gave the grandkids plenty of video games, RC cars, action figures, dolls, and stuffed animals.

MY MOUNTAINS

It was their way of showing the kids that their grandparents were absolutely devoted to and committed to them. It didn't take long for all of us parents to give up our protest. Every time a kid unwrapped a shiny new toy from Grandma and Grandpa, we would simply smile with gratitude.

Plus, Linda was a trendsetter and moneymaker. She had invested in Apple stock right when the company went public in the '80s. To ensure her investment succeeded, she pushed all her grandkids into idolatry and made them computer and video game nerds. After owning Apple, a lot of it, for over 40 years, her strategy continues to pay off as her grandchildren still play these games... with her. Yes, Grandma plays World of Warcraft with her grandkids. She has all the best avatars and the highest levels of accessories, mounts, and weapons. They always want her on their team when battling other gamers.

She still upgrades many of her grandchildren's computers every few years at Christmas. So generous, right? Well, yes, but she's not fooling anyone. We all know she's mostly looking out for her investments. Louis also invested in stocks successfully for many years, and his returns were admirable, but Linda beat all of his picks with one winner (and her recruitment strategy). No one is complaining, though. New Apple gear at Christmas is always a crowd-pleaser.

The grandparents more than made up for materialism and video game addictions by providing us all with the most amazing places to vacation together out in nature. This was before Airbnb. If you wanted a vacation place, you bought it or built your own. Louis made an enormous commitment to his fifteen grandkids when he built his own log cabin at Bishop Creek, high in the Eastern Sierras of Central California. It overlooks a pond that mirrors the rugged peaks of the High Sierras, and it is within walking distance of Louis' most enjoyable fishing creeks. The back deck allowed us to gaze up at a beautiful waterfall that we all felt was our very own.

Red plaid curtains, pillows, and comforters decorated the cabin's interior. It had real leather sofas and real wool carpeting. It seemed spacious, but when all three families were there together, every inch of floor had a mattress or sleeping bag on it at night.

Just a short walk down the road was Habegger's resort, an RV campsite. Habegger's had a pond where almost every cousin learned to fish. Keagan and a few other cousins felt like serious fishermen after catching a few trout in that heavily stocked pond fished by every camper in that RV park. I, too, felt like a serious fisherman one day after Louis took me down the creek, bushwhacking endlessly to find a tiny puddle no bigger than a kitchen sink to pull a native brown trout out of. I even bought myself a popsicle at the camp store after catching that brown trout.

For many years, we took family vacations at the Bishop Creek cabin. Each of the families loved camping, but this was camping in complete luxury by our standards. We would never have been able to do something like that without the initiative and generosity of Louis and Linda to create the experience. But as comfortable as it was for our families, it was a lot of work for the grandparents, especially King Louis. He spent considerable time repairing broken pipes and getting rid of bats so we all could enjoy the cabin. He loved fishing, but he gave up much of his private fishing time to untangle kids' fishing lines or pull wet children out of the creek.

No one had more fun than the fifteen grandchildren, first with each other, then with Grandma. Linda was the master of imagination. She made it magical by doing little things like putting tiny signs on holes in the logs for the homes of Flora, Fauna, and Merryweather, the fairies in the story *Sleeping Beauty*. It only took a couple of forays into the woods with Grandma before the cousin's imagination took over and created forts, towns, stores, trails, rules, teams, currency, characters, and wild stories. And when a cousin got hurt playing amidst the natural dangers of the woods and a freezing-cold creek, they picked each other up, dried each other off, or administered first aid. Before long, they became keen wilderness cubs, knowing what to do and not do out in nature and how to employ the maximum amount of imagination.

Boredom was not a concept for these kids. If it got dark, they moved the make-believe inside. If they got tired, they fell asleep right where they were for a nap while the older kids went on playing. Bedtime required tearing them away from each other to brush their teeth and put on pajamas. I think all of us would agree that the times spent together at the cabin were among the most beautiful and memorable moments for our young families.

If any of Linda's daughters carried on the legacy of imagination, it was Michele—at least in my opinion. Her initiative and imagination served her well when she was a preschool teacher for a few years in college. It was also helpful during the summer she worked at Tom Sawyer Day Camp, a very prestigious day camp for preschool-aged children near Los Angeles.

I witnessed her at work many times, and she was completely natural with little kids. She was an absolute master at keeping children engaged in activities. She could make up games on the fly and knew how to get every child involved. Our own children developed great respect for their mom's ability to start something fun.

In fact, this character trait was one of Michele's biggest strengths for homeschooling our six kids. And thankfully, she absolutely loved the job. Homeschooling was her career for 25 years, and it brought her deep fulfillment. The kids' younger years of school were the most fun for her.

She thoroughly enjoyed teaching the kids to read. Each child learned to read from the classic book, Teach Your Child to Read in 100 Easy Lessons. As the oldest child, Keagan was the first to finish the book. I got to read a few lessons with him, too. When Kailey was ready to read, Michele and I didn't have to do as many lessons with her because Keagan wanted to help. With Sawyer, I might have done one or two lessons, and Michele only a handful more because Keagan and Kailey were all about it.

And if I remember correctly, I don't think either parent taught Sydney, Kassidy, or Sully to read. The older kids had mastered all the techniques. Reading was the center of schooling in our home. All the kids read daily.

We often read a wonderful novel together, even outside of school time. I loved reading *The Scottish Chiefs* by Jane Porter to all the kids. It is a historical novel relating the heroic feats of William Wallace and Robert the Bruce.

After we finished that book, Michele, Minette, and Melissa organized a medieval banquet for the whole family. Louis and Linda were the king and queen, of course, and all the boy cousins participated in games of bravery and combat, wearing homemade armor and brandishing their swords. The girl cousins were maidens wearing wreaths upon their lovely, braided hair. They would dance with their assigned squires. At the end of the evening, King Louis knighted the squires in a very serious ceremony.

During these early homeschool years, I worked hard to grow my construction business and was making a little money for the first time in my life. Most days, I still feared where the money for groceries would come from after the current contract ended, kind of like that feeling I had at the financial aid office with Mrs. Roach in college. We all learned a great deal about trusting God during that time, and sure enough, we never did go hungry.

One strategy I used to drum up business was going around to property managers and leaving my business card with them. One day, a man called me for a bid on remodeling his restaurant. I gave him a good price, so he hired my crew, and we got started right away.

The job went well, and the restaurant owner was pleased with the results. He said he had lots of friends he could recommend to me. I was thrilled to finally develop a referral network.

I got a lot of work through those contacts. Almost all of it was in a gated community called "The Country" in Diamond Bar, California. This really was a great area for a young contractor to get into, because it was a very affluent neighborhood. I did several extensive additions to homes there.

But I had a lot to learn in business negotiations with people from different cultures. Most of these jobs were for Indian and Chinese businessmen. They loved to negotiate the price of the jobs. Even after signing a contract and sometimes even after I finished the job, they would want to renegotiate even more. Eventually, the property manager who got me started with this group of people pulled me aside and coached me on how it worked with his culture.

"You have to 'do business' with us, or we don't feel satisfied in completing a deal," he explained. "When you give us a price, plan on not getting paid that price. Then, when you're all done with the job and give a nice discount, we feel great about the job. It's that easy." After that, I became better at working with different people and bringing in more profit. Over time, we even saved up some money, and I decided it was time to put that money to work for us.

I read the popular book, *Rich Dad Poor Dad*, by Robert T. Kiyosaki, and decided I was ready to start a new business that would get me out of the rat race, and I had found just the right thing—something I could do at home with the kids.

Our house on Bluehaven Drive was a half-acre, and a designated horse property. I don't know how you would fit horses on such a small piece of land, and we didn't try. But the lot was perfect for a different animal—worms. Yep, you read that right. My new lucrative business venture was going to be a worm farm.

I had seen a news report on TV of an old blind man who was making a fortune raising and selling worms, so I went out to his mansion over in Hollywood to see what it was all about. When I got there, this guy was lying in moist soil full of worms. Worms were crawling all over him. As ridiculous a sight as it was, there were investors from South America visiting his farm alongside me. They wouldn't have traveled all that way if there wasn't something to it. It had to be the real deal.

I was convinced that we could raise worms just as successfully. How hard could it be? I bought the starter pack and then spent $8,000 to build all these raised beds to breed worms. That was a ton of money for us at that time. We'd never spent money like that. I convinced Michele this was an "investment." I was taking initiative, and I was sure I was going to impress Michele and her parents with my resolve and brilliant business acumen.

Initially, her intuition questioned everything about it. Her parents questioned everything about it, too. But Michele put her trust in me. She even bought me overalls, so I'd look like a farmer. Now it was time to dig in—literally. After working construction all day, I'd come home, put on my overalls, and tend to my worms. On hot days, Michele would bring me ice-cold lemonade.

My "farm" consisted of twelve, four-by-eight-foot boxes that were about three feet off the ground. They all had lids to keep the heat in when it was cold. I'd monitor the temperature in each box, keeping a journal of it all. I built a special conical, motorized screen machine to sift the worms out of the soil so I could gather them. Keagan and Kailey would help me shovel horse manure into the beds to keep the soil fresh and nutritious for the worms.

After many months of hard work from all of us, we were ready to launch our agricultural business with the first harvest of our worms. We had grown a product to take to market. It felt like a true farm.

Until it didn't.

Our farm didn't yield a single worm. Keagan and Kailey helped me shovel what seemed like endless cubic yards of soil into the conical machine. With each sift, I grew increasingly concerned. We found no worms—no live ones, at least.

My mind flashed back to the hundreds of worms crawling all over the old blind man as the South American investors looked on with excitement. Wait, were they really investors? Come to think of it, they looked suspiciously like local gardeners. Were they really from South America or just down the road?

Suddenly, I realized someone had conned me. What I believed was the next big thing was just a big bust. Michele never made me feel guilty with a bunch of I-told-you-sos, but I learned my lesson: Trust her intuition. It felt strange to abandon something I had spent months working on, but I couldn't let that one failure define me. I had to learn to pick myself up, look for the lessons in the mess, and keep going, no matter how embarrassing it was. Life was about finding the courage to try again, and I wasn't ready to give up. In fact, I was a little excited about what else I could try one day. So much for becoming independently wealthy. I needed to learn what due diligence meant before my next venture.

After the failed harvest, our yard had a dozen useless boxes spread out in it. I painted them white to please Michele. In the months that followed, Keagan invented various games of tag among and on top of those boxes. The worm farm ended up becoming an excellent playground for our kids and their cousins.

Having Michele's parents, siblings, and nieces and nephews all living within a few miles of us made our years of living in the big city very rewarding and fulfilling, but most things eventually change, and this did too.

THE BLESSEDNESS OF FAMILY

One day, Minette's family announced they were leaving California and moving to Missouri for Tony's job. He was going to work for Christ in Youth and start taking high school and college kids on mission trips all over the world.

We were now down five cousins. It took some time, but the remaining cousins slowly adjusted to the change. Thankfully, Melissa's family still lived right next door to King Louis and Linda, so it was very convenient for us to visit all of them with one stop. Grandpa's pastures were still just as magical as playgrounds for all the remaining cousins.

As the families scattered, I couldn't help but feel a twinge of sadness. These were the people who had shaped me, who had become part of the rhythm of my everyday life. I was sure going to miss them. But it didn't take long for me to realize something important—our bond wasn't dependent on proximity. We had built something stronger than just physical closeness. Our family would evolve, yes, but the foundation we had built together would remain with us, no matter how far apart we were. Plus, in a way clever enough to suit the entire clan, Melissa figured out how the families could stay in touch.

"I have breaking news, Mom. The tree swing has broken off! How are we going to tell all the cousins?" Meagan asked her mother as she attempted to catch her breath after running into the house one morning.

Louis had put up a tire swing on a large tree branch in his horse pasture. This tree was down in a dry creek where much of the fort-building and day-trading went on among the cousins when they were together playing. The swing was an iconic part of the whole outside world the cousins played in. One cousin or another was always sitting in that tire as someone was hustling the others.

During a big windstorm the day before, the branch holding the swing broke off. As Meagan was walking across the pasture that morning, she immediately saw the damage and came running back home to report the news.

This is where the resourceful homeschool mom power kicked in.

"How about we write an article about it, like in a real newspaper, Meagan?" Melissa suggested. "We'll need a statement from the property owner and any eyewitnesses."

"Maybe Grandpa will have a statement," Meagan replied.

"I have my notepad. Can I go and write it down if he does?" asked Molly.

"Great idea!" Melissa answered.

In record time, Meagan and Molly burst through their grandparents' patio door. The two girls were bouncing up and down with their big news.

"Grandpa, Grandpa! The tree swing is broken down!" they exclaimed.

"Oh, is it?" Louis replied.

"We need a statement from you so we can tell all the cousins about it. Can you give us a statement?"

"Let me go have a look."

After setting his newspaper down and taking another sip of his coffee, he slid open the patio door, walked over to the edge of the yard, and slowly descended the three levels of terracing. He curiously looked the tree over.

"Yep, it looks like the tree swing has indeed broken off. It will take a little time to clean up today for sure."

"Is that your statement, Grandpa?"

"Uh, huh."

"Hurry, Meagan, I wrote down Grandpa's statement, and now we've got to ask Mom what to do next."

With this, the Cousin Courier was founded, and the broken tire swing was to be its first story ever. Melissa helped the girls add a few other articles for the premier issue, which debuted in August 1994.

In that inaugural issue, everyone learned of the death of our cat, Jemimah. The inaugural issue reported Minette and Tony's family's successful move from Southern California to Missouri. Michele announced her pregnancy with Sully, and the twins' one-year birthday party was covered. After that first issue, Melissa asked Michele and Minette to help produce the next issues, and for many years, each family and the grandparents received the much-anticipated monthly edition.

In one issue, we reluctantly reported on a forgotten infant incident. As the oldest among our kids at nine years old, Keagan was Michele's helper for many things, so it made sense for him to write the article.

The story goes that one day, we loaded all our children, including four in car seats, into the car to go swimming at Grandpa and Grandma's. Michele had a few errands to run on the way there, but she felt rushed—she wanted to be on time for the other cousins who were eager to swim with our kids.

One of Michele's errands was to the drive-up window at the bank. As Michele was waiting for the teller to return to the window, Keagan was just about to comment on how quiet it was in the car that day, but before his words came out, Michele let out "the scream," the same one Minette unleashed that day I told her about buying an engagement ring for Michele.

Because it was so startling and loud, the bank teller dropped to the floor in terror. The kids in the car began frantically scanning the area around the minivan, looking for the monster that was about to attack their vehicle. Some of them started crying.

The entire bank heard Michele through the drive-up microphone, and the teller finally shut off her mic to keep someone from calling the police, thinking they might be getting robbed. By the time the scream stopped, Michele switched to crying, and it took a while for Keagan to understand that she was trying to say: She had forgotten Sully at home!

When they got to the house, she drove all the way into the garage and shut the garage door, instead of just pulling into the driveway, because when she ran in the house and came back out with Sully, she didn't want anybody to see she had forgotten a baby at home.

As mortifying as this was, Michele knew her family would want to know the story, so why not include it in the Cousin Courier? One of our kids was bound to spill the beans, anyway.

Over time, Michele, Minette, and their kids added new columns like Prayers & Praises to the newsletter. We chronicled Melissa's carpal tunnel surgery, Clancy's broken finger, and Michele's ear surgery, and asked the family to pray for healing. Every family had missionaries they requested prayer for, as well as other extended family members.

When Uncle Tony finished another mission trip or when I finally got enough construction work, we gave thanks throughout the family. Major blessings, such as the births of new cousins—Hudson, Sully, Cooper, and Bliss—were first announced in our Cousin Courier.

The cousins wrote articles about the adventures they had during family vacations. As more of them began playing sports, they gave detailed accounts of goals scored and new friends made. Every cousin had some kind of pet during those years, and each of them had their story told in the Courier. Pet rats, lizards, snakes, and bunnies came and went rather quickly, but they were all dear to someone.

As the family spread out over time, the Cousin Courier became even more vital for keeping us all connected. These moves were drastic changes, especially for the cousins, as all three of the families became separated by considerable distances. Whenever one family visited another, the Cousin Courier detailed the trip. These family get-togethers were huge events for the cousins.

Michele added a new section early on called The People's Choice Awards, where we could share our favorite books, movies, and music. In March 1996, Michele recommended *Parents and Children* by Charlotte M. Mason. Her favorite line from the book was, "God forbid that we should ever lose sight of the blessedness of family life."

I had read *The Adventures of Tom Sawyer* to the kids, and we started using a line from it around our house to be gracious to those who were struggling with worm farms or bad behavior: "Let us draw the curtain of charity over the rest of this scene." That was a book I wholeheartedly recommended in The People's Choice Awards.

Kailey's recommendation for one month was *The Cabin Faced West* by Jean Fritz. In February 1997, Clancy wrote that on a visit with Auntie 'Chele, they got to watch the movie, *The Inn of the Sixth Happiness*, a story based on the life of a missionary in China, Gladys Aylward. He loved it because it really happened and it honored God. This might have influenced his new little brother getting the name Hudson after another famous missionary to China, Hudson Taylor.

The Quotable Quotes section was added shortly after. This was where the moms would write down the crazy or silly things their little kids said. Many of them were inside jokes that required a lot of context into the personalities of the speaker, but our families all had the insider knowledge to appreciate each quote. The Quotable Quotes section became the Sunday comics for our entire family. Everyone would go right to that section when they received their newest Cousin Courier issue. I'm so glad these three moms kept a record of these memories. Here are some of my personal favorites:

Keagan, while looking at a Picasso painting, "Yikes! What happened here?"

Kailey, walking past a churro cart at Disneyland, "Yum, did you hear that smell?"

Kassidy, to her mother, who was falling asleep during story time, "Mommy, please read straightly."

Molly, asking to be excused after dinner, "Mom, may I be forgiven?"

Molly's reaction to new baby brother, Jordan, "I mean, we should make a wallpaper printout of this kid!"

Clancy, trying to take Dawson to the bathroom on an airplane, "Mom, there are no bathrooms back there. There's only a vacant."

Keagan to Uncle Joel, who had just swerved to miss an oncoming car, "Wow, that was great! My dad would have hit him!"

Reilly, after fixing a broken lamp with duct tape, "All these years spent with Keagan have sure paid off!"

Kassidy holding her throat, "Ow, it weally huwts. I think I have stwep neck!"

Clancy to Keagan, who had tummy troubles, "You should try that Gas-X, or is it Fart-X?"

Sully, telling us what his new friend, Noah, was wearing, "Noah and the Ark has overalls just like me!"

Keagan, trying to help his Auntie 'Lissa serve all the little kids at dinner time, "It can be a little hectic at mealtimes, but life is worth living when the little ones are down for a nap."

Dawson, after his mom gave him a huge hug and kiss, "Hmmm, I really like women!"

Jordan, "Mom, this dinner is so good, I'm going to pray twice!"

Kailey, "Sully, you be careful up there. If you fall, you could break your head!"

Sully, "Oh, that's okay. Daddy could hammer it back on again."

Molly, "Mom, what does 'estimate' mean again? Oh! Now I remember, you just had to glare at me for a moment."

Kailey, "Yuck! My bubble popped, and it got stuck all over my downer lip."

Sydney, to her twin sister Kassidy, "Come when your mother calls. Yep, Kass, that's what it says in my Bible right here in chapter 1999."

Dawson to his mom, "When this little Cooper's grown up, I don't know which face he's gonna have—mine, yours, or Dad's."

Sawyer's new dinner prayer: "Much obliged."

Young Dawson to his mom at bedtime, "When I'm 12, will you be my grandma?"

Kailey, "Daddy, Daddy! I get to be in the July 4th parade for St. Patrick's Day!"

Poems and songs were often added to the Cousin Courier as well.

Here's my favorite: Sydney's Song
By God's grace and my grit,
I know that I can do it!
By God's grace and my grit,
I will surely stick to it.
Work before play all through the day.
Quick and cheerful to obey,
With all my heart, I'll sing this song,
And give the glory to my God.

CHAPTER 6:

The Call of the Mountains

When my construction business started seeing some success, it was largely because I had a good crew. Scott, Corey, Tom, and I enjoyed working together. Tom was tall and rugged, but soft on the inside once you got to know him. He smoked all the time and blamed it on his time in the Army. He was older than Scott and Corey.

Scott was Corey's sidekick. He was the youngest but had experience in construction because he worked for his dad's electrical business growing up. He wanted to learn framing and the rest of construction, but he mostly wanted to have fun doing whatever Corey was doing. My brother-in-law, Tony, recommended Corey to me. Corey was active in Tony's college-aged church group. He didn't go to college, and he was a bit older than the actual college students, but he fit in well with the young single adults there, especially the ladies.

Corey was way cool. He had a long blond ponytail, and even though having a ponytail or man-bun wasn't popular back then, he made it look good. When he pulled his shirt off at work on a really hot day, none of us were surprised to see he was jacked. He and Scott would go to lift weights after a full day of framing a house. When he kept his shirt off and drove to the gym after work in his fully restored, bright red Willy's jeep, he was the iconic cool California beach dude.

Corey was a very respectful worker. We worked alongside each other extremely well. He was one of those people I easily collaborated with. When faced with a problem, neither of us complained or blamed anyone; we just wanted to figure it out.

The crew members all got to know Michele and the kids, as we would have BBQs and holiday parties together at our house. I think they enjoyed being around our large young family. All our children got to know them and played in our big yard with them. The crew became an extension of our family.

On one big remodel job, we had an electrician working with us who was not part of our crew. He was very overweight, with a huge mop of curly brown hair on his head. He spoke with a thick Creole accent, having moved to Los Angeles from Louisiana. When he spoke to someone, he had to tilt his head up to see through his coke-bottle glasses that rested below where they should sit normally because he was too lazy to push them up.

One day, while the electrician was working in a stairwell, Corey called Tom, Scott, and me over to look at something.

"I've seen butt crack before, but this is the best one ever!" he whispered, directing our view toward the electrician.

In that stairwell, bending over an electrical outlet in the wall, this poor guy couldn't have been exposing any more butt crack than he was. He didn't seem like the kind of guy who was aware of it, either.

"I'm embarrassed for him. We should all match him, so he doesn't feel conspicuous around us," Corey recommended.

We followed Corey's lead, backed away quietly, and pulled our pants way down under our framing belts. It was difficult to work that way, but we didn't want the guy to feel bad about being the only one who couldn't keep his pants up.

A few jobs later, we had a huge project working for a dear family from church. It was the biggest project we ever had up to that point. They wanted a very nice guest house on their property. They also wanted a sports court, a 3,000-square-foot bird aviary, and lots of beautiful landscaping and patterned concrete paths. All of it had to be done in time for their oldest son's big wedding. As the completion deadline was looming, I was picturing having to work nights to finish on time. My stress levels were high, and I needed my crew to focus and work diligently. Typically, this wasn't a problem.

One day, Scott and Corey didn't show up to work. These two were always the first to arrive. They loved their jobs and were very conscientious about this deadline. Why would they do this to me now with the wedding just a few weeks away?

I got angry thinking of all the goofing off they must have done the night before. I was going through many things I wanted to say to them when they arrived. When Scott finally showed up at 11 a.m., I was pretty heated in my head.

As Scott approached me and I was ready to let him have it, I could see his bloodshot eyes. He'd been crying. He said, "Corey was murdered last night," unable to lift his head and look at me.

I was completely dumbfounded. I must not have heard him right.

"We were at Bible study, then he went to an ATM to get some cash on his way to meet us at Taco Bell. Some gang-banger kid put a gun to his head and shot him." Scott stuttered out in sobbing syllables.

The murder filled the news later that day. Surveillance video from the bank recorded the entire incident. The authorities believed it was a gang initiation thing because it was unlikely to be theft. Corey was only getting $20 out of the ATM. And you know why he needed that cash? He had just given the last few bucks he had on him to a missionary who told their Bible study group about his work among the poor.

Corey's murder broke our hearts. It was so traumatic for everyone who knew him. Corey's death crushed his family. His mother never fully recovered from it. Scott and I spent two days driving the neighborhood nearby to find the murderer based on the mugshot we saw on the news. I guess we believed we were going to catch the guy and get some kind of revenge, but we came to our senses, realizing nothing good could come of us finding him. Corey was gone, and nothing could change that.

In the following days and weeks, I worked in silence, my mind regularly returning to Corey. I felt his absence as an unfillable void. I questioned everything—how could something so senseless happen? How could such a vibrant life be snuffed out so fast? How could someone take a life so flippantly?

It seemed so pointless to work hard, be generous, and take care of my health. Doing all the right things guaranteed nothing for Corey, so why would they guarantee anything for me? I wondered how life could have a purpose if it could so randomly be taken away. I felt confused, heartbroken, and far from God. His reasons for all of this left me uneasy because I didn't understand them.

I knew life had to go on, and it did, but it didn't feel the same anymore. It felt colder. Emptier. Working with my construction crew was never the same. There was no more joking around or showing off to each other while raising a wall. We still had deadlines and responsibilities, but work wasn't fun anymore. Corey was the glue.

It wasn't long after that Tom found work elsewhere. Scott stayed on longer but eventually went back to work with his dad. Corey's death also sparked the next big change for our family.

MY MOUNTAINS

On the way home from Corey's memorial service, Michele and I started talking seriously about finding a better place to call home and raise our family. It wasn't just because of Corey's murder. On more than one night around our home, the L.A. County sheriff's helicopter would circle with loudspeakers, saying to stay in our homes because a dangerous person was in our neighborhood. Michele would literally huddle in the living room with all six of our kids, reading by candlelight so we could keep the house dark.

Despite being near our family, Michele and I longed for the mountains. We both felt it—the pull of those beautiful, wild mountains. Wild sounds dangerous, but wild has rules that aren't hard to see and learn. People bring a huge element of unexpectedness. People are random and creative beings. The mountains are predictable. I felt more comfortable abiding by the rules of the wild mountains than the rules of living in a crowded city.

Corey and I daydreamed about moving to the mountains together to build log cabins. He said if my family ever returned to the mountains, he was absolutely coming with us. So, the mountains became a symbol of everything we hoped for—peace, a fresh start, the chance to build something new, not just for us but for our children, and a way to honor Corey. We didn't know at all what lay ahead for us, but we believed in the possibility that our next chapter of life could be even better.

We took out one of those big paper roadmap books of the USA and started looking at places we could go. I remember trying to find the least populated place I could on the map, an area where no big highways went through. A place without helicopters or gangs or traffic or smog.

One place I noted was the southwest corner of Colorado. No interstate was nearby. There was no international airport. There were only a couple of small towns, including Pagosa Springs. It stood out to me because it was near a ski area called Wolf Creek. The internet was only just beginning, so we couldn't really look up a lot of details. We had to go visit!

King Louis owned a lot with storage spaces for 450 RVs and trailers. Sometimes, if the renter didn't pay and didn't respond to his notices, he eventually took possession of the RV.

There was one such repo of a 1979 motorhome, thirty feet long, with a 454 V8 engine. It had a busted-out window, and the carpet was rotten, but King Louis said we could have it if we wanted to put some work into it and get it off the lot.

So my brother-in-law, Joel, and I got to work. We put in new carpet, had a little engine work done, bought some new tires, and, just like Louis always did, tidied it up with a wire brush and some black spray paint. We now had a fine motor home and an easier way to explore the areas we were considering moving to.

Michele and I and the six kids planned a three-week trip to find a new place to call home. We got that big old motor home all loaded up for eight of us to live in for a while. The kids kept a journal of our travels.

First, we went to Iowa to visit my sister, Carolyn, and her family. They were working at a church camp. We wanted to see cousins, and we wanted to see America, including the Midwest. From there, we backtracked to Colorado to see my mother, April. Recently widowed, April had moved to Colorado Springs. We spent some extra time exploring that area since it was close to my mother and in the mountains, and we heard people from California were moving there in droves.

Finally, we went to explore the Pagosa Springs area that we had seen on the map a few months earlier. We entered the area from the east over Wolf Creek Pass, which must be the best-named mountain pass in America. You summit the pass at 10,850 feet above sea level. Wolf Creek ski area, famous for receiving the most natural snow of any ski area in Colorado, rests just before you crest the pass. Then you come down into the West Fork of the San Juan River.

That valley is arguably the most beautiful valley in the entire Rocky Mountains. It was fall when we drove through, and aspen groves abounded with golden brilliance in every direction. Mixed in and contrasting were the pine and fir evergreens of different hues—some more blue, some more green. The valley floor was still lush even in the waning season because of the river running through it. Everywhere we looked was magnificent and spectacular.

Once in Pagosa, we had some engine trouble that waylaid us for a few days, so we rented a car and stayed at the High Country Lodge east of town. Despite the carburetor problem, the time Keagan accidentally locked the keys in the trunk of the rental car, and the early winter snowstorm we drove through on the way out of town, everyone agreed that the time in and around Pagosa Springs was immensely satisfying to our curiosity. We all wanted to move to Pagosa Springs.

That whole winter, we couldn't stop thinking about that little mountain hideout and getting out of the big city. The following summer, Michele and I returned to Pagosa to look for land. Despite our excitement, it was a frightening experience for us. There were plenty of reasons we almost didn't go.

This was our first trip ever away from the kids. We'd never invested in property other than our own home. We worried we'd be stuck with a piece of property we couldn't do anything with, or buy something in a bad area, with awful neighbors, or drill a dry well and have no water.

As soon as we set foot on the property Michele found, we knew it was the one. The blue-painted wooden sign said Lot 181 in white letters. There was only one other house within sight of the lot at the time. The afternoon thunderstorms had created a lush green pastureland bordered by mature pine trees and gambrel oak bushes. Standing on the property looking north gave us a view of the magnificent

Pagosa Peak, a coveted view we learned later. We walked slowly all around the property, brushing the tops of the wild wheatgrass with our fingers, taking slow, deep, relaxing breaths while out on the land. We stood there imagining having our very own home for our family there. It was a dream location and still is to this day.

On June 8, 1998, our 13th Anniversary, we bought the land.

Michele immediately started thinking about house plans. We went to Barnes & Noble and began looking through dozens of design books. They featured pretty pictures of all kinds of houses. From there, you could purchase the complete architectural plans. Michele was most taken by the Carolina Farmhouse style—the kind with wrap-around covered porches and cute dormers on the roof. She found one she liked best and changed its name to Ambleside. Ambleside was going to be our dream home in the Rocky Mountains.

Around the same time, Minette and Tony were also looking to build their own custom home in Carthage, Missouri. They had been in Missouri a couple of years and were ready to move out of their cold, creaky, 100-year-old house and into something that could withstand the wear and tear of their own six children. I don't know whether Minette and Tony didn't care to find something different or it just fit their family perfectly, too, but they built the exact same house we did. Or maybe it was the other way around. I don't know. Their strange magic isn't part of our natural world.

A few months after closing on the land, we stuffed every nook and cranny of the motorhome to return to Pagosa and start working on Ambleside. We set up our motor home on our very own mountain property and lived in it while we worked. As we began clearing the building site, we discovered black mud. Black mud, we learned later, was something many parts of Pagosa were famous for. It stuck to everything when it got wet and didn't wash off. Instead, water activated its super adhesive properties.

The biggest challenge with the mud was when our six young kids left the motorhome to help build or play. They would return with mud caked so thick on their shoes, they couldn't walk in them. We lined up a neat row of their shoes outside the motorhome every evening at dinner time, and the next morning, we'd spend a few minutes banging and scraping off the dried mud.

Our job for those two weeks was to lay the foundation of our house. I chose a type of concrete forms that looked like large Lego blocks. They were white foam pieces that even the littlest ones could carry to me to stack.

Keagan, now thirteen, was a Lego savant, and he was all about building these STEM walls with me. Kailey helped by watching Sully and the twins. If she got Sully occupied with a stick or lump of mud, she'd help the twins carry blocks to me and Keagan and Michele. Sawyer helped a little, watched mostly, played in the mud with Sully, but struggled to focus on the mission. Sawyer spent most of his childhood watching and thinking.

Despite the mud and the hard manual labor, we felt confident we'd made the right choice to move. The mountains were intoxicating. The peace of being in the forest was so soothing compared to the constant droning of freeway noise in Los Angeles. Looking up and outward, taking in the expansive views of mountains, clouds, and sky, filled our souls with a huge breath of fresh air.

After the two weeks had passed, we took a picture of our big white Lego project in the middle of the black mud. We banged off all the shoes one more time and loaded them up in the motorhome. Going back to Los Angeles was tough because we knew it would be a while before we could call Pagosa home. I still had to finish a large custom home in Arcadia, California. It was a big job and had a long way to go.

Thankfully, I had a strong crew again. After Scott and Tom left, my Guatemalan brothers from Angeles Crest Christian Camp, Byron and Elvis, joined the team. They introduced me to their cousins, Edwin and Axcel, who also came to work for me.

Still, that last job in Arcadia was really tough to finish. The homeowner kept adding stuff and changing the scope of the work while I was getting increasingly desperate to finish the job. I so wanted to put all my attention on our plans to move to Colorado.

The homeowner then added to the tension. At the end, when I desperately needed to get my last payment, he sued me for petty things he claimed were problems. During the whole fiasco, I learned he did this regularly to avoid paying full price.

In a panic, I had King Louis come see the progress and give me advice on what to do.

"Do you think any of his claims are true?" I asked him. "He wants me to redo these things that aren't even done incorrectly."

"Well, you're right, it looks fine to me, but it wouldn't take too much extra work. I think you just have to buckle down and redo it," he replied.

"But that's not right! Why should I have to redo it?"

Louis looked me straight in the eye and said matter-of-factly, "Chris, you're just gonna have to do it."

That was the kick in the pants I needed to get the work done. So I did it. I still had to settle on reducing the last payment to half, but the homeowner dropped the lawsuit, and we were finally free to get on the road to Pagosa.

In the summer of 1999, we sold our beloved house on Blue Haven Drive (along with all its worm boxes) and headed to Pagosa Springs, this time for good. We were more than ready for our dream of living up high in the Rocky Mountains.

It was harder than we knew for Joel, Melissa, and their kids to see their cousins move away. First, it was Minette and Tony and their kids, and now we were moving away, too. That left their kids,

Megan, Molly, and Jordan, with no cousins nearby for the first time. Molly was Kailey's best friend, Jordan was Sawyer's best friend, and Megan was everybody's best friend.

People do a lot of adventurous things in life so they can come back and tell their friends and family all about it. This adventure felt different. We were leaving our tribe behind. We felt a bit like pioneers or colonists who left their families and countries for a new life, knowing they probably wouldn't be returning to share it with anyone. As excited as we were, it was scary to go so far away from everything and everyone we knew. It was incredibly bittersweet for all of us.

Plus, we were nervous that our big family might drop into this small town like a cannonball in a hot tub and wreak havoc. Were people going to like us? Would it be easy to make friends? How long would we feel like outsiders? Locals can tell when a family is new to town. And worse, we were from California; Californians have a poor reputation in a lot of states. We didn't want to come across like some Big City know-it-alls. We just wanted a safe place to raise our family.

The first few months felt like a breath of fresh air. No expectations, no pressures to meet anyone's standards. It was just us—our family—finally free to live at our own pace. We had a rare chance to build, not just our house but ourselves. And as the quiet stillness beneath the mountain peaks gave me respite, I also realized something: This was the first time in years that I had the space to really think about who I wanted to be—not just as a husband and father, but as a man. The mountains gave me that. God gave me that.

We had to stay focused, though, and finish the house. We all worked sunup to sundown, but we weren't moving along nearly as fast as I planned. It became apparent that we would not get this house built by ourselves over the summer. In fact, camping on our property and building our dream house kind of fell apart after only two weeks.

Framing a house is the fun part. Progress is evident quickly as walls stand up, and you can see door and window openings. Then add the roof—voilà! It looks like a building. But this needed a crew of several experienced framers. It'd be safe to say my children, 13, 11, 9, 6, 6, and 3, lied about their experience on their resumes. Even Michele had fudged her construction experience a bit.

In Pagosa Springs, the monsoon rainy season arrives at the beginning of July. Some summers are particularly wet. The summer of 1999 was one of them. Coming from dry Southern California, we loved the rain. Every afternoon, a thunderstorm would open up and cool everything down. However, thunderstorms are not so great for construction work. We would spend an hour each morning sweeping out the standing water so we could get to work. In the afternoon, the rain often cut our day short.

Remember the black mud? Yeah, that continued to try our patience. Michele and I quickly developed a mud-management protocol for ourselves. But the kids' protocol was the complete opposite: to get as much mud on themselves and everything around them. The white exterior of the motorhome was a perfect canvas for black mural drawings. The nearby pond was a particularly fun way to mix more water with the mud, making it easier to smear all over their clothes.

We had planned on more traditional flooring in the new house, like brick or hardwood. When the kids got most of the freshly poured concrete fully coated with black mud, however, we considered just calling it a stained concrete finish. And you can probably imagine what the inside of our motorhome looked like after a couple of weeks of this. Now double that.

One afternoon, Michele said, "I don't think we'll be able to live here in the motorhome for the entire summer." (Actually, she said, "I cannot live in this motorhome one more day!") So she quickly found us a delightful spot at the Riverside Campground. It had gravel campsites (a big upgrade) and showers. Michele loved it there. It worked great.

Still, as much as all of us tried, there was no way we were going to finish the house before winter. Michele decided we needed to find a rental home to live in for our first winter. She started calling around, but every call went the same way. The landlord either hung up after she said we have six kids, or if they would let her tell them more, they slammed the phone down after she said we had a 75-pound Alaskan Malamute that sheds horribly in the spring. If she got past those enormous hurdles, they still turned us down when they found out we had no references because we had never rented a house before.

Michele realized she needed to lead with other things. She would now start with a friendly conversation to get them to stay on the phone for at least a few moments. She would talk to them about how we were building a beautiful custom home and how we were so looking forward to moving our cute young family into it as soon as possible. This strategy worked! She finally found a three-bed, two-bath place on Dragoon Court. It wasn't as good as our house at Angeles Crest Camp, but it was not surrounded by black mud, and it would serve us through the winter.

Progress on the house slowed even more when school started in the fall. I lost my "crew" (of children) and my foreman (Michele) overnight. It was time to enlist professional help, so I picked up the phone and called my last framing guys from California and offered them a lot of money to come out for just two weeks and help me get the roof on. I made sure to sell it as a wonderful camping trip they could enjoy and also get paid for. So, they agreed to come. These guys were awesome. They were born and raised in East L.A., a very tough area, but they were Jehovah's Witnesses, which meant they were an impressive combination of hard workers with street smarts who also didn't mess around. They didn't drink or smoke and were extremely respectful.

We cleaned up the motorhome as best we could so they could stay in it on our lot. Brilliant plan, right? Well, there was one thing we didn't plan for—their fear of the wilderness. The first mistake I made was having them arrive at the property at night. When the sun went down, our lot was pitch black. There were (and still are) no streetlights. Yes, they had lived in some of the most crime-ridden neighborhoods in America, but the lightless nighttime was terrifying to them.

"This is safe darkness here, guys. You don't have to worry. There are no gangs or drive-by shootings. No sirens or helicopters. Even the wild animals out here just want to be left alone," I explained.

At the mention of "wild animals," their eyes grew to the size of saucers. Each of them immediately stepped back a half step and frantically peered out beyond me into the dark. They slept little that first night, and you could tell they were much relieved in the daylight.

The next day, they rolled out their hoses and cords to do something familiar and comfortable—work. But as they worked alongside me, I noticed they were slower and less focused than I'd remembered. I could tell they were uneasy the whole time.

I brought them groceries and stayed until after dark, using every bit of diplomacy to convince them to stay and finish this job out here in the serene, tranquil mountain paradise. It was so peaceful and safe out here. My efforts worked for the time being, and they agreed to stay. I felt confident another night would prove to them that nothing bad was going to happen.

Was I right? Nope. I was wrong. Very wrong.

"Hermano Chris, we will go home now, please?" said Jorge, the oldest brother, as I arrived the next morning.

They were all standing at the entrance to the driveway with their extension cords all rolled up and all their luggage packed. They were wearing their clean traveling clothes and didn't look at all like they intended to stay and work.

"Come look," said Jorge.

He pointed to the motor home, indicating that I lead the way. He followed, but as we approached the motorhome, he kept his distance, as if it were haunted.

I immediately noticed the screens on the windows were torn up. Massive muddy paw prints decorated the sides of the vehicle. Jorge didn't have to say anything; I knew what happened. That night, a bear came and rocked the motorhome, trying to get in. It could probably smell the crew's food inside. I forced myself to control my gut laugh, imagining these tough street guys all quivering in the motorhome the whole night, terrified like characters in the movie *The Night of the Grizzly*. I pictured them banging pots and pans and screaming in Spanish at that hungry bear while trying not to break down crying or pee their pants. But there was nothing funny about it to them. They refused to work another day and insisted on going home immediately. They were done!

Once again, my Guatemalan brothers came to the rescue. First, Byron moved to Pagosa, then his brother, Elvis, then their cousins Edwin and Axcel. I now had the best construction crew in town! We did almost all the trades ourselves. It took almost another full year, but we finally finished the house. We did it!

There was still touch-up painting to be done and a bunch of trim carpentry. But we moved in anyway. We had the biggest house in our lives and were thrilled with it. We put the homeschool room in the formal dining room. The upstairs had two bedrooms; a boy's bedroom and a girl's bedroom. There was a wood-burning stove in the great room. We lit a fire in that stove every night to be cozy and warm that winter in our mountain dream home. Now Michele could do her favorite part: Fill up all the bookshelves throughout the house.

By the time we got everything finished up, including a yard with grass to keep the black mud away for good, our kids were between the ages of eight and sixteen. We were in our prime family years. Homeschooling was firing on all cylinders. All of us were making friends. The kids were all playing sports. Keagan was loving the Powerhouse youth group. Kailey and the twins had their own horse. The twins graduated to the A-team in the prestigious Durango Soccer Club. Sawyer was learning the violin, and Sully was everyone's favorite little buddy. These were the best years for our family. Every day was full to the brim with adventure and discovering how to live well.

It was tiring, though, especially for Michele. One afternoon, Michele was reading to the kids about George Washington's great escape across the Delaware River and preparing dinner in between chapters. Whenever she would sit back down to read, she kept getting sleepy. At one point, she dozed off but kept trying to read and inserted food words into the narrative. Something like, "So Washington crossed the Delaware with his twelve pizzas... All the kids turned abruptly and stared at her, wondering what the heck she was talking about. At least we knew they were paying attention!

One thing that helped was sharing the load with other homeschool families. Michele took the lead in organizing a very active homeschool co-op. She recruited other parents to teach music, dance, art, and language so we could all benefit from helping each other out. Many of our lifelong friendships came from our homeschool group.

As if she weren't already doing enough, our church asked Michele to be the preschool director. I think because she was a homeschool teacher, and all our kids spent time in the church nursery helping out.

She was happy to help and did this job for many years. It's hard to believe that she had time to hold down a job while homeschooling our kids, but she did. She slid effortlessly into it, just like she did back in her college days at the preschool and the Tom Sawyer Day Camp. She was absolutely in her element, loving on little kids, and that delight never faded. It was a wonder to watch her do something so joyfully.

But that was just who Michele was. She was warm, welcoming, nurturing, kind, and cheerful. She rarely complained and seldom worried. In those early years of my construction business, when it was trying to get off the ground, she would faithfully turn to prayer. During one terrible season, I finished a couple of homes, but there just wasn't any profit at the end, so we had almost no money.

Michele remained steadfast. She knew the situation was serious, but she always trusted God would provide. And He did. Always. We even set up an Ebenezer Stone—a "stone of help" to remind us of all the times God reached down to lend a helping hand.

This one time, sitting around our table, we ate the last of the food from our pantry and fridge—literally. A family of eight goes through a lot of food for each meal. Michele was frugal and resourceful, but this time, we were out of food completely. Thankfully, her commitment to caring for others came back to help us in our time of need.

Michele loved baking pumpkin muffins and banana chipper cookies for other people. It was how she showed love. Even with such a big family, she always baked extra. There were many times that she asked me to deliver these treats to our neighbors. They were so pleasantly surprised. I would feel like such an imposter accepting their thanks; I did nothing!

On this one day, after scraping the bottom of the peanut butter jar and spreading it on the last heels of the bread, a neighbor she had befriended knocked on the door and announced that they were moving—that same day, in fact. The neighbor wanted to know if we could use any of the food from her fridge and pantry, as they couldn't take any of it. It took a moment for us to fix our faces from the shock and close the mouths of each child before we happily accepted the offer.

"We'll leave the house unlocked when we leave this evening. Just go right in and take everything you can use," our neighbor told us.

"Oh, and make sure you get everything out of the garage, too!"

After she left, nobody around our table said a word. We had literally just said grace, thanking God that we had this meal and were trusting Him for the next. Michele and I cried. All the kids were stunned. The younger ones didn't understand why someone would just give us all their food. But we were in for an even bigger surprise. When we went over and began emptying the fridge, we couldn't believe what we found. It wasn't just a carton of milk and half a bottle of old mustard. It appeared she and her husband ate like royalty. We didn't realize anyone had this much food in their home. Our family of eight kept the stores of food to a practical level in our house. Not them, they had steaks, not just flank steaks or cube steaks but ribeyes, filets, and top sirloins. I don't think we had ever, in our 15 years of marriage, bought anything like that for our family.

It wasn't just one fridge either; the freezer out in the garage was full too! As we were emptying it, one kid asked, "Can we have all these buckets that say three months' food supply for a family of four?"

Michele and I didn't understand the question until we flipped on the rest of the lights. This couple had some sort of business where they sold food for the end times. Their garage was full of these buckets and cans, and they had left it all for us. I still have cans of that food in my attic.

Without God's provision and Michele's generous approach to life, I'm not sure what we would've done in that situation. As I watched my children gorge on plentiful food in the coming months, my eyes often misted over with tears. I couldn't have been more grateful. Another event for our Ebenezer Stone.

From there, things only got better in the coming years as we enjoyed many outdoor adventures, joyful family traditions, and a few funny mishaps.

On one of those small adventures, Michele was on the floor in the throes of laughter, Sydney was frozen with embarrassment, Keagan had completely left the building, and the rest of us were giggling nervously.

All the other restaurant patrons, having stood up and gotten ready to run for their lives, were not laughing, however. They were looking for more napkins, wiping up their spills, standing their chairs back up, and recovering from the trauma Michele just inflicted on them.

We just finished dinner at a small diner in Cuba, New Mexico, on the way home from a soccer tournament in Albuquerque. Sydney and Kassidy played really well. The coach put Kassidy in several positions, but she never left the pitch because she played every position better than almost any other player on the team. Sydney was a consummate forward. She waited on the wing, or up front, until all the pieces lined up just right for a lightning attack, then ran faster than any other person in the tournament to score.

The drive home after the tournament was only four hours long, but it necessitated a meal stop. Cuba was the only town along the way big enough to have a restaurant in it, but it's by no means a city. It's a small, isolated community of mostly old New Mexican stock and Native Americans, both very suspicious of outsiders.

The restaurant was full of these locals when we walked in. It must have been a sight to see all eight of us out-of-towners pile into this diner, but we didn't care. We were all starved after a whole day on the soccer fields, and some good, authentic New Mexican food was just the thing.

The restaurant was traditionally outfitted in its regional décor, as in, there wasn't any. Unlike big city chain restaurants that fill their walls with collectibles, antiques, and art, Cuba rejected that approach. We're talking barren white plaster walls like an old military hospital.

Well, there was one decoration on one wall—a solitary calavera ("sugar skull") mask likely hung just in time for Halloween and Día de los Muertos. We noticed it on the way in but thought little of it. We were hungry travelers in need of a meal.

Sydney and Keagan, who were too cool for school at this point in their lives, were thankful when the food came because everyone kept silent and minded their manners. I think we even got a mildly grateful nod from one elderly patron who appreciated our quiet, controlled kids.

Our family motto was "leave while you're having fun," so once everyone gulped down the delicious food, it was time to head out with our dignity intact. We all kept our heads down as we got up to leave and walked through this intimidating crowd. So far, so good.

Sydney was on the verge of complete relief, about to head outside of the restaurant, when she noticed her mom intrigued by the calavera. Sydney's amygdala "Oh crap" meter instantly came online as she watched her mother approach something Sydney knew was not what it appeared to be. Michele went up close to check it out. It was right at the level of her face. It was creepy, and we couldn't understand why Michele would want to investigate it more carefully. Suddenly, the mask screamed and jumped out from the wall at her. The sudden action of the mask caught Michele completely unaware. To say she jumped a little would be thoroughly understating it.

Michele fought back at it with a scream of her own. You know, "the scream."

Our whole family knew the scream well by that point. Even Sully was old enough to instantly know it was just Mom…again. I was preparing for the chainsaw murderer bursting in the front door. For a scream like that, any horror was possible.

Although already mortified, poor Sydney knew it was about to get worse. What was coming would eclipse what everyone had just heard. Even though she was standing among her remaining four siblings, she was certain these upset strangers were staring only at her.

Michele eventually ran out of air with the scream. As she drew in her next breath, she realized how much she must have alarmed everyone. So to remedy the situation, she followed up with her infamous gut laugh, which needed to match or surpass the sheer scope of the scream. Surely that would put people back at ease, right?

To everyone's surprise but mine and the kids,' the gut laugh could last longer than the scream and resulted in her falling to the floor. Michele's scene completely canceled out all our kids' quiet, polite behavior from the entire previous hour.

As we scrambled to pick her up, we felt a dark shadow fall over us as everyone grimaced in our direction; we were clearly no longer welcome. We quickly skedaddled out of that place, buckled the kids in the car as fast as we could, and drove off, never to return to that restaurant again!

I don't know when most husbands become the knight in shining armor their wives thought they were marrying, but for me, it wasn't during or right after the wedding. It wasn't after our first anniversary, either. I needed lots more time to grow into my chain mail and polish my helmet. During the first couple of years with Keagan and Kailey as babies, I think my armor glimmered a bit as I learned to be a dad. After Sawyer was born, I had to step it up a notch. Having three children is a test of cunning and ingenuity because the parents are now outnumbered. Resourcefulness and strategic thinking are skills you need to cultivate. You plan your trips to the store more carefully. You preload the car with multiple fallback options: extra clothing, a variety of toys, plenty of snacks, and supplies for any kind of weather. As our family grew to four, then five instantly, and then finally six children, I had to think a lot more about those around me than myself. If someone's water gets spilled, I'd volunteer mine. If someone ran out of food, I'd offer mine. If the kids woke up during the night . . . well, Michele took care of that most of the time. I wasn't a knight yet, remember? I still had a ways to go.

With Michele's constant cheerleading, tenacity, and love, I gained more and more confidence as a husband and father. I slowly shed some outer layers of selfishness and foolish pride. Much of this transformation resulted from the focused effort Michele and I put into our marriage. It was the primary relationship in our lives. Not our children. She and I were the core of the family. The kids just made it bigger.

When the kids were younger, Michele and I had "couch time" every day when I got home from work. After a quick hug for each kid, I'd request they go back to what they were doing so I could spend 10 minutes sitting on the couch with Michele and catching up with her.

Each marriage class or retreat we attended became the content of the next marriage class we would then lead for others. One memorable one was *Love and Respect* by Emmerson Eggerichs. His teaching really clarified how to love my wife the way she needed to feel loved. And it showed Michele how to respect me the way I needed to feel respected.

Belonging to the family we created together became my life's most enduring blessing. As a young man, I was not capable of grasping how rewarding it would be. When Michele looked up into my eyes in that small cabin and said, "Let's start having kids," I had no idea what we were heading into. Perhaps because I am a guy, or my childhood home, broken by divorce and fighting, prevented me from anticipating what happened in my life. It is only by the grace of God and the partnership of a devoted wife that I ended up with a family like mine.

Michele and I enjoyed many adventures together—winter camping where the creek flooded our tent at night, backpacking trips that tested our physical fitness, mountain biking at high speeds down steep trails, and four-wheeling in the most beautiful high country America has to offer. But the one adventure that surpassed them all by far was building a family. My drive home each day after work or after a business trip was always one with a longing to be reunited with my wife and kids. My clan, my people. The ones always up for an adventure. The ones I could figure out life with.

During these years, my construction business was constantly up and down, and it was becoming clear that the industry was not my best fit. I loved creating things and winning contracts and working outdoors with my hands, but I did not have the tenacity or the profit margin to finish one job to perfection and then patiently wait to start the next one. I wanted projects to just be done, maybe because the last stages of the build were where I usually lost money. It felt like most projects limped along to completion while I waited on subcontractors, materials, and favorable weather. But mostly, I made enough to support my large family, so I stuck with it.

Michele had a motto that everyone needed to "pull their weight," so whenever we were in a season of less income, she would take on work where she could. At one point, that included some paid childcare in our home. She watched the two young daughters of a doctor whose son was on the soccer team I coached. The doctor really liked our family and felt comfortable enough to ask Michele if he could pay her to watch his girls during his workday. Our family practically adopted his daughters, Carina and Carlie. Carina was a darling towhead two-year-old when she started coming to our home. She was almost a little cousin to our kids, who played with her every chance they got. A year or two later, Carlie was born. Sadly, she had severe birth defects, and she needed special care throughout the day. Michele was naturally up for the challenge.

Even though we all knew it was a strong possibility, we were crushed when Carlie passed away from complications of her condition at just a few years old. Our family felt so honored to have been a part of her brief life. Carlie's quiet strength and generous spirit helped our kids learn to be less self-centered and think about others' needs ahead of their own. And she helped all of us prepare for what it would be like when Michele's twin sister had a special-needs baby.

Since the day she was born, Minette and Tony's red-headed daughter, Bliss, has been a beautiful blessing to our whole extended family and countless people at the children's hospital in Kansas City. She has especially shaped the lives of her sister and four brothers, three of whom pursued careers in healthcare.

Bliss's daily battle to live has been a powerful example of strength, perseverance, sacrifice, and commitment, not just from her, but from the whole family. Minette has spent a large part of each of the last 21 years living at the children's hospital with Bliss, but she's done so without complaint. Back at their house, you'd hardly notice the extra work they all do for Bliss because they do it so seamlessly and generously. They've made it a part of their life.

Bliss could be in the living room on a breathing machine, feeding tube, and various other monitors, but it seems like no big deal while they host a BBQ or Bible study. They don't treat caring for her like a chore or inconvenience, even though I'm sure it's very difficult. They've been able to grow from their trials and the many times they've almost lost Bliss. Along the way, they haven't stopped having fun or lost their joy. Watching their family has been one way our family has learned to be far more generous in serving others and not fear helping those in need. When we entered our next season of uncertainty, we found that helping others in our community would come back to save us.

CHAPTER 7:
Angels in the Making

Miss Ada lived one street over from our house. She and her husband moved into their mountain retirement home a year or two before us. They attended our church and were very involved there. Her husband and I were elders together, and Miss Ada and I were on the missions committee. More notably, Miss Ada worked with the youth group. She was in her seventies but still had plenty of vim and vigor to work with teenagers. This probably came from the many years she served as a youth minister during her life in Texas. She and Michele were kindred spirits. I think Miss Ada could see Michele's genuine faith and kindness. She also loved Michele's pumpkin muffins delivered to her house occasionally, by me or one of our kids.

Shortly after our friendship began, Miss Ada lost her husband to natural causes. Her three children lived out of state and only visited occasionally, but she was so energetic and full of life, so it wasn't odd that she continued living in her mountain home. Miss Ada continued to work with the youth group, of which our middle kids were now members. They could all tell she was a rockstar church lady, the good old Texas type, and they had great respect for her.

Several of us at the church decided we'd look out for Miss Ada now that her husband was gone. Michele was the most excited for this task, and we lived closest to her, so we got very involved and attached to her. Michele eagerly looked forward to showering Miss Ada with gifts and encouragement.

It wasn't even a full year after her husband's death that we realized something was changing for Miss Ada. For a few years, she, Michele, and I served hot dogs at our church's annual Halloween party. We had another wonderful party that year, but the next day at church, Miss Ada mentioned the event the night before and asked why we weren't there. We thought she was joking, suggesting that we didn't pull our weight that evening, but she was serious. She had no memory of us being there.

The next Sunday was very concerning. Miss Ada had always been a very classy lady for as long as we'd known her. She always carefully styled her beautiful silver hair and went around town dressed to the nines. But that day, she wore a black sweatsuit to church, and she hadn't groomed her hair.

The situation shocked and embarrassed Michele. She knew Miss Ada would never go out in public without looking her best. Michele felt so bad for her, she quickly rushed her out of church and took her home to change and groom her. We lacked experience in caring for the elderly, but we believed Miss Ada suffered from memory loss.

From then on, our family took a bigger role in caring for Miss Ada, especially Michele. Each Sunday, Michele helped her get ready for church. Our boys shoveled her driveway and sidewalk every time it snowed. We frequently called Miss Ada's children to keep them updated, and we discreetly informed concerned church members about what was happening.

Eventually, Michele started going to visit her every day to do small things around the house and make sure she was eating, taking her pills, and getting dressed and groomed. That's how we found out Miss Ada was only eating hot dogs and drinking Diet Coke. Her basement was stocked floor to ceiling with Diet Cokes, and her fridge only had hot dogs in it. We felt it was important that Miss Ada eat better, so Michele started grocery shopping for her and either arranging for church members to make meals or preparing meals herself.

One cold winter morning, Michele arrived early to get Miss Ada out of bed and dressed for her women's Bible study. When she walked into the house, she saw the entire ceiling of the great room charred black with soot. She rushed into the bedroom expecting something awful, but Miss Ada was all smiles when greeting Michele.

It turns out Miss Ada had lit a fire in her fireplace and inadvertently closed the flue before going to bed. As the fire burned, all the smoke filled the main part of the house. Thankfully, the bedroom door was shut and kept the smoke out of Miss Ada's room. We were so grateful that our dear friend was alive and smiling that morning.

As the weeks went by, Miss Ada started calling Michele, saying she was lost while driving somewhere. Our little town of Pagosa Springs has one highway going through it, east to west, and some neighborhood streets. It is very hard to get lost. Michele offered her rides whenever she wanted to go somewhere, but Miss Ada would still get in her car and drive away from her house, only to end up lost. After some persistent discussion, Michele convinced Miss Ada to stop driving.

The care we gave Miss Ada wasn't easy on us, Michele in particular, and there were days when it didn't seem like we were helping enough. But there was something deeply meaningful in those acts of service beyond just meeting her daily needs. We weren't only caring for her body—we were preserving her dignity and her spirit. In these actions, I saw the resilience of my family in refusing to give up, no matter the obstacles. And in those moments, I felt a deeper sense of faith in our ability to rise above the hardest challenges together.

In the fall of 2010, Michele drove our middle son, Sawyer, back to school at Ozark Christian College in Joplin, Missouri. I stayed at home trying to sell every piece of construction equipment I had, just so we could make ends meet. The Great Recession had hit us hard.

A few years prior, King Louis had asked me if I wanted to develop some property in Pagosa. Thrilled at the opportunity, I eagerly accepted. I spent a couple of years finding the land, getting an architect, and drawing up one of the largest, nicest condo developments the town had ever seen. It was a wonderful experience to bring an important housing development to our town. But as the economy took a nosedive in 2007 and 2008, so did our project. The construction industry in our region dropped by 90 percent. We had to lay off all our workers, even our dear Guatemalan friends.

In the meantime, four of the condos were under construction and didn't have roofs yet. Not knowing how long they would sit idle, I didn't want them to deteriorate to the point of being unsellable, so I used two-thirds of our savings to get the roofs done.

We eventually had to put the unfinished development on the market for a quarter of the value we put into it. We sold the condos at such a loss that I couldn't even reimburse our savings I'd depleted. Michele's babysitting money was the only way we put food on the table. But that would not keep us going forever, and I was at a loss for what we'd do next.

Even in the uncertainty, Michele still selflessly focused on the needs of others. On her way through Oklahoma with Sawyer, she heard an advertisement on the radio for Visiting Angels Home Care. She quickly called me and asked me to find out if they could start helping Miss Ada. Miss Ada needed more help than Michele could provide, especially while she was still homeschooling three kids, babysitting, and running the church preschool. I tried to find Visiting Angels in our area, but to no avail. I looked for other companies that provided services like that, but there wasn't much. A solitary home care nurse I found was fully booked. Durango had nothing either.

I called Michele back with the bad news. Discouraged that there was no help for Miss Ada and overwhelmed by our financial predicament, she began crying in the car. My heart shattered instantly. I knew my work crisis was putting extra pressure on Michele, but I hadn't realized how much. We began praying together, begging God to show us a way forward.

Shortly after we hung up the phone, God immediately started showing her the way. He put an intriguing idea in Michele's head: What if we started a Visiting Angels? She mulled it over for the rest of her drive, and when she got home, she was eager to tell me all about it.

My first inclination was to dig in my heels and refuse to hear any more of it. I wasn't about to take a "desk job." My identity was a construction worker and a mountain man. I was rugged and tough, remember?

"Chris, I couldn't care less about this identity you've created for yourself."

"But, Lord, I work with my hands, and I like that about myself. It's who you created me to be."

"I created you to be my child; that's the only identity that matters. Besides, didn't this rugged and tough identity leave you unemployed and broke?"

"Ouch. OK, fair enough, but I don't know the first thing about the home care industry. What if this plan lets me down?"

"The only thing that won't let you down is me. Do you trust me to be with you no matter what happens—good or bad?"

"Well, yes, of course, but I'm responsible for my family, right? As a husband and a father, I can't afford to be reckless."

"The only thing that'd be reckless is hanging onto something that is no longer part of my plan for you. Michele doesn't care about your old identity, and neither do your kids. They love you regardless of what you do for a living."

"But I don't feel ready for my life to take a different direction, Lord."

"I know. I don't need you to be ready. I need you to trust my timing. You have no construction prospects on the horizon, and the situation is already wearing you and Michele down. But I've used her gifts of creativity and problem-solving to spark an idea. Wouldn't it be foolish to resist, at least considering it?"

"Yes, I suppose so."

"I won't promise that this will be easy or that everything will go how you'd like, but I will promise to be with you every step of the way."

It wasn't easy to consider that my life needed to take a different direction. But as I faced the reality of needing to evolve, I realized resilience wouldn't come from sticking to what I knew—it would come from adapting, learning and trusting this fresh path that held potential for growth. Even though it was a leap of faith, I believed that hard work and God's help could build something beyond what we thought possible.

When Michele got home, we did a bunch of research on Visiting Angels and all the other franchises that did home care. We narrowed it down from there, and Visiting Angels stayed toward the top of our list. It looked to be a solid organization with a strong reputation. We also really liked the name. It fit with our faith and felt good to Michele, thinking of being a visiting angel to someone.

Michele called her dad to see what he thought, and he was happy to help us explore the options. Our contact at Visiting Angels headquarters advised us to go look at the franchise in Glendora,

California. Louis agreed to be our liaison in California and schedule a visit to the Glendora location.

When Louis called to make an appointment, the owner, Lindsey, said she was too busy. King Louis showed up anyway and waited in the lobby to talk with her. It was humorous to picture our King Louis being made to wait in a lobby after being denied an appointment. Thankfully, Lindsey did finally talk with him. They got along fabulously. Both were no-nonsense, savvy businesspeople. He called us back and said that if we could run an operation like Lindsey's, it could be great.

This would be an all-in gamble. We would play all our chips on our last bet. Buying a franchise is expensive. Even if we sold off all our heavy equipment and leftover building supplies and gutted the rest of our savings, we'd still barely have enough to afford it. We prayed about it, did more research, prayed again, and pushed our last chips out into the middle of the table to play the game.

No business begins without hiccups, and ours was no exception. One big hiccup was getting our Colorado state health license. We already paid all the money to get the franchise going, but then we had to wait a few months for the license to come. This was nerve-racking because we knew that when first starting a business, you don't make money for yourself right away. You have to pay all the bills first. Then you have to pay the employees. Every month that went by meant even longer until we'd see any income. And did I mention we really needed to earn money?

While waiting for the license, we flew to Pennsylvania, spending money we didn't have to complete the training on how to start and run a home care business. Afterwards, we felt nervous and still had lots of questions, but our instructors assured us we were prepared.

When we got home, the next challenge was finding office space. Fortunately, a good friend allowed us to use a space he had in downtown Pagosa. It was a 10-foot-by-10-foot room, more of a closet than an office, but we were grateful for it. Michele enjoyed joking that she really enjoyed working from my lap, since we both had to share one computer for scheduling, payroll, marketing, and emails.

Finally, the day arrived for our state survey. This was when a health inspector came down from Denver to review everything and test us on our qualifications to run a home care business. As our luck would have it, they didn't send down just some regular inspector. Instead, the head of the health department came down to our rural part of Colorado. No pressure.

Michele and I sat nervously across the table from the head of the health department as she started going through her checklists. Not surprisingly, Michele quickly won her over, and our excitement grew as she checked more and more off her list. Visiting Angels had prepared us well for setting up this business. This was the last step. Almost there. Just stamp the paper and we'll be on our way.

"Just one more question here. In your submission packet, I didn't see any of your credentials as a medical practitioner. Which one of you is the licensed RN?" she asked, smiling back and forth at each of us.

Awkward pause.

Michele and I smiled back at her for a moment, our eyes blinking absently while our brains tried to process the question. We then turned our heads towards each other and sat there staring at one another helplessly. We didn't know one of us had to be a registered nurse to do this business. Either we missed that in reading everything, or it was some new rule.

We chuckled nervously while we scrambled to find something to say, but it was looking like this whole thing was a bust. She'd discovered we were both imposters. It's not like either of us could become an RN overnight.

Was this another worm farm? It sure felt like it. We had no other prospects. The economy was still awful. There weren't any jobs that fed a family of eight with some kids in college, especially in our small mountain town. And every bit of the money we had left was used to buy this franchise.

It felt like all our chips were being swept off the blackjack table and given to the house as we watched the wrong card flip over. What were we going to do now? And how were we going to find care for dear Miss Ada?

It seemed like an hour passed as the chief inspector stared at us expectantly.

"Neither of us is a nurse," Michele finally confessed.

Another awkward pause. Then the inspector's face softened as she tilted her head and smiled at us.

"You know what? It's OK. I really like you," she said as she addressed Michele. "I think even without the RN, you will be excellent at this. Plus, we really need providers in this part of the state."

With that, the inspector stamped the license!

Our mouths fell open. Nobody ever gets a pass from the health department, building department, or IRS. Was this a first? Why didn't I bring Michele to all the hundreds of building inspections I had to endure with my construction business?

The sequence of events had been incredible. We just happened to have an elderly neighbor who needed home care beyond what we could provide. We just happened to hear a radio ad about a home care company for seniors. We just happened to be totally unemployed and desperately needing income. We just happened to have the exact amount of money needed to buy the franchise. We just happened to get an exemption from the chief health inspector, who just happened to feel generous that day.

No way was all that just a random coincidence. Not a chance! After overcoming my shock, my mind returned to my conversation with God, humbling me to tears. Indeed, he was with us every step of the way. This was another blessing—with more to come—that couldn't have come from anything other than God's sovereign work in our lives.

From day one, Michele and I knew we had to succeed in this. Otherwise, we'd be facing the frightening possibility of bankruptcy. We also didn't want to disappoint King Louis, who had given us his vote of confidence.

Michele insisted we do everything the Visiting Angels franchise told us to do, including her reading every bit of material Visiting Angels provided, and me reading every word of what our health license allowed us to do. This involved reviewing our performance daily, weekly, and monthly. Accurate data collection across all measurable business aspects informed our decision-making process. It meant hiring a third-party company to regularly poll our employees and customers to see if we were really delivering the best service possible. It meant always striving for excellence in every aspect of the business. Michele put herself in charge of hiring, which was no small undertaking. She had just spent 25 years homeschooling. She had no connections to a professional network, particularly in home care. How was she going to find caregivers to join our little operation?

With her trademark resourcefulness, she came up with a winning strategy—tapping into the strong network of homeschool moms she had nurtured over the years. She called around and asked if anyone would like a part-time job to care for Miss Ada and maybe some others.

Most of these women didn't have recent professional experience, but homeschool moms have skills! For starters, they're enterprising and industrious. They take initiative every day, writing their own lesson plans, selecting books to study, and making the learning environment successful for their kids.

These weren't idle housewives. They developed a keen sense of ownership over whatever they did. It was for their own kids! And they were extremely comfortable and confident working in a home setting. They were perfect for this business.

LuAnn was one of the first homeschool moms we hired. We couldn't believe she agreed to try it. She was such a good sport to jump in with us, especially because she already had a couple of part-time jobs, and I think she made more money at those than with us. Good thing she and Michele were close friends.

Not surprisingly, Michele was amazing at her roles. She dove into learning all about caring for others in their home. She studied dementia and palliative care and learned how to transfer patients and set up medication reminders. Prospective clients instantly felt loved and at ease when she walked into their home, a skill she possessed naturally.

Our license required us to write up a care plan for each client based on their needs and schedule and keep logs of everything we did in the home. I would not have been the right person to do that or even to check on other people doing that. Michele was perfect for it. This was mostly due to her fastidious ability to follow instructions and manage details. I think the state health department should have issued weekly gold stars for how well she did that kind of thing. The highlight of those early days for Michele was finally having a way to help Miss Ada. Michele was proud to accomplish the goal of seeing Miss Ada get the professional, consistent care she needed. Our kids were a little relieved as well.

I will admit that I wasn't nearly as enthusiastic as Michele in the beginning. To be honest, I had a hard time thinking of it as a proper business; my ego was still struggling to let go. Working from a desk and using a computer were foreign enough, let alone immersing myself in the world of elder care. But I had made a commitment to go all in on this and work my hardest to make it succeed. I was going to have to push through the discomfort of the transition.

With Michele handling personnel, I took on the responsibilities related to marketing and accounting. Visiting Angels corporate taught us that, in the early stages, marketing should focus mainly on speaking directly with hospital staff who work with elderly patients and their families. I spent hours upon hours cold-calling hospitals and clinics to set up meetings with surgeons, physical therapists, hospice care specialists, and discharge nurses—anyone who might come in contact with patients in need of in-home care services.

At first, Michele didn't want to come with me to any of those meetings; she had no interest in that part. So once I had a few lined up, I switched my wardrobe from construction attire—flannel shirts and torn jeans stained with paint and joist glue—to collared shirts and khaki pants (from the thrift store) that made me look like a healthcare professional. With as much confidence as I could muster, I'd waltz into meetings and deliver a well-practiced pitch. I was reasonably successful in my interactions with medical professionals, but I knew Michele was the magic sauce for our company. People would like her right away, no matter the setting. Using shameless flattery, I finally convinced her to come with me to at least some meetings, and it didn't take long to see that was the right move.

Even when hospital staff were skeptical, Michele would quickly win them over. Her best tactic was bringing them homemade pumpkin muffins or banana chipper cookies, which they would devour while she delivered the most heart-warming sales pitch they'd ever heard. Her knees would knock the whole time, but she was so sweet and winsome. People found it very hard to say no to her.

Another part of the marketing plan was advertising. Based on advice from Visiting Angels corporate, I started by wrapping our family car with a full advertising decal. At this time in Pagosa, no other business had done this. It turned out to be a lot more effective than I could've expected.

Michele got her driver's license as a teenager, but it took her four attempts. In her adult life, she was successful in getting where she wanted to go, but often with a few bumps and scratches. More than once, she backed out of the garage and ripped off the side mirror, only to overcompensate while pulling back in and tear off the mirror on the other side. The beautiful, blue angel car wrap drew attention all on its own, but with Michele behind the wheel, it was impossible to miss. People can't help but notice your ad when you swerve in front of them or stop suddenly for no reason, or veer off the road a little now and then. But, hey, all publicity is good publicity, right?

With marketing and advertising generating interest, the next hurdle was turning an interested party into a paying client. But here's where the blurred line between home care and healthcare became a challenge for us.

In-home care provides assistance with the activities of daily living; it's not considered "medical" care. Still, when we met with a prospective client to discuss their needs, they inevitably told us about all their health issues. We were so far out of our depth in this area, it was comical. Michele and I would look at each other and try not to laugh, as they would mention another medical acronym we had no clue about. I mean, we didn't even know what the words meant.

Thankfully, LuAnn had experience earlier in life as a medical assistant, so she was more comfortable with the terminology. She helped cover for our inexperience in those early days. And Michele wasted no time getting up to speed. She would write down every unfamiliar term during each visit so she could Google it later to learn what it meant. She would then read all about it and develop a home care plan that accommodated the specific needs of someone with that health condition.

We also got a lot of help from Visiting Angels' headquarters. So many times, we'd call them up and ask what to do. They patiently held our hands as our confidence gradually grew. Some people think we were courageous to start a new business we knew nothing about, but with a franchise, it doesn't take as much courage as you'd think. Being backed by a corporation allowed us to get up and go far faster than we ever could have done by ourselves. We experienced tremendous growth rapidly.

When we bought our franchise, we bought a territory that was protected and dedicated to us. No other Visiting Angels could operate in our territory. A typical territory had a population of 200,000+ people, but our territory was rural. A rural territory is one with only 100,000. And by operating out of our little Pagosa Springs, we weren't even reaching 25% of our territory. We realized that in order for the business to be viable, we needed to expand beyond our small town. Pagosa just wasn't enough of a market.

After only a few months in business, I told Michele we had to expand to Durango somehow. Durango is our "big city" neighbor. It is four times the size of Pagosa. Businesses from Durango might expand to little Pagosa if they thought it might be worth a morsel of growth, but players in Pagosa rarely attempted to expand into Durango.

Michele was skeptical about expanding; she didn't see how we could do that while living an hour's drive away. And she was right; the only way we could swing it would be to hire more help. The problem was that money was still tight. We had only just started paying Michele a very modest salary, and I still had received no pay yet. But we had enough to buy groceries now, and we really needed to grow the business, so we ended up hiring someone new to help us branch out into Durango.

Michele wasn't willing to grow the business if it meant sacrificing quality care, though. She believed that not only was it the right thing to do for our clients, but it was great for business. And once again, her intuition was spot on. We decided that excellence would be our driving force and primary core value.

Soon, this culture of excellence started catching on, especially for how Michele supported the staff. Her greatest love was giving encouragement to others, but she didn't just gush it out without merit or genuine kindness. She had an acute sense of what people needed and when they needed it.

For example, when she gave a card to someone, which she did often, she squeezed her own words into the card's printed message. They were beautiful and sweet embellishments, thoughtful and fitting just for that person. She had a whole cupboard full of cards for every occasion, so she would always be ready.

I'm convinced our Visiting Angels would not have become the success it is without this company culture Michele created. Employees felt supported and cherished, which spilled over into the care they provided our clients. The company challenged employees to do excellent work and provided a clear mission.

As our reputation for quality in-home care spread, our business exploded. A few months after opening in Durango, I started receiving a paycheck myself. At the Visiting Angels national conference the following year, we received the award for the fastest-growing new franchise in the country.

This growth required ramping up our hiring and training processes to get more caregivers out into the field quickly. Michele took the lead in training and discovered she loved it. It was a lot like teaching, so all those homeschooling years came in handy.

In the beginning, we had a hard time rejecting anyone who applied to work for us because we thought, with our training, anyone could be a good caregiver. Quickly, we realized our perspective was incorrect. We came to understand that our priority had to be our clients. They and their families were paying us to find a safe, skilled, and reliable caregiver. It didn't really matter that we found it unpleasant to turn away candidates and disappoint someone who wanted a job. Clients were relying on us to find only the very best.

Over time, Michele and I got much better at being selective. One way we did this was by drug testing. Before then, we were both naïve enough to think that only people with a criminal record or those living on the streets did drugs, and that those individuals would never even consider applying for a job with us. But Visiting Angels corporate advised us to do drug testing, so we followed their guidance, and boy, did we learn quickly how common drug use is.

On that first day of surprise drug testing, we had four trainees, and they all seemed viable and ready to work. Just before she started the training session, Michele announced we would do a drug test first. Two ladies stood up and immediately walked out, never to be seen again. One other person failed the drug test. Only one out of four passed!

From then on, we would test every job candidate before they attended Michele's training. It was part of refining our hiring process so we could continue pursuing excellence for all aspects of the business.

With better and better hiring practices, Michele turned her full attention to the training program. Visiting Angels provided a franchise operations manual that contained all the training material for our caregivers, but Michele wanted to take it to the next level. The manual outlined The Basic 12, which were the primary rules caregivers needed to follow in their work. For example, communication was one of The Basic 12. Employees needed to answer their phone when their employer called.

Michele made sure there was nothing "basic" about The Basic 12. In the PowerPoint presentation, she added clip art of a little kitten or a bell ringing to help people remember a specific point. I hardly remember The Basic 12 myself, but I remember the kittens and bells.

She didn't stop with fun embellishments, though. Michele continued to add substantive material over the years. When we started the franchise, new employees went through about three to four hours of classroom training. Employees now attend two full days of classroom training, then go out and shadow experienced caregivers for two more days before taking their first shift. They also have follow-up trainings throughout the year to learn even more skills and become highly trained Care Specialists.

One of the specialized trainings the Visiting Angels headquarters developed was a simple presentation on Palliative Care. Michele noted that this aspect of care really needed some formal training material, so she took what headquarters provided and jazzed it up to be more robust and effective. As soon as she started using it, she saw tremendous confidence develop in our caregivers. They now had actionable tactics for helping those with chronic conditions or who were developing additional health issues but didn't have family who could identify that something was causing pain or distress.

Around that time, the Visiting Angels franchise hired a young lady who started a program where franchises could enter a competition with their best business practice. The winner would then present it to all the other franchises at the national convention. Michele hates the limelight, but she couldn't help entering her enhanced palliative care training program to show how it was helping our caregivers and clients. She won the Best Practice Competition that year and then had to present it to the national organization. She practiced and practiced, but for her, this was just like school, so she aced it. Her PowerPoint was perfect. She was lively, fun to listen to, and at ease in front of hundreds of people. What could go wrong?

Well, me, apparently. My job during her presentation was to manage the PowerPoint slides. She wanted to focus on her presentation and not have to worry about the computer part. We had a signal worked out where she would nod, and I would advance to the next slide. Simple enough.

I wasn't too embarrassed when, in front of hundreds, she gave me a little reprimand for not keeping up with her. But after the second or third time, she asked if I could just give the remote to LuAnn, who now had a job as Michele's assistant. Then, I might have been a little embarrassed.

Afterward, she claimed I wasn't paying attention; I say she was more nervous than she would admit and wasn't giving me that exact nod we agreed on. Either way, I maintain I did her a favor. Even now, after many years, the part of her presentation that endeared her to the audience was our cute little argument over the remote.

A few months after we opened in Durango, the Southern Ute Indian Tribe called us. The gentleman said his name was Tom and that he'd like to talk with me about Visiting Angels. We knew about the Southern Ute Indian Tribe, which was between Pagosa Springs and Durango, but had never considered it as an area that needed home care services.

At the time of Tom's call, we had been doing Visiting Angels for only five months. We were still feeling very much like imposters in the home care space. We had a decent hiring process and a solid training program developing, and we knew how to get a client started with in-home care, but I still felt like we barely knew what we were doing.

But I didn't see any harm in talking to Tom, so I drove out to Ignacio, where the tribal headquarters were. I had never spent any time in their town, and I didn't know quite what to expect. They had their own health clinic, tribal museum, and heritage center. Their schools and government centers were impressive modern facilities. Their town pleasantly surprised me.

Someone escorted me up the stairs to a very professional board meeting room when I arrived. I thought I was meeting with just Tom, maybe in his office. When I entered the room, there were six other people. They introduced themselves as the director of tribal health, the chief medical officer, the long-term care director, the tribal CEO, and the top leader of all of it—the chief of the Tribe! They started by asking me a few questions about my experience, and I told them the truth. We were very new to this. I also emphasized to them that my franchise was one of the best and largest in the country and that I was committed to making this work and learning whatever was necessary to meet their community's needs.

They told me they had tried the only other provider in the region, but that provider found the Tribe too difficult and too far away to service. Then they cut right to the chase and asked me if we could provide all the long-term care for their tribal elders.

For a moment, I hesitated.

If the home-care company before me couldn't do it, maybe I can't either, I thought.

But I couldn't say that. I couldn't convey a lack of confidence.

Maybe I should ask for some time to think about it.

I grew worried they would realize I was stalling and change their minds.

The answer is yes, Chris, say yes. Stop overthinking it. You have a big client basically throwing themselves at you. Just say yes already!

"Of course!" I said like I wasn't scared.

"OK, great! We can start out with one or two of our elders and slowly work in the others," someone said.

"Oh, that would be perfect," I replied, not any less scared.

"We look forward to getting started," someone else said.

It was that simple. The meeting didn't last long, and I didn't have time to think much about the challenges we would inevitably face. I was just excited about this opportunity and grateful they reached out.

When I told Michele about the meeting, she was equally excited, if not more so. I started checking out all the books on the Southern Ute Indian Tribe I could get my hands on, and we dove into reading them. I collected books on many other Native American tribes, as well. We really wanted this to work. I wanted to know these people as well as I could and understand their culture. We were dedicated to serving their elders, regardless of distance or cultural differences.

Reading about the Tribe wasn't the same as actually working with them, though. It was quickly evident that we were providing care for people who had a much different background from our own. Even though they lived just one town over, the Tribe had traditions, rules, and a history that made its people unique. Their experiences made it difficult for them to trust outsiders, which presented challenges for providing a service as intimate as in-home care.

We were already accustomed to working in someone else's home. We already understood that a person's home is where they let down their guard, where they kick off their shoes and relax, where they share meals with relatives, even where they yell at their kids or their spouse. It is a private and safe castle. We were the intruders.

When a client realizes they'll have a stranger staying in their house all day and sometimes all night, it is very uncomfortable, sometimes even threatening. Their home is no longer the private place where they can let down their guard. It's a daily reminder to them that things aren't going great in their lives. People only need home care when they can't feed themselves, or drive, or keep their house clean, or remember to do all the things they need to stay safe and healthy.

Our clients are sometimes lonely and scared, but also often ill, weak, or in pain, so they are mentally, emotionally, and physically stressed. They have to humble themselves to allow their caregiver to see their real life. They have to adjust to someone helping them, often with things that are quite personal, like bathing or going to the bathroom. There is no more privacy for them. It's a very vulnerable position to be in.

And it's not easy for the caregiver either. No matter how confident and experienced they are, it is always awkward to arrive at someone's home for the first time and take charge of their household—the schedule, the meals, the cleaning, the medications, etc. It's difficult to deal with the forgetfulness, the grumpiness, the stubbornness, the messiness, and the downright meanness of people who are no longer the best version of themselves.

With the Tribe, many of these difficulties were stronger than usual. Added to the mix were the differences in values, traditions, and customs. Michele's usual method of showering people with care, compassion, and companionship did not win over tribal families as quickly and easily as she was used to. The challenge was undeniable, but Michele and I were determined to rise to it.

We saw this as a door God was opening for us to be His servants to a community that was very isolated and historically oppressed. Here we had a group of people who lived just a short drive from our town who wanted us to come tend to the needs of their elders.

How often does an opportunity like that come? We felt like we were acting like missionaries. We couldn't have been more thrilled by the challenge.

Being missionaries was something Michele and I both gave up on in college. We went in with high ideals, but neither of us felt the draw to stay with it. One big issue we both had was the fact that we'd need to raise money for all our financial needs for the rest of our lives. Michele's parents supported other missionaries, but she felt strongly that she should pay her own way and not depend on others for a living.

For me, it was more about proving myself capable of producing an income. I was extremely poor when I left my parents' house, and the hardship of that stuck with me. My stepfather was in ministry work, and it was a struggle for him financially. I didn't want the same for myself.

But the main reason for us not pursuing missionary work was the pull of Michele's family. This was true for me as much as for her. I knew how rare and precious it was. I couldn't imagine us ever setting that aside to live and work overseas.

There was always a tug on our hearts for people who didn't know Jesus. The stories of well-known missionaries intrigued us, and we read them to our kids at the dinner table—stories like Bruchko and Peace Child. We also collected every movie of missionary stories we could find—movies like Inn of the Sixth Happiness and End of the Spear. Our family's heroes were missionaries like Brother Andrew, Don Richardson, Richard Wurmbrand, and Jonathan and Sarah Edwards. What adventures these people had!

We supported modern missionaries from our own community. We served on our church's missions committee. Our close missionary friends were wonderful to hear from. We even built a large studio apartment above our garage for missionaries to come furlough with us or just enjoy a stay in the mountains. Many have used it.

Our work with the Southern Ute Indian Tribe rejuvenated this passion for missions. Many of them didn't have a relationship with Christ, so we took a missionary approach to their care. We prayed that caring for their physical needs would open the door to spiritual conversations.

One of our first Ute clients was a lovely lady who suffered a serious injury and was immobile. She was bedbound or in a wheelchair. Michele pulled out all the stops to give this woman everything she needed 24/7. It takes a lot of work to figure out everything that is needed for a client at this level of care, but Michele did.

This client had various family members living with her and coming in and out of her house, which was a little difficult for our caregivers to navigate, but the real dilemma was her husband. Shortly after we began caring for this lady, he moved back in after getting out of jail. He had served his time for violent offenses and had recently been released from prison.

His behavior made our caregivers feel uncomfortable being in the same house as him all night. He would cuss them out and threaten them. This house was in a very rural area; the only neighbors were a good distance away. Cell service wasn't reliable either. We couldn't expect our employees to do their jobs if they didn't feel safe. We emailed and called the house several times to request that he stop intimidating our caregivers, but nothing worked. Finally, we set up an in-person meeting. Perhaps it would be more effective than emails or phone messages. Michele was planning to sit down with this client and her husband, but after all that had transpired, she was understandably apprehensive about interacting with the husband. She asked me to join her, which I agreed to do, but honestly, I was scared too.

Still, I knew I had to go.

I wasn't about to let Michele be scared or get hurt trying to help this client and our employees. I was ready to take one for the team. That said, we took the precaution of notifying the police that we were going to this house and may need help if they didn't hear from us in an hour. Our drive to the house was long and quiet, taking us past herds of deer and elk emerging in the evening twilight. The scenery was much more serene than we were. We pulled up to the house, said a prayer, and walked apprehensively up the wheelchair ramp to the door.

The husband didn't give us any greeting when he opened the door; he just let us in, then went and sat down. We sat down after him, Michele and I on one side of the table and our client and her husband on the other. He had very dark brown eyes, a long braid, and was wearing a headband and a white tank top. Clearly, he seemed prepared for this meeting. Prepared to beat our brains in, we thought. I don't remember ever being that scared before in my life.

I gulped and held my breath. I'm sure the fear was visible on my face. Michele must have been afraid, too, but she didn't show it. She seemed brave. After waiting a few moments for some simple, hospitable greeting that would never come, Michele began gently explaining why we needed to have his understanding and cooperation in keeping our employees safe. No one else said anything while she talked. I'm sure she was nervous and uncomfortable, but she handled it like a pro. I stared at her the whole time she spoke, so I wouldn't have to look at him. His stare made me feel like he was about to jump across the table. After Michele finished speaking, we just sat there silently for a long, awkward moment. I was attempting to steel myself for whatever blow was about to come at us.

"When you first came into my house, all I wanted to do was grab your throat in my hands and strangle you guys, but after listening to you and thinking about my wife's needs, I respect you, and I will look after your employees' safety from now on," he said, breaking the silence.

Michele and I remained frozen, trying to process the words "strangle" and "respect" in the same sentence. Well, that was probably about as good a response as we were going to get. Our sighs of relief were audible. We then followed them up with the most nervous, awkward laugh of our lives. I'm not saying we became best friends with this guy after that, but he was a man of his word, and we never had problems with him again.

One of Michele's most dear clients in the Tribe was a much-venerated elder who was very resistant to having other people in her home, especially white people. Frequently, she scolded Michele and our caregivers for some minor perceived offense, which we attributed simply to Michele being white. We concluded this because she said as much. This woman had been forced from her home as a child to attend the missionary school. The missionaries of that time forced the Tribe to give up their language and culture. Understandably, this woman was very bitter toward anyone who resembled those missionaries.

But God had a plan to give this lady a different experience with his church. By His grace, Michele came at the end of this lady's life and showed her the love of Jesus authentically. Michele didn't pile on insensitive or unjust expectations, and she didn't pressure her to abandon her cultural identity. She just showed her kindness, compassion, gentleness, and patience.

The lady ended up giving her life to Christ just weeks before she died. Incredible! I groan at all the fruitless work of misguided missionaries who completely undermined their own efforts because they lost sight of what Christ's love looks like!

For many years, Michele managed these kinds of cases herself, but this wasn't sustainable. After a while, she asked the Tribe if there was some kind of cross-cultural training our employees could participate in so we wouldn't unnecessarily offend any clients and damage the relationship we were building. They happily put a program together, and our caregivers started attending the culture training before working with tribal clients.

The cross-cultural training helped quite a bit, but we still had clients here and there who challenged us and our staff. One gentleman was probably the hardest case we had with the Tribe. He was not that old, but he had lived a very hard life. He was frail and dying of alcohol poisoning. The biggest problem was that he was very inappropriate toward our female caregivers (most of our caregivers were women). From day one, he would make crude remarks and request offensive favors. If he got a caregiver who didn't put up with his behavior, he would call the office and ask for them to be fired. He would then demand another "Fallen Angel," as he called it. Fortunately, he could not physically act on his words, but it was unacceptable. He made the working environment stressful and unsafe for every single employee we put on his case. And we put more on his case than any other. Eventually, we had over seventy-five employees refuse to return to his house.

He was married, but this only made the situation worse. His wife didn't live with him, but she would come by now and then. When she was around, she abused our caregivers, too. If our caregiver was confidently handling her client, his wife would feel challenged by her and kick them out of the house because she was jealous. This meant that our client would go without taking his medications and not get any food. It was a desperate situation. It was such a dark, oppressive place.

Michele and I went to visit him countless times to persuade him to stop behaving as he did with our caregivers. Much to my relief, when Michele visited him, he did not mistreat her. He seemed to respect Michele's sincere desire to help him and knew he needed her help.

After a visit from Michele, he would change his behavior for a few days, or, if we were lucky, a few weeks. But eventually, he would return to his old ways, and we'd have to draw up a new behavior agreement.

For two years, Michele and LuAnn worked tirelessly to staff this case, usually with a new employee, knowing it was going to be awful for her. They knew that after a day or two of harassment, threats, or being kicked out, our caregiver would be too scared to return or would quit. It was a situation we were no longer willing to subject our staff to, so we needed to come up with a solution quickly. Once again, Michele's creativity, compassion, and intuition came to our rescue.

Michele loved to celebrate holidays and birthdays more than anyone I ever knew. This went for employees and Visiting Angels' clients as well. Everyone always got a card and a gift of some kind. For Michele, this was not a chore or task to check off; it was with joy that she got to do this.

When this challenging client's birthday rolled around, Michele wanted to surprise him with a party, so she asked him to come to the office. I don't think he had any clue what she was up to. She and LuAnn decorated the office with balloons and streamers, making it look really festive.

When he walked in with his latest caregiver, all of us yelled, "Happy birthday!" We got him so good! The surprise completely overwhelmed him. He began crying tears of joy. We then presented him with a cake with his name on it. I think cake was the only food he liked. He smiled with delight as he took his first bite. I had never seen him happy like that. I had never even seen him content or slightly happy. He never gave out compliments. If he joked, it was at someone else's expense. But at this party, his countenance totally changed. He told us with sincerity that this was the best day of his entire life. He said no one ever threw him a birthday party. It was the first birthday party in his life. This man, who didn't like white people, was miserable from his disease, and only wanted to objectify women, was now smiling at all of us with sincere joy. I believe Michele, with her intuitive love for people, made him feel valued and celebrated for the first time in his life. For Michele, this was a simple birthday party that took little effort. For him, he said it was the best day of his life.

When he died a few weeks later, we all felt peace in knowing we had accomplished getting at least a hint of Christ's love through to one of the most spiritually lost people we had ever known.

After several years of successfully providing care for the Tribe, we had a client who so disliked Visiting Angels being in her home that she tried to use her influence as a tribal elder to get rid of us. Michele, LuAnn, I, and another manager all had meetings with her to address her concerns, but it was clear her distress came more from her predicament than from us. Besides other health concerns, she was a diabetic who had to have her foot amputated. She was also upset about no longer being able to help her children and grandchildren. Visiting Angels was simply an easy target for all her angst. Being a tribal elder, she had easy access to the tribal council and the Executive Officer, which she used to press her complaints. More than once, she wrote letters to the editor of the local newspaper disparaging our caregivers and company. Although unfounded, this negative publicity threatened our business, despite the satisfaction of all our other clients. As we feared, her campaign against us eventually had its desired effect: The Tribe requested bids from other companies for all its in-home care. The tribal leaders felt pressure to take some kind of action.

The news deeply hurt Michele and me. We remained committed to serving the Tribe when no other care provider would. Hiring and training caregivers to meet the specific needs of tribal elders consumed countless hours of our time. We spent a considerable amount of extra time and money doing additional things for the Tribe's clients, who were especially demanding. And when we lost employees because of ill-treatment from clients, we had to scramble to find new caregivers who were willing to give it a shot.

It was especially hurtful to Michele. She had been unflagging in her effort to care for the challenging clients. She was insistent we could always find a way to succeed with these difficult situations that needed real hands-on care and Jesus' love.

For many years, our resolve was at the expense of our employees and our business. We were worn down from hiring literally hundreds of employees who were arbitrarily tossed out of homes and found different work. Those 400 well-meaning caregivers who needed a job, went through training, and really wanted to succeed at caregiving were summarily discarded. Clients often injured caregivers who remained, emotionally if not physically. Those who made it for any length of time were truly extraordinary souls.

Plus, the Tribe now accounted for about 40 percent of our total business. If we were to lose it, we would have to restructure our entire business. We would have to lay off many employees, not only caregivers but also managers and administrative staff.

As the one in charge of our finances, I immediately started calculating how we could cut costs. I considered lowering the prices of our services to just cover our costs so we could survive with the fewest number of layoffs. I thought maybe this would buy us some time to come up with a long-term solution.

But harder than any of that was knowing we could lose the relationships we worked so hard to build. We believed God had given us this unique opportunity to minister to the Tribe, and that we had effectively become missionaries in our own backyard. We also believed that God's work with the Tribe was far from done and that he still wanted to use us as part of his plan there.

We decided we wouldn't go down without a fight, so I drew up a very comprehensive and professional bid. Because we had been working closely with the Tribe for the previous six years, I knew exactly what I needed to address in the bid. I also made sure my bid was the first one they received. I had a lot of experience from my construction years in preparing and submitting a competitive bid. We were also the only ones to submit a bid before the deadline. Surely all this meant we would win the contract.

We didn't. We felt devastated.

The company they chose was our new competitor. We saw this competitor at various health conferences and in the community, and in the beginning, we got along just fine. They had been civil initially, but over time, they began actively trying to hire our employees out from under us. This is not an ethical practice, and in some cases, it's illegal.

We sent a few stern letters to this new provider to stop soliciting our employees, but I'm not sure it deterred them much. It seemed they didn't have any qualms about walking into homes and taking all our well-trained, experienced employees. We felt like we had done everything we could to be professional and provide the best care possible, and now it was being stripped away.

Even though we lost the bid, we still had to cooperate with a plan to transition all the care we provided over to the new company and their caregivers. It was going to take a couple of months to do this, and it was going to be very disruptive for the clients. They were all going to have to adjust to a new caregiver in their home. We made every effort to professionally cooperate in all of this, but there was only so much we could do to minimize the disruption.

After a little over a month, we noticed we weren't really losing many clients yet. Unsure what that meant, we asked the Tribe what was happening in this transition period, but we didn't get a response for quite some time. Finally, we were called in for a meeting with tribal leaders. They told us the people in the community were all rising up in protest of switching from Visiting Angels to this other company. The few that had transitioned were very unhappy with the poor quality of care from the new provider. They all wanted their Angels back!

The tribal officials humbly asked if we would come back. They discarded our previous bid and asked us to name our price to sustain care for their elders indefinitely. This was music to our ears! For all the previous years, we had been offering a discounted rate to the Tribe to ensure we wouldn't lose them. But delivering care to them was far more expensive than it was for any other client due to all the extra training and troubleshooting required and the enormous turnover of staff.

We reset our price to reflect all of this, asked for overtime pay when needed (we had been paying out of pocket for overtime), and charged mileage to travel to some of the more remote clients. The Tribe readily agreed to all our terms. There was simply no denying that their people loved our Angels. In fact, they even sang our praises in their local newspaper, unraveling the earlier bad press.

There is no doubt in my mind that we prevailed in this situation because of the culture of excellence we worked so hard to establish. Our hard work, dedication, and deep resolve to show Jesus' love saved the day.

Having stability in the business again took a tremendous weight off our shoulders. And we were going to need that more than we knew. Our family was in for its biggest challenge yet.

CHAPTER 8:

The Weight of a Son

Michele's perspective on what was beautiful in life and how to live well always instructed and delighted me. She wasn't afraid to pursue her dreams, and she was resilient in the face of difficulty. I trusted her completely; if she believed it was time for our next adventure, I would dive into it with her.

I think that's the main reason I went along with the idea to start having kids when she sprang it on me that snowy February evening. I didn't think I was anywhere close to being ready to be a father, but like I said, God's timing and Michele's intuition never led me astray. Pregnancy for Michele wasn't without its challenges. Michele had awful morning sickness for the full nine months. She got an extra layer of awfulness because this was when we were living and working at Angeles Crest Christian Camp with that winding mountain road. I had nothing to complain about, though. The only thing I had to put up with was sitting in the driver's seat, resting my eyes at a turnout along the highway. She bore the experience so well. She took good care of herself and got through all the difficulties of pregnancy like a champ.

On November 24, 1986, Michele gave birth to our first child, Keagan Christopher. Michele's preparedness for motherhood astonished me. She took to all the feeding, changing, and strange noises and faces this child made like a savant. I felt like I witnessed an absolute miracle when Keagan was born. Becoming a father for the first time was the most profound experience of my life. I instantly fell in love with Keagan, making it easy to put aside any worries about being too young or inexperienced. I couldn't get enough of being his dad. It overwhelmed my heart with love for another human being like nothing ever before or since.

Michele's intentionality in becoming a parent was so helpful to our family's success in those early years. As a young mother, she was full of energy and eager to learn everything she could. She studied all kinds of books on babies and how to raise them. She learned every step of child development and was ready when the time came.

When Keagan was just a few months old, she knew to have blanket time, so he would learn to hold his head up correctly. When he began moving around, she made sure we childproofed everything. When he was playing, she would stay ahead of him by giving him a different toy and putting away the previous one.

This is where the family motto of "quit while you're having fun" got its start. Michele always stayed ahead of the kids' activities so they wouldn't get bored or cranky or mischievous. If a child was contentedly engaged in something, it was almost time to change it. She didn't fix things that weren't broken, but Michele's intuition told her when a good time was about to end.

This skill was most evident when we were at Grandma's house or visiting friends. We aimed to be the first ones to leave, so it wouldn't be our kids who fell apart. I was so grateful that I could follow Michele's lead on things like this. Her instinct for parenthood and her deep, selfless love for our family made it so much easier for me to transition into fatherhood. Her unwavering faith in me gave me the confidence to overcome my fears and focus on loving our kids more than I ever imagined was possible.

Keagan fit right into our lifestyle from the day he was born. He was a mountain cub as much as he was a boy. I took him everywhere I could while working around camp in the middle of the Angeles National Forest. When he was young, you could find him on my back, or shoulders, or in my arms.

One time, he and I were taking the little, secret, back trail to the dining hall from our house. The light was quickly fading as the sun set, making for a comfortable, relaxing short walk to dinner. Keagan was riding up on my shoulders, and I was telling the story from his baby book, *We're Going on a Bear Hunt*, and acting out the pictures. "Can't go over it, can't go around it…must go through it." I had that book memorized. My head was down as I focused on the trail, and I wasn't able to lift my head to look ahead very well.

Suddenly, in a quiet part of the story, Keagan blurted out, "Bear!" and pointed his little finger straight ahead. He wasn't much older than one and had said nothing other than "Dadda," so I was excited to hear his new word.

Then, in the following instant, it dawned on me that he might not just be repeating a word from the story. After all, we were in a remote area of the mountains at dusk. We had bears all the time at camp. I stopped dead in my tracks and looked up as best I could. There was a full-grown bear on the trail just yards in front of us. It had stopped walking also and was staring back at us. It's hard to say who was more frozen, me or the bear. Keagan remained completely silent, almost instinctively. If it had been a momma bear with cubs, it would've been my role to back away, give her the trail. But I was the daddy bear with the cub, and the bear seemed to realize that.

He dropped his head and turned into the thick manzanita bushes, giving us leave to continue on our way.

Mountain living continued to shape Keagan as he grew up in a cabin in the woods surrounded by camp friends, trees to climb, and ropes to swing on every day. All the strange and seemingly otherworldly aspects of mountain life left an impression on him. For instance, there was a hermit named Dennis who lived out in the woods somewhere fairly close by, and he would come into camp occasionally for some company. Sometimes he would do odd jobs to earn a little cash, but he lived off the land, eating squirrels and lizards and plants. Each year, the government allotted the camp surplus food, such as #10 cans of peanut butter, 40-pound blocks of cheddar cheese, tuna, and flour. We would give Dennis a can or two sometimes.

Dennis was always respectful and kind, but mysterious. He never revealed where he lived, but we never felt threatened by him. He was a Vietnam veteran and was just more comfortable living on his own in the woods, away from society. Keagan was so intrigued by Dennis. Dennis taught him how to make a snare out of long grass to catch lizards. Keagan would then teach campers this amazing skill. Even decades later, people still remember him for this.

Keagan also learned to be a little mischievous at camp. The camp staff gave him a lot of attention and helped him form a few strange habits. In fact, as more of his cousins were born, describing his behavior as mischievous toward them would be a little too kind.

When Keagan was a toddler, he would walk up to a cousin and just knock them over for no apparent reason. He would do this at the church preschool, also, and sometimes in public to a random fellow toddler, if he felt like it. We didn't know what got into him! It's like he was curious to see what happened when he shoved someone.

His cousin Meagan, so kind and sweet (and still completely is), didn't take offense at this behavior. Clancy didn't get it either but just stayed out of Keagan's way as much as possible. Later, even though Clancy found his courage and matched him in size, he maintained his vigilance when playing with Keagan.

One time during a season when the kids were studying Roman history, Keagan appointed himself as Nero and deemed everyone else his slaves. Reilly, one of Minette's daughters, said he secretly told her he wouldn't torture her too badly, only the others. He was so good at the role, and everyone kept in line. But before you think he was the only tyrannical cousin, as soon as Keagan was tired of being a despot and wandering off, the next oldest kid in line would announce their succession.

Outside of trying to steer Keagan away from his bully-like tendencies, he was a joy to raise. Michele, Keagan, and I journeyed through life together as a trio, at least for quite a few years. We were young when he was born, and he went through everything with us.

He was also such a big help to the family. After Michele gave birth to Sully, our youngest, there were several months when Sully was very sick, and Keagan was right by Michele's side, fetching anything she or Sully needed. When we built our custom home in Pagosa Springs, Keagan did the most work of all the kids by far. Though he enjoyed his return to mountain life after five city years, he found making friends in the new town somewhat difficult. He felt unaccepted as the new kid, but as his dad, I could tell his peers thought he was cool. He paved the way for his five siblings, so when they went to Pagosa High School, they were automatically cool because they were Keagan's brothers and sisters.

But as with any child, there were several challenges in raising Keagan. None of these ever diminished our love for him, but some scared the hell out of us, and others brought us heartache. One such instance was when Keagan was just out of high school. He was dating a beautiful girl named Tamara. The two of them were hanging out with some friends at a gas station in town, late Saturday night, when an older guy from out of town approached Keagan and picked a fight with him.

Maybe Keagan wanted to show off in front of his girlfriend or whatever, but at one point, he felt he needed to hit this guy and ended up knocking him out cold with one punch. Someone called an ambulance, and they took the unconscious guy away. Keagan's friends thought it might be good for him to leave before the police came, so he left.

News quickly spread that a guy from out of town got into a fight, was taken to the hospital, and died that evening. Keagan came to me and Michele with this terrifying news. We made some inquiries, and it seemed Keagan could face manslaughter or murder charges.

Michele and I were in such anguish as to what to do. Should we help him, hide him, or wait it out? We didn't know if we should call the hospital, the police, or no one at all. We took Keagan to a lawyer nearby in Durango. He agreed to do an investigation to find out if there would be criminal charges.

After three agonizing days, the lawyer told us a young man had died that night after being involved in an altercation at a gas station, but it was a different person at a different gas station. The guy Keagan punched received treatment for a concussion and was discharged. The mother of that young man asked Keagan to pay for the hospital bill, but at least Keagan stayed out of jail! Now, after all these years, the incident seems so small, but at the time, we thought our son might spend the rest of his life behind bars! We thought our lives would be over.

Thankfully, this kind of thing wasn't a regular occurrence with Keagan. During his high school years, I think he kept out of a lot of trouble working alongside me when he wasn't in school. He gained useful experience doing construction work and was very good at the hustle on a construction site. He had an artistic bent, too, and loved doing creative carpentry and metalwork as well. His biggest strength was crafting woodwork and metalwork, such as custom bumpers for his and other people's trucks, art for a friend's new store, or custom post bases for our porch.

In one home he worked on, he created a custom art balustrade for a sweeping, curving balcony above the great room. Using sheet metal, he cut out plant and animal shapes—moose, elk, cat tails, pine and aspen trees, bears, and foxes. As artistic as it was, he skillfully kept it all to code for safety. When the owner came in to see it, she burst out crying because she couldn't believe how beautiful it was.

The last home Keagan worked on was a custom home near Durango. The entry to the home had a lot of extra space, too much for a foyer, but not enough for another room. They asked Keagan's boss, Darin, to come up with something creative and unique for that space.

By this time, Darin had gained a lot of confidence in Keagan's work, so he gave him free rein to unleash his creativity. Keagan came up with a design for a center-pole-supported spiral staircase with railings of metal made to look like oversized barbed wire. This led up to an open loft overlooking the entryway. In the loft, he placed an old, open-air horse-drawn carriage and surrounded it with a small library and some additional seating. The owners just loved Keagan's work, and the house won the local home show that year.

Years after all our children were born, Michele needed to have a hysterectomy. She had developed severe fibroids that were painful and causing complications. It took some effort to get our insurance to cover the procedure, but once it did, we quickly scheduled the surgery, and it went very well. We were both so relieved to finally get her the help she had been waiting for.

As Michele lay recovering in the hospital room in Durango, Keagan dropped by after work to pay us a visit. Keagan was living in Durango, working construction, and dating Cheyenne, who was a student at Fort Lewis College. He had finished junior college and decided to just get on with working on the things he liked to do. He was making his way on his own as an adult.

We were so glad to see Keagan that day. He went right to Michele and hugged her and said how happy he was that the procedure was successful. I was relaxing in the reclining chair beside Michele, but Keagan never sat down. He just paced around the room as we talked about what he was building at work and about how things were going with Cheyenne. He waited for a pause in the conversation and finally made an announcement.

He was going to have a baby!

"Oh, no, no, no," I said to myself quietly. Michele blurted out the same words, only much louder.

Having children out of wedlock felt like the cardinal sin for my Christian homeschool family. A big part of the reason we homeschooled our children was so we could influence them more than society did when it came to these major pitfalls in life. I was an elder in our church, and Michele and I taught marriage classes and child-raising classes there. Keagan's announcement made us feel like total hypocrites. We were certain this huge failure in our parenting would cause our spiritual FICO scores to plummet. How were we going to show our faces at church again?

Keagan respected us and knew this would be a heavy blow. He did his best to admit his failure and take seriously the reality of becoming a father. He'd been telling us he wanted to marry Cheyenne, whom he truly loved. He also didn't expect us to feel sorry for him or fix anything. Excited and ready, he planned to take responsibility and start a family.

After he left the room, I looked at Michele for a long moment. She was crying, and I felt like I might join her. I didn't know what to do. We'd just gotten her healthy, and then, suddenly, another crisis hit. I turned away, saying nothing, but my mind was in turmoil.

We sincerely wanted to live for God. We went to Bible college, worked in the camping ministry for 10 years, taught our kids the Bible at home their whole lives, and were very involved in our church. By all accounts, we did the "right" things—the things that mean life should go our way. The things that are supposed to protect our kids from obvious, careless mistakes like this. This wasn't supposed to happen to us.

Then an epiphany struck me.

It was never supposed to be about life going our way. The way we lived our lives and raised our children was about loving Jesus and obediently following Him, not about getting rewarded for being "good" Christians and having everybody look up to us because of how great we were doing.

Our kids were growing up, going out into the real world, making their own choices, and experiencing real consequences. We had to learn how to operate in such a paradigm, one in which we didn't have complete control (we never really did anyway). We had to trust that God would see our children through whatever happened in their lives, just as He always saw us through.

The choices they made didn't mean we were "bad" parents or that our kids were "bad" Christians; it meant they were human. They were sinful and broken, just like all of us. The fallout of their "mistakes" seemed so much more like an opportunity for Jesus to pull them in close and show them how much He loved them.

This revelation didn't take away all my worry for Keagan or for us, but it helped me realize what I was supposed to do—for now, at least.

"I'm not really sure what to do, but I am sure what not to do," I said to Michele.

With tears running down her cheeks, she looked at me expectantly.

"We can't scold Keagan or scare him with horror stories about all that could go wrong. We can't turn our backs on him or treat him like we're embarrassed by him. None of that will do any good. It'll just push him away," I continued.

Michele closed her eyes and nodded slowly.

"I just want to toss my piety out this window and love that new child more than anything else."

When I finished speaking, Michele cried harder, but now with a bit of relief. We both knew we couldn't fix or take responsibility for Keagan's actions. But we could pray that becoming parents would push them right into the Lord's embrace more than anything else ever had.

In July 2013, Keagan and Cheyenne's son, Kai, was born, and the three of them moved into the apartment above our garage. That September, Keagan and Cheyenne had a beautiful outdoor wedding at the Mill Creek Ranch in Pagosa Springs. Keagan committed to being a good husband and father, focusing on making responsible life choices. One of those was to attend a Dave Ramsey Financial Peace University class with his sister, Kailey, and brother-in-law, Kyle.

On October 30th, they were all coming to our house for dinner after this class. It wasn't quite snowing that evening, but the roads had their first patches of ice for the season. Cheyenne was driving separately from Keagan, as they had each gone straight to the class after work. Kyle and Kailey were following behind Keagan.

Suddenly, Keagan's red pickup hit an icy spot on the road and fishtailed. Having plenty of experience driving in the mountains, this was probably something Keagan could have recovered from, but then, just as quickly, he hit a dry patch of road while going sixty miles per hour. This instantly flipped the truck. Because Keagan wasn't wearing a seat belt, the impact threw him from the vehicle. Right as he hit the ground, the truck landed directly on top of him, barely missing his head. The truck continued to flip many more times beyond where Keagan lay, crushed.

Kyle was driving right behind him and saw the whole thing happen. He jumped into action, called 911, and went to help Keagan. He scrambled over to the drainage ditch on the side of the highway and found Keagan trying to drag himself out of the ditch with his arms. It was clear he couldn't use his legs.

Keagan was in complete shock but hadn't lost consciousness. He told Kyle he didn't understand why he was struggling so much to breathe. That's what was panicking him most. He could also tell something was wrong with his legs. The ambulance came quickly and took him right to Mercy Regional Hospital, where he had first told us he was going to be a father less than a year ago.

As soon as we heard of the accident, the whole family quickly mobilized and drove to the hospital in Durango. We all knew the situation was bad, terrible. By the time we arrived, it was now late into the evening. We were all by ourselves in a waiting room with pastel yellow walls, no decorations or windows, and only a few chairs. We were all sobbing and praying and so scared.

Keagan was the biggest fighter we knew, but we didn't know if he could make it through this one. We wondered, even if Keagan survived, how would a brand-new marriage with a very young son go forward? What was that going to look like? I thought more of Cheyenne than anyone else. She just got married to him and had a baby only a couple of months before that. How bad off could a new marriage start? Although it felt like ages, it didn't take long for the ER doctor to come in and speak to us. He didn't mince words.

"Keagan is alive, but we have intubated him because his left lung has collapsed, and all his internal organs are up in that lung cavity. He needs immediate transfer to a tier-one trauma hospital in Denver; we cannot treat him here. The life flight crews are starting the helicopter right now," he said.

He let that sink in for an appropriate amount of time. Once the gasps and whimpers calmed down enough for him to continue, he had more to share.

"Keagan's spinal cord is completely severed as well, and his pelvis is crushed. If he survives the night, he will never be able to walk again. I know I'm telling you extremely difficult information, and I'm so sorry, but we do not expect him to survive this flight to the hospital in Denver. If you are praying people, now is the time."

The doctor then quietly but quickly removed himself from the room where he had just detonated an atomic bomb. Subdued sobbing turned into outright wailing as we tried to force the news into our brains. These were the most severe injuries I'd ever heard of in an accident. This was the most traumatic thing our family had ever faced. Surely it was a nightmare. We were going to wake up, right? I closed my eyes for a moment, praying that when I opened them, none of this would be real. I then gulped down a painful breath and willed my eyes to open again.

It was all too real.

I looked around the room at everyone. Most of the people I loved were in that room, and they were hanging on by a thread. Their cries of anguish stabbed me like a hundred daggers all at once. I felt I needed to lead my family, to be strong for them, but I could barely stand. I started hugging whoever was near me because I was afraid I'd collapse without someone holding me up.

I couldn't get the image out of my mind of my son's body lying torn apart and crushed on a hospital bed, his life slowly draining out of him. The only thing I could do was fall to my knees and start praying, so that's what I did. The rest of the family quickly followed suit, our bowed heads forming a circle around the crater left in the bomb's wake.

When Cheyenne, Michele, and I finally saw Keagan, he was intubated and unable to talk. He was restrained on the gurney in the ambulance bay. The big roll-up doors were open, and just outside, the life flight helicopter's blades were whirring.

He was desperately waving his fingers, indicating he wanted to write something to us. A nurse ran and got a pad of paper and a pen. He could not bend his head forward to see the paper, but while looking into our eyes, he concentrated on moving his restrained wrist to write:

"I love you."

CHAPTER 9:

Uphill in the Dark

That was all he had time to communicate as the medical team quickly rolled him out the door. As they were loading him into the aircraft, a nurse came up behind Cheyenne and put her arms underneath her and hugged her tightly from behind. It seemed merely an act of compassion until the doctor started speaking to her.

"We'll hope for the best, but you need to be prepared that Keagan will not be alive by the time this helicopter lands in Denver," he said directly.

It was then clear that the nurse was not only hugging Cheyenne to comfort her but also to ensure she wouldn't collapse and hurt herself if she passed out. Then she loaded up into the aircraft to go with Keagan. Cheyenne would be at his side the whole flight.

It was now about 11 o'clock at night, and Michele and I were making the six-hour drive to Denver. We were absolutely sick with dread as we drove what seemed like endless miles of black asphalt on a foggy, dark, moonless night. A couple of hours later, somewhere on I-25 south of Pueblo, I pulled over, unable to drive. I felt like I was going to pass out and throw up at the same time. Exiting our Toyota, I walked to the front and into the headlights' light. I needed to see something other than blackness. I choked back my nausea, then allowed myself to weep for a moment, only to stop and choke back another round of nausea. When I had gathered myself enough to get back in the car, Michele took my hand to pray in hopes it would give us enough strength to keep driving. Her eyes were red and swollen from crying, but her grip on my hand was firm and steady. I knew she must have been praying the whole way so far.

Sitting in our car in the dark on the side of the road, we began calling out to God.

"God, help us get to the hospital soon," I said.

"God keep Keagan alive…. please," Michele asked.

"God, let Keagan die peacefully, if that's what you have in mind."

"God, we don't know what to ask for."

"God, please take care of Cheyenne and little Kai."

"God, we're not ready to give up on Keagan. Please don't give up on Keagan!"

I don't remember whether we didn't know what else to pray or we just felt we needed to drive again, but as we resumed our dark journey, I let my mind really talk to God.

Why does this need to happen, God? What good can come from it? Keagan is just beginning his family and trying to do it right. He has a three-month-old son. Don't do this to his little boy.

Keagan is so full of adventure. Take someone who contributes nothing to this world, not my son.

"Do I pray for his death so he doesn't have to suffer?"

"Are you sure you know what you're doing?"

"Can't you just make our car suddenly appear in Denver so I don't have to keep driving through the darkest night of my life?"

"Are you listening, Lord?"

I heard nothing in response. The silence was deafening.

When we arrived at St. Anthony Hospital, we rushed to be with Cheyenne, not knowing if she was holding it together. To everyone's surprise and relief, Keagan had survived the flight and was still fighting for his life. The medical team was working feverishly to save him.

They opened up his entire abdomen and pulled all his organs down and out from his left lung cavity. Then they put them in a football-like pouch outside of his body. The trauma caused the organs to swell, preventing them from fitting in his body, so they remained outside him for several days until the swelling subsided. Then, they worked on getting his left lung re-inflated and functioning.

Every few hours, the entire team of doctors—the Spine surgeon, the Pulmonologist, the lead trauma Nurse, the Gastroenterologist, and some others—would have a mission huddle. I had the privilege of standing in on these meetings, which were fascinating, heart-wrenching, and hopeful all at once. I felt grateful that all these brilliant people were putting their minds together to make the best decisions for my son.

At one point, the pulmonologist was arguing to extubate and let Keagan's lungs determine if he would live. Because I was focused on his severed spine, I raised the issue. All these impressive medical experts turned and looked at me all at once, blank stares on their faces. Did I ask a dumb question? I mean, a severed spine seemed pretty serious to me! After an awkward silence, one of them responded with mild irritation, "That doesn't matter right now," and they all turned back to their huddle. I didn't interrupt anymore after that.

For many days after that first night, Keagan was still in very critical condition, so we rarely left his side. Staying at the hospital for days on end caused us to lose all sense of time. Fluorescent lights and little time outdoors made us completely unaware of whether it was day or night. Hospital food wasn't exactly energizing, and lack of sleep took a toll on our already frayed nerves. It was utterly exhausting on every level imaginable.

One of the few things that helped us get through that time was that we knew tons of people were praying for all of us. Text messages were flooding in from everybody we knew. This gave us a glimmer of hope and a respite from the distress, even if only for a few moments.

As difficult as it was for us, it was awful for Keagan. They restrained his arms to prevent him from pulling out the breathing tube, and he couldn't move his legs or lower body. Even with the pain meds he was on, I knew he was trying to grasp the extent of his injuries and assess whether he would ever walk again.

He desperately wanted to talk but couldn't because of the breathing tube. It took a couple of days for his eyes to not be wide with fear when he was awake. When he did wake, he just kept writing, "I love you," to Cheyenne and Michele. I can't really imagine how difficult it must have been to experience that pain and fear and lack of control.

Despite all this, Keagan's will to live was fierce. Even as his crushed body seemed beyond repair, his heart remained steadfast. He wasn't just fighting for himself—he was fighting for Cheyenne, for Kai, for all of us. I could see the determination in his eyes, a determination that made me believe in something greater than just physical strength. It was faith—faith in a future he could still have, faith in a big, miraculous God. That hope kept him pushing forward, and it kept all of us believing. He needed every ounce of resolve to make it.

After several days, the team of doctors finally relented to the pulmonologist and extubated Keagan. They pulled the long breathing tube out from his throat and lungs. We all took an enormous sigh of relief as his once-collapsed lung worked on its own. This was the biggest sign so far that he may survive.

Then they hatched the football package they made of all his organs and put them back into his body. Then his severed spine, right? Not yet. His large pelvis bone was smashed. They called it an "open book" fracture. To put the two "wings" back in place, they put a rod the width of the pelvis from one front tip to the other, bolting it back together. His neck was also fractured, but they considered that a minor injury to address later.

I never heard of someone's spine being severed. The spine is surrounded by large, strong muscles. Thankfully, Keagan's lead surgeon was one of the foremost spinal experts in the world. He did a very ingenious and experimental surgery on Keagan.

The accident severed his spine at L2/3. This is where the spinal column changes to the cauda equina. His cauda equina didn't get cut like a typical spinal cord injury. It kind of got shredded instead. Picture a pipe with a thousand tiny telephone wires running through it. When a backhoe accidentally digs up the pipe, you have those hundreds of little telephone wires torn, some cut, others with bare metal, and all twisted and tangled. Those little wires would be the nerves to Keagan's lower extremities, all mangled and damaged.

They opened up his entire back from top to bottom, like gutting a fish from the wrong side. Then, they took a hydraulic spreader and pulled his body lengthwise. The rods stretched his spine so they could realign the two parts. They mixed some cadaver bone and medical magic powder together, I think, with bubble gum or something, so it would stay together. They hoped it would regrow that bone and fuse together. Then they bolted two titanium rods on each side that ran the entire length of his spine.

Eventually, during yet another surgery, they opened up his neck and put rods in there to fuse those vertebrae together, too. He also had a broken femur and other "minor" injuries, but these were never formally treated as they would heal on their own while he recuperated. He couldn't feel those below his waist anyway, so I guess it was no big deal.

After Keagan's most critical days, Michele and I had to pause long enough to figure out what we were going to do about Visiting Angels. We were only two and a half years into our new business, and it was going very well, but the two of us essentially ran everything. Michele was starting new clients, interviewing and training new caregivers, and I was doing all the billing, payroll, and marketing.

Thankfully, we had amazing help. LuAnn, our very first homeschool mom, was already assisting Michele, and Katrina, another fantastic caregiver, had recently come into the office to help with scheduling. We called them to report on Keagan regularly and talk about the business. They were leading the prayer efforts and helping keep our work people updated. We asked if LuAnn would take over all of Michele's duties and if Katrina would take over LuAnn's. They graciously and bravely agreed. We all decided that if we hired a new scheduler, and I continued doing payroll and billing from the hospital lobby, we could keep the business going with minor interruption to our clients.

Keagan stayed at the trauma hospital for about a month. Although our business was running a profit, it wasn't enough for us to stop working altogether, and certainly not enough to take a few months off and live in hotels and eat out every meal. I wasn't worrying too much about money yet, but we were using our credit card an awful lot. During our days and nights at St. Anthony's, we got to know a particular nun who worked in administration. She built a special bond with our family and visited us frequently when we ate in the cafeteria. She often said hello to me while I did billing and payroll in the hospital lobby, where the internet worked best. In addition, she provided timely updates on Keagan's case.

One day, she came to us and said that a benefactor, the Applewood family, had donated a house to their Catholic charity for use by families who have longer stays at the hospital. She said she thought we might benefit from this home and asked if we'd like to stay there. We excitedly expressed interest and our deep thanks. Having a place to stay nearby would be such a blessing, as we were having all Keagan's brothers and sisters come visit as much as they could. Plus, it was Thanksgiving season, and who wants to celebrate that at a hospital? Even in the midst of this tragedy, God was around, taking care of us.

After receiving the house, we quickly invited all the kids to stay with us for the holiday. Sully and Sawyer came in from Missouri, where they were going to college. Sydney, Kassidy, and Kailey came with their young families. We just wanted to be together, even though it meant many of us would sleep on the living room floor. Having a big dinner was not our priority. Being together was. We needed to be together for this one.

To our immense surprise, the Applewood family had a gourmet catering company deliver a full Thanksgiving dinner for our entire family. It was one of the kindest things anyone has ever done for us. We figured we'd just be having food from the hospital cafeteria or buying a precooked meal from the grocery store. There's nothing quite like celebrating Thanksgiving during such a profoundly challenging time. You'd think it'd be difficult to feel gratitude, but it's quite the opposite. So many other things rush into focus that you're deeply thankful for. The tragedy sucks out the tranquil tide of daily life and contentment. Then a tidal wave of things you take for granted rushes in to fill the void and engulf you in gratitude.

Our extended family, and our new family with Cheyenne and little Kai, were overwhelmed by the kindness and support of so many dear friends. We didn't yet know Keagan's prognosis, but at that Thanksgiving dinner, we realized how grateful we were that he was still with us.

Toward the end of Keagan's time at St. Anthony's, the discharge nurse came around to advise us of our options for rehab. We learned that Craig Hospital in Denver was the best place to go for his type of injuries, so that's where we wanted him to go. The problem was that Keagan was uninsured, and Craig had limited slots for Medicaid patients, all of which were full. We repeatedly asked about Craig, but they denied us each time. It looked like it would not happen, but at the last minute, an opening came up, and Keagan's social worker jumped on it for him. Again, God's provision was undeniable.

All along, we were told he wouldn't walk again. Years later, now that seems like no big deal, but then it was scary. It'd be an enormous change for him, his new wife, and his three-month-old son. Living in a wheelchair was such a hard thing to imagine, and Keagan would have to go through a lot of physical therapy to learn how to do that.

This made us especially grateful that he was going to Craig. The doctors, nurses, and therapists there were top-notch. Because of their ability to think on their feet, they creatively came up with effective therapy for Keagan's unique needs. They were so engaged with their patients. Many of the therapists were about the same age as Keagan, and he became good friends with them.

We were especially grateful for how the staff helped Keagan learn to be his own independent person again, including teaching him how to move forward on an emotional level. They even had classes for Cheyenne and him to attend together. We all loved the care and treatment he received there.

At Craig, one floor was for spinal injuries, and another floor was for traumatic brain injuries. There were a lot of patients there with sports injuries from activities like skiing, CrossFit, and bicycling. Keagan loved interacting with these other patients and encouraging them in their recovery. They were just his type. The outlook for all of them was life-altering; they were facing permanent disability. But more important were the many incredible stories of survival, resilience, and hope.

One patient was a top CrossFit athlete who one day had the barbell come down on him and snap his spine. Another patient had flipped an ATV and broken his back. One guy had fallen off an eighth-floor balcony and landed in a palm tree. One older gentleman had fallen into a tree well while skiing. He broke his back and was paralyzed but could breathe. Thankfully, he always skied with his dog, and his dog stayed by his side for hours until someone saw the dog and came over to investigate.

While at Craig Rehab Hospital, marijuana was becoming legalized in America, and Colorado was one of the first states to do so. Keagan's lead doctor at rehab was Dr. "B." He took Michele and me aside and told us we needed to change our view of marijuana and allow it to be a part of Keagan's life, as it might end up being the one thing that saved his life.

During the months of rehab, thankfulness replaced our fear and worry. Keagan's recovery was looking promising as he learned how he would live as a paraplegic in a wheelchair. Cheyenne's employer, Wells Fargo, gave her lots of time off to get situated again, and Michele and I continued to be grateful for all our Visiting Angels' team and the way they filled in the gaps.

In fact, this experience convinced us to go further down that road of allowing others to use their strengths and grow into increased responsibility in our business. When we returned home, Michele decided to work only part-time. This would free her up to help Keagan and Cheyenne, who would continue living with us for a while.

As we were nearing the discharge day from Craig, I had our house remodeled to accommodate Keagan's wheelchair. Some good friends who worked construction with Keagan and me went in and remodeled our master bathroom to make it handicap accessible. We put in a concrete parking spot and sidewalk to the back patio so he would have a ground-level, covered entrance into our house. We also made our office/library into Kai's bedroom. Michele and I moved upstairs into the light green girl's room.

Keagan's employer, Darin, and his wife, Erin, came to the hospital one day with blueprints of a large expansion to their shop that would accommodate Keagan's wheelchair. When it was done, Keagan could stay in the shop to work since he wouldn't be able to get around job sites any longer. The expansion included a welding shop where he could continue his more artistic metal work for the custom homes they built. Keagan was thrilled; the gift was incomparable, allowing him to continue working and contributing. Darin and Erin gave him such a bright outlook on getting back to his life. Keagan loved to work.

When he finally got to leave the rehab hospital in the spring of 2014, he was so excited to learn to live in this wheelchair and be the coolest paraplegic in town. He didn't have unrealistic expectations, but he had a lot of things in mind to try. One of these activities was hunting, mountain lion hunting, specifically. His buddies were all avid hunters, and they were starting their own guiding and outfitting company.

Keagan wanted so much to be a part of it, so he spent a lot of time calling and texting them about where they were looking for and finding game. He had spent a fair amount of time out in the woods with them before, so he knew the area pretty well. He became a sort of command post. When we had friends come to town for hunting season, Keagan would tell them where to find game, and he was surprisingly successful in locating Bear, Elk, and Mountain lions.

In the early winter of that year, his good friend, Luke, got a group of friends together to take Keagan out to hunt a mountain lion. It had only been a little over a year since his accident, and only 9 months since leaving the hospital, but he was extremely excited and determined to make it happen. It wouldn't be easy, though. Mountain lions hang out in rugged terrain, and hunting season for these cats is in the winter when snow covers the ground. But these guys were determined to help Keagan get a lion. If anyone could do it, it was these guys. They had dogs that tracked the lions and snowmobiles to get out into the woods. They were all very experienced and prepared. One guy was the world record holder for the largest mountain lion ever taken. He broke President Teddy Roosevelt's long-standing record.

One morning after it had snowed lightly, they found a track worth chasing. Luke came and bundled up Keagan, gathered his wheelchair and heating packs for his feet and hands, and took him out. They got only so far by snowmobile because of the fallen trees in that area, so they loaded him up in a sled and took turns pulling him through the snow to get a little farther along the cat's trail. When that didn't work anymore, they started taking turns carrying him by piggyback with snowshoes on.

The dogs were doing a good job of treeing the lion, but then the cat would jump to a nearby tree, scramble down, and run until the dogs caught up and treed it again. Each time they'd get Keagan there, the lion would have just escaped.

It was near dark when they finally got the lion treed and Keagan there at the same time. It was quite a moment for Keagan, a paraplegic out in extremely rough terrain hunting a mountain lion. With one leg in a rigid brace, he could lean up against a nearby tree and prop himself up for the shot. All this had to be done smoothly, not to scare the cat, yet quickly, so it wouldn't escape again.

He drew his .45-caliber Glock pistol, quickly aimed, and hit the lion with the first shot.

Everyone cheered! They pulled the dogs back and got Keagan over to the fallen lion. He held it up to his body, feeling the warmth of it, and got all the trophy pictures. By this time, the sun had set, and twilight was fading. They had gone deep into heavy woods with snow on the ground; in no time, the temperature would plummet. It was time to get out of there.

Getting game out of the forest after a hunt is often the most work of the entire ordeal. But they didn't just have to get a 100-pound Mountain Lion out of there; they had to get Keagan out of there, too. One condition of his paraplegia was that his body didn't regulate the temperature in his legs properly. He had those little packets of hand warmers, which were not nearly enough, so they had to stop many times, gather wood, and light a fire to warm him up.

At 11 o'clock that night, they all staggered into our living room, elated by the success of the hunt. Surrounding our warm fire, they told us the entire story and showed us the pictures, and brought the actual mountain lion into our house. But something wasn't right with Keagan. Even though he was sitting by the fire, he was still shivering, and his skin was purple. Everyone agreed he was probably hypothermic, so we took him right to the emergency room. The ER staff was able to get him warm and rehydrated, but it took several days for his pain to subside enough to be tolerable. He was miserable.

Unfortunately, this wasn't new or unexpected. By this time, he had already found he could not work in Darin's shop. The pain from his injuries would build up too much during the day, and he could not return to work for a few days until it settled down. This was just the beginning of his long, brutal fight against debilitating pain.

For almost eight years, Cheyenne, Michele, and I watched helplessly as Keagan would convulse in pain daily. At night, it seemed to be the worst. Our nights were restless, as his hard breathing and sometimes soft crying would often awaken us. It was heartbreaking to watch him suffer like a man beaten and wanting to give up and not have any ideas or solutions to offer or try.

Michele gave up so much to help him. She devoted herself to watching Kai and then also Liam when he came along. Most days, she stayed home with Keagan to help him around the house and assist him in any way possible. She shared in his episodes of pain more than any of us. I know that this took a big toll on her.

We chased down every new treatment for pain or something that could allow him to walk again. There were so many experimental robotic leg braces and self-balancing wheelchairs. There were electronic spinal devices that could mask the pain or reroute brain signals so he could walk. Experimental things on social media became vapors that disappeared when you tried to grasp them. The pain specialists with little experience made empty promises. The experienced pain specialists admitted they had nothing to help him. We went to doctor after doctor. Each time they had to "evaluate" him. Keagan had to tell them what happened, what treatments he was doing or had tried, and relive the entire ordeal all over again. I remember the last physical therapist we tried, in mid-conversation, he sighed, dropped his head, and wheeled out. He didn't say thank you or goodbye. I could tell by his countenance that he was done with doctors. I was kind of proud of him just calling it when there was no use in sitting through it all again.

As a family, we tried to accommodate Keagan's marijuana use. He was vaping pot constantly throughout the day and night. When the pain seizures hit him, he would still cringe and tighten up terribly, but it reduced his anxiety. The big issue was that he was constantly stoned, and this prevented him from doing much. He couldn't reliably take care of his one-year-old and three-year-old boys. Driving safely was impossible for him. He would pass out while watching TV. He spent most of the day hunched over in his wheelchair. This took a big toll on his marriage.

One day, Cheyenne found a bag of cocaine in Keagan's wallet. Keagan was still under the effects of the cocaine when we confronted him. We asked him what else he was hiding from us. He pulled a bottle of vodka out of our own couch! Cheyenne went and looked through his car and found another bag of cocaine. He acted completely like a homeless addict and denied everything we were showing him. His illegal drug use resulted in our telling him he couldn't live with us. We called the police. We wanted Keagan to know how shocked and serious we were about having illegal drugs in our house. The deputies were high school buddies of Keagan's and were very kind in dealing with him. The amount of cocaine he possessed could have resulted in a class two felony charge. But they didn't take him to jail. We wanted them to take him to jail, so they would cut off his supply. But they didn't take him. I knew he was also buying extra Oxys from friends. I enforced boundaries with Keagan. Kicking him out of our house, I thought, would be enough to straighten him out.

I never felt so awful as a dad as when I drove him to a hotel, paid for a couple of nights, and told him he had to figure it out, but he couldn't do illegal drugs in our house, especially with his children living there. Usually, as a parent, you know the path your children should take; they just have to figure it out for themselves. But this time, I didn't know what he should do, or how he was going to make it just one more day. He was in a wheelchair. I didn't give him his car because he was stoned. We had just taken away all his "extra" meds, and Cheyenne wasn't going with him. We sat in the hotel room and cried together for a long time. He seemed to respect what I was doing. As I left, he was sweating profusely as he was coming off all the "extra" drugs he was on. I was picturing the hotel calling me in the morning with awful news. It was a dead end in my head, and I had no idea how to fix it.

But Michele did. She knew it was time for a rehab program. Despite her momentary perplexity at getting Keagan out of the house, she refused to abandon her son. She did this with confidence, like her intuition was supernatural or something. Resourcefulness was one of Michele's special talents. She found the best rehab place Keagan could go to. She didn't just pick the first one she could find. To ensure they understood his needs, she thoroughly questioned them about wheelchair accessibility and the necessity of his pain medication. Keagan was at first understanding and agreeable to going. After several days in the hotel, we allowed Keagan to return to our house if he promised to go to rehab. But as the date of departure neared, he got cold feet. I think he was talking to friends and looking online to see if they would detox him. Because he was an addict, his body was telling him not to go. At this point, Michele was fearing for her safety in her own home when I was away during the day at work. We called the place and delayed his arrival once or twice. We had arranged for one of his high school friends, who was a pilot and had a small Cessna, to fly him down. Finally, one evening, while I was out of town for work, Michele called me from a locked bedroom upstairs, fearing for her safety. Keagan was refusing to go to rehab and was yelling and trying to hit her with anything he could get his hands on. We called someone who could help. Keagan's hunting buddy and best friend, Luke. Luke modestly told me later he "helped" Keagan get packed up and "helped" Keagan get out of the house and onto that airplane. I know he made things happen, and appreciated him getting Keagan down to rehab.

Upon arrival, they take vitals and admissions stuff, and then... detox. Detox was probably the second worst experience of his life after his accident. Detox was in a "cell." They designed the room to be suicide-proof. Three days into Keagan's detox, the staff realized his pain was causing dangerously high blood pressure and heart rate, necessitating an immediate resumption of his OxyContin and Oxycodone. Yes, he was an addict, but there was no alternative.

Thankfully, we learned that detoxing from OxyContin and Oxycodone, even for a few days, essentially resets your tolerance to the drugs, allowing them to perform at renewed effectiveness. This allowed Keagan to stay for a few months and take part in a lot of excellent classes and good rehabbing. Cheyenne, Michele, and I went down to visit him during family week. He introduced us to all his new friends, who he said were the ones "really" messed up. I incredulously recall looking at him, thinking, "Are you that unaware of why you're here?" You're one of them. I know it meant a lot to him to have our support that week. It was helpful for us, too. We learned from the staff how important it was to set clear boundaries with Keagan. There was a particular group session with eight other patients and their families where Cheyenne wrote and then read aloud to Keagan that she couldn't have him in the house if he used too much marijuana or other drugs. It was unsafe for her, Kai, and Liam. Our class instructor said we had to state a boundary we would keep and follow through. They sat face to face, holding hands, when they told each other their boundaries and commitments. When I did mine, I bawled and hardly got the words out. It was about the same as Cheyenne's. All the other parents, the really messed-up ones, ended up crying too.

Keagan completed his rehab and was in a good spot again. He learned a lot and was equipped and committed to getting back to his family. He resumed his gratitude journaling. He promised Cheyenne he wouldn't do extra drugs anymore. For the sake of his family, his desire for success was strong. Keagan had designed and was working on a custom home that was wheelchair accessible and could fit his whole family.

While he was in rehab, I took charge of getting his house finished up. His younger brother, Sawyer, brought his family out for a couple of months to help. His brothers-in-law also jumped in to get it done. Shortly after he returned, Cheyenne and their boys had a home of their own for the first time in their married life. His new house was downtown in the older district of Pagosa, just a half block from the San Juan River that flows through town. They could walk to parks, along the paved river trails, and even get to coffee shops and the movie theater without driving. Keagan could wheel over to Liam's preschool and pick him up after school. After they moved out of our house, Michele and I felt we could take a deep breath since the accident five years ago.

With Keagan settled in his new house, we booked an extended stay at a boutique condo near the end of the road on the North Shore of Kauai. This was a rainforest paradise. The weather in a rainforest is the most wonderful weather in the world. We took naps listening to the pitter-patter of the rain each afternoon, then got up to an afternoon cup of coffee and sat on the porch, looking at the waterfalls in the high cliffs. Michele and I paddle boarded up the canal, relaxed on world-famous beaches like Ke'e and Tunnels, and hiked the Na Pali Coast. Michele struggled with her balance while hiking. It must be from all the stress, I thought, and I was right…in part.

Keagan and Cheyenne lived in their custom home by the river for a little over two years. Our families did a lot of things together, like watching the July 4th fireworks from his backyard, regular walks along the river, and birthday parties Cheyenne loved putting on. With Keagan's younger sister, Kassidy, and her husband, Blake, living next door, their two sons got to spend time with Keagan's boys often. Other people's lives always seem OK, until one day it comes out, and it's not. In December 2020, Cheyenne made the hard decision to leave Keagan and stick to the boundaries she set during family week at his rehab. He had been drinking and using drugs. It was as bad as ever. For most of those two years, Cheyenne quietly struggled, repeatedly adapting to keep things going. We knew he wasn't doing this to intentionally hurt his family, and he knew he was going down the wrong path again, but he truly had no way to get relief from his pain. Still, his behavior endangered the boys, and he was a miserable person to live with because he was passed out most of the time. Cheyenne filed for divorce and tried to get a mutual agreement on how to take care of the boys. Cheyenne was brokenhearted on one hand because she knew Keagan was a wonderful dad if sober. But if not, he was nothing but a danger to them. I tried to mediate a couple of times, and I could see the damage was too deep for Cheyenne. She made up her mind and had to move on. But she really wished there was a way to co-parent. There really wasn't. She couldn't leave them with him.

Without Cheyenne at the house, I started going over more to help Keagan with things he couldn't do, like shoveling snow or mowing the lawn. Plus, I knew he was lonely and needed someone to talk to. His house was slowly becoming more and more unkempt. Every dish in the cupboard was piled up in his sink. He would start a crazy new bumper on his car, tear it apart, and then lose parts and not be able to put it back together. So, he would be without a car. He shouldn't have been driving anyway, but his garage would be full of all kinds of pieces he could no longer put back together. Before, I had always loved any time he and I could do something together. He would show me his art projects, or we'd talk about new business ideas. Now it was only time with an addict, high and hardly coherent. He'd cry about it and then ramble about stuff that made no sense. His battle with pain was winning. During those six months after Cheyenne left him, he was leaving us some voicemails and texts that were alarmingly suicidal. It became increasingly difficult to stop by and hang out or help him with little things. It was always stressful, and I didn't know what to do. Michele could not visit him at his house anymore. Cheyenne was completely out of the picture. I was trying to run a business, but I was about the only one who could help him and be emotionally available to him. When I'd visit, I would do some dishes and clear his wheelchair pathways. It was hard to keep the house from looking like a hoarder lived there. He was often passed out. It was a grueling emotional visit if he was awake. We would go round and round about how hopeless his situation was. I'd pray with him. He and I would cry together. I'd remind him about how important he was to his sons. I was behind in the situation the whole time. He was ahead of me with what he was experiencing and his hopeless heartache. He was hurtling toward a cliff he could see. I was following, not chasing, as I couldn't see the cliff that was out in front of him. We made several calls to the police, asking them to conduct "Wellness" checks. We were afraid to be the ones who found him injured—or worse.

Our last time spent with Keagan was unusually memorable. It captured so much of our lives with him in a simple evening at our house. Keagan and his boys came over to our house for dinner. This was in July, the thunderstorm season, and that night was right on queue. As gray clouds tumbled quickly across the sky, the setting sun painted their edges with shades of orange, pink, and purple. Lightning in the distance jaggedly split the horizon, sending out deep rumbles of thunder we could feel as much as hear. To us, it was as beautiful as a July evening could get; we loved summer thunderstorms more than almost anything, maybe just slightly more than a heavy snowstorm in the winter. The afternoon rains on the dry ground release this delightful odor called petrichor. We snuggled up on the front porch, and rumbles of thunder caused us to pull the blankets up under our chins in delight. Our house has a perfect view of the North range, which includes the namesake peak of Pagosa Springs, Pagosa Peak. These afternoon storms usually correspond delightfully with afternoon coffee. Michele needed her special "I'm in my Happy Place" mug, which is meticulously prepared with warmed milk and a dash of coffee. With her extra plush blanket and pillows, she was all set for this BIG show. Michele will tolerate this event alone, or even enjoy my companionship, but snuggling little ones and clutching them at each peal of the thunder is magical for a grandma. Even Keagan rolled his wheelchair up next to his mother's seat. That day, as the clouds grew darker and the rain began, Liam wrestled himself out of the pile of blankets and arms and took the stage at the front of our porch with outstretched arms and exclaimed, "Great show today, God!"

With that, Keagan smiled and was momentarily at peace, enjoying the company of his mom, his dad, and his boys. But as the clouds slowly started weeping, I couldn't help but think of what awaited Keagan when he went home. Without Cheyenne, without his boys, he was alone with all his pain, tormented by a body that had become his prison; he just wanted to leave it all behind. The next day, he would.

There were times it didn't feel like God was running this thing. We knew in our heads He was in control and loved Keagan more than we ever could, but we couldn't understand why God would allow him to survive such a horrific accident only to be in constant, unbearable pain. As much as we wanted it to make sense, none of it did. It still doesn't.

I've often thought back to my prayers that night on the drive to the trauma hospital. Why was God silent? Why did he feel so far away as we drove through the dark? I don't know, and I'm not sure

I'll ever know. But I know: on that drive, I was calling out to God for answers; instead, He gave me strength. I couldn't see this future, this long, difficult journey ahead, but I wasn't alone.

And in hindsight, God answered our prayers. Keagan survived. His life didn't look how any of us wanted, but he had more time with Cheyenne, Kai, and the rest of us. He brought Liam into the world and into our family. I don't know why God allowed so much pain in Keagan's life, and I don't know why he was quiet that terrible night, but I know we've never been alone. We've never been alone in any of it.

Keagan didn't doubt God, and I think he submitted to his pain better than I did. His attempts at getting relief from his pain took him down a path to addiction and loneliness. He couldn't bear his physical pain anymore. None of us knew what to do and kind of stood and watched, wishing we could help. Keagan's suffering puzzled me and is continuing to stretch my faith in God. I know God is intimately involved in everything of my life; my work, my marriage, my family, my fun times, my hard times. I'm glad it is this personal, because I was asking God questions that were very uncomfortable and upsetting. Ones that don't have pretty, churchy answers. I could not see a solution for Keagan. Death seemed like the only thing for him. My Bible doesn't have a chapter and verse for this one.

I often compared Keagan's suffering to that of Jesus. I'm not sure why I did this, and maybe it's not a wise thing to do, but I struggled with the idea so often preached that Jesus suffered more than any human. It was difficult for me to see it that way. They arrested Jesus and brutally beat him. Lots of people get beaten up every day. But His beatings lasted only an afternoon. Then they made Him carry a heavy wooden cross up a hill. That's hard, I'm sure, but Navy SEALS carry big logs, in the sand, up and down the beach at BUDS training all night long. Then they nailed Him to that heavy cross and let Him die. OK, now you're talking about actual pain and injuries you aren't ever going to recover from. But then He died… within 24 hours of the start of it all. It was over. All over and done. No more pain or suffering. But there are and have been millions of humans in the history of this world who have rotted in jail for years, been the victim of a random murder, suffered cruel torture, or lived in a life of slavery.

When Jesus was betrayed and arrested, He found Himself alone. As He went through His beatings and crucifixion on the cross, His disciples and followers abandoned Him. His Father abandoned Him as He died on the cross. He said, "My God, why have you forsaken me?" He was alone. As Jesus hung dying, His Father and everyone else completely abandoned Him. Jesus had no one and no road home. God turned away from Him. Perhaps Jesus suffered more than any human after all. Keagan knew God was not abandoning him. Keagan was running to God. God was the only thing Keagan thought could help him. Someone was still with Keagan. He had a road home.

CHAPTER 10:

Above Tree Line

Having children might be the one part of life in which we didn't follow our policy of quitting while we were having fun. Early on, Michele told me she wanted eight kids. I barely grasped the concept of being a father at all, nor the chaos of six kids in the house. Neither of us considered the long-term health implications Michele would face from childbearing.

Her first health issue was shortly after all six kids were born—she started losing her hearing. She had otosclerosis, a condition often linked to repeated pregnancies in which extra calcium builds up on the ear bones. A specialist recommended an outpatient procedure where the surgeon would go in and gently scrape off the excess calcium.

In that small, pale blue hospital waiting room, I waited longer than I was told it would take. A lot longer. Finally, the surgeon hustled into the waiting room like he'd just jogged across the hospital. Sweat stained a large area of his scrubs, and he was panting for air.

"The procedure went badly, and I broke her ear bones," he unloaded awkwardly.

I was waiting for the rest of the sentence, but he just stood there, catching his breath and staring at me through his thick glasses.

"OK…but it's all fixed now, right?" I finally asked him to give me more information.

"Well, we had to do an emergency stapedectomy."

He was no longer looking me in the eye. His sheepish expression resembled that of a school kid caught misbehaving.

"What's a stapedectomy? Please explain. I'm getting a little concerned!" I said, raising my voice at the end as I lost patience.

"It means we had to completely remove her broken ear bones and make a prosthesis, which we put in. This should be as good or better a solution for her hearing."

He wasn't convincing me at all. He was still giving me the school-kid look, like something else was wrong. I narrowed my eyes and crossed my arms, waiting for him to tell me the truth.

"She is experiencing significant vertigo and is throwing up. She's very uncomfortable at the moment."

And that's all I needed to know, I guess, because he immediately turned and left the room, saying nothing else. I had to go find someone else to tell me what to do next, where my wife was, and if she could go home or not. For a year, she battled to recover. The vertigo did eventually subside, but then tinnitus took over. These conditions can literally drive people insane, but Michele fought hard to recover. It took several years, but thankfully, she eventually recovered for the most part.

But it wasn't just childbearing that took a toll on Michele's health; it was also the stress of working and homeschooling simultaneously, which was a lot for her. She always took her responsibilities seriously, and although I wouldn't call her a perfectionist, she put herself completely into anything and everything she did.

The stresses of adult children may have been the most stressful thing she went through. The grief of seeing Keagan suffer and lose him was intense for many years. During that time, we also became estranged from our daughter, Kassidy. Doctors diagnosed her with a brain tumor that was causing some paralysis and loss of vision. The surgery removed the tumor but left her with seizures. Her doctors told her to stay home quietly and not do anything. After weeks, then months of this, she got stir crazy and started playing video games and spending tons of time on social media. We believed she became addicted to digital media. As we grew more and more concerned, her husband, Blake, stumbled across her social media feed, revealing inappropriate conversations and photos. We could also piece together unfaithful meetups with some of these people. Our entire family, from in-laws to grandparents, brothers and sisters, all agreed to do an intervention to get her help at a rehab facility for media addiction. She agreed to go but immediately left the facility and would not take part. She came home and tried to live separately from Blake but eventually left town and stopped communicating with anybody in her family.

Also around this time, our other twin daughter, Sydney, went through a difficult divorce after finally fleeing her abusive husband. Sydney moved in with us for a time, as we helped her recover and adjust. As I watched Michele continue to give her all to everything and everyone, I suspected she was paying the price in her body. I'd always admired her strength and drive, but now, it was becoming clear the woman who had carried our family was struggling. Her resilience wasn't able to keep up with her drive. She wasn't regulating her drive to match what life was throwing at her, but what would she cut out?

For a while, we both tried to ignore it. Maybe that's all she would get. She's had a full share of unexpected, undeserved trials already. But when a new family member joined us, we could no longer pretend everything would resolve itself.

In the summer of 2017, Michele became dead set on getting a dog. She found a breeder she liked in Pueblo, Colorado, who had a litter of Australian Labradoodles. She was over the moon!

When the day arrived that she could get her dog, Michele drove there and passed whatever tests the breeder had for her. When she arrived back home, she brought in the cutest little chocolaty-brown puppy I've ever seen. She announced that the dog's name was Padgette, French for "little page/helper."

This puppy quickly took on Michele's personality and love for other people, which was important because Michele wanted to train her to be a visitation dog for our elderly clients. When Padgette was about six months old, Michele enrolled her in a service dog school in Durango.

The program required Michele to do quite a bit of training at home with Padgette, which she was very committed to doing. At the dog school in Durango, this included Michele walking Padgette on a close leash. On a couple of occasions, doing this, Michele lost her balance. At first, she suspected her ear problems, but that seemed odd since she had experienced little vertigo for years.

Padgette completed the basic obedience training and was starting the more advanced part, but Michele had to pull out because she couldn't take all the walking and turning. Padgette didn't end up becoming a vest-wearing service dog, but she got enough training to be a very sweet and loving companion.

At this stage, we just kept hoping and praying Michele was experiencing something temporary and treatable. Losing her balance wasn't horrible; it was just one more thing she had to deal with. To help, she started buying canes. She eventually had up to thirty different canes. She even had a Gandalf staff and a

Stormtrooper cane. A fan favorite was the pink glitter one. The need for a cane didn't bother Michele, because she turned it into another shopping opportunity.

But difficulty walking was only the beginning. Michele had an operation in 2018 to control severe acid reflux, but it also didn't go well, and we believe it caused some kind of damage to her vagus nerve.

Shortly after that procedure, Michele began losing weight, and we couldn't slow it down. The discovery of being at or below her best weight quickly turned alarming. She felt nauseated constantly and just didn't want to eat. She tried eating all sorts of specialty foods, going on a vegetarian diet, taking extra vitamins, and more, but nothing made much of a difference. Finally, a test revealed she'd developed severe gastroparesis, a condition that slows or stops the movement of food from the stomach to the intestines. Her stomach was only operating at 10% of normal, and she was slowly starving. We switched her diet to mostly liquids, and thankfully, her weight stopped decreasing.

However, the lack of nutrients started causing other problems. Without adequate vitamins B and E, Michele began experiencing neuropathy from her waist down. Not only is neuropathy painful, but it is also dangerous and can lead to amputation of the feet and lower extremities.

After some frustrating trial and error with vitamin shots and pills, the neuropathy subsided, much to Michele's relief. But overall, her condition was not improving.

Many visits to multiple specialists and dozens of medical tests later, we started running out of options to explore. Her symptoms continued to get worse, and her doctors were not sure how to diagnose her. We went to three different neurologists and still found no answers, so she did her own research.

She discovered a new therapy that relied on a portable neuromodulation stimulator (PoNS). It uses a mouthpiece to deliver neurostimulation while the patient performs exercises like walking and balancing. The goal was to reset the patient's coordination or bypass the parts of the brain that weren't working properly anymore. This therapy was not yet approved in the United States, but it was in Canada, and Michele wanted to give it a shot.

We planned for her to receive the PoNS treatment in Canada, but there was one big complication: the COVID-19 pandemic. Canada still had a closed border. Thankfully, after much research, we found exemptions in the travel restrictions for medical treatments. We read everything on the government websites and did everything necessary to comply with the travel restrictions. We booked our flights and hotel rooms. Everything looked good, and we were ready to go.

When the day came for the trip, we boarded the flight from Durango to Denver, where we would get on another flight directly to Vancouver, British Columbia. The pandemic still made travel confusing and difficult, so we felt encouraged when we reached Denver without problems and found the Air Canada desk to check in for our next flight.

"I'm sorry, but I'm afraid you haven't followed the guidelines, so I can't let you on this flight," the desk clerk told us.

"What?! We haven't? How is that possible?" I asked with frustrated confusion. The situation completely threw me off. The plane was already boarding, so we had little time.

"Follow all these guidelines to travel from the U.S. to Canada," the clerk replied, showing us a long list of requirements.

"But some of these don't apply to us," Michele said. "We're traveling for a medical treatment. Your regulations clearly state there are exceptions for medical treatments. Is there someone else we can talk to?"

She called her supervisor, but that didn't get us anywhere. Nobody seemed to be confident in the rules, as they were changing all the time. It was a hectic few moments as the plane was about to close its doors.

In the end, they refused to allow us on the plane. We were heartbroken that Michele didn't receive the treatment we had hoped for. We had to wait at the airport for five hours for a flight back to Durango. In the meantime, we texted all the kids and extended family about our discouraging news. Keagan and several other kids responded, expressing their disappointment. The family had been praying this trip would be a turning point for Michele's health.

No one suspected that by the next day, this setback would barely be a blip on the radar. We never imagined that would be the last text we got from Keagan. He took his life that evening.

A month after his death, the border to Canada was going to reopen completely, so we paid for airline tickets again, hoping to be the first Americans to get into Canada. Just to be safe, we flew to Seattle so we could rent a car and drive across the border. We didn't want to deal with the same Air Canada clerk at the Denver airport again.

The road from Vancouver up to Squamish was one of the most beautiful drives we'd ever made. Squamish is at the northern tip of the island-dotted Howe Sound, and surrounded by mountains like the Stawamus Chief, a huge granite monolith. The beauty of British Columbia astounded us.

The town of Squamish was so quaint. We watched them filming Hallmark Christmas movies most days when we drove into town for Michele's therapy sessions. It was summer, but they were making it winter by hauling actual snow down from Whistler Mountain. The people in town looked at us like real foreigners because they hadn't seen international travelers in a couple of years.

After the many months of closures during the pandemic, we enjoyed just getting out in town. Despite Michele's inability to eat solid foods, I was happy she joined me for meals. We couldn't do the walking and hiking that we'd always done on vacation because Michele couldn't go very far, even with a cane. But the focus of this trip was not vacation; it was getting Michele treated.

She dove right into her PoNS therapy sessions with Nicole, her newly certified therapist, who had her do all sorts of balance work and treadmill work. After the first week, Michele felt like an athlete in serious training. She had her different exercise outfits, and she'd put her hair up in a ponytail for her daily therapy workouts. While she gained a little stamina, her balance remained unchanged. She persevered through the next week, but it became clear toward the end of the second week that the treatment was not working. In fact, during the last few days, Michele was feeling terrible, worse than when we arrived. Feeling totally discouraged, we headed back to the U.S.

When we returned home, we talked with our nephew, Clancy, a Doctor of Physical Therapy, and with Michele's neurologist. They both agreed that the PoNS therapy had probably taxed her brain too much, and they recommended she take a few months to rest and recover. We didn't know it then, but her brain was dying off. The therapy had no chance of helping because it was trying to retrain parts of her brain that were shutting down.

So she rested. In fact, she spent the next four months resting. This was difficult for her as she had always been full of energy and determination to work hard, but she was willing to do whatever it took to get better.

We wanted so badly to fix her problem, so we continued to study what could be causing her to decline. Her neurologist kept exploring the nutritional deficiency issue, so sure that it had to be the culprit, but based on Michele's research, she suspected it was Multiple System Atrophy (MSA).

When she mentioned this, her neurologist adamantly rejected the idea. She felt embarrassed to keep bringing it up to him. He couldn't get past how healthy Michele appeared to be and the fact that she was still so young. To him, a nutritional deficiency caused by gastroparesis had to be the cause. But to his credit, he advised us to get a second and maybe even a third opinion.

He referred us to a specialist in Denver. After some testing, the specialist told us it could be autonomic ataxia, but she wasn't very convincing in her reasoning. Her office said they'd get back to us later with next steps. After several weeks of waiting, we checked in. We called and left messages but couldn't get a call back. One day, we got a notice that the doctor was retiring, so we would work with her physician's assistant going forward. We grabbed the earliest appointment we could, which was several weeks out.

When the physician's assistant finally met with us, it was clear she hadn't read Michele's file. She had absolutely no idea of what tests were done and no plan of action. We asked her several questions, but she gave us no answers, so when the clinic asked us to schedule a follow-up appointment, we declined. That path was going nowhere.

The PoNS, the neurologist, and now this specialist, provided nothing useful, leaving Michele disappointed, frustrated, and exhausted. Not only did it seem like the medical community didn't have answers, but it seemed like they didn't care. The mental and emotional battle was almost as tough as the physical one.

Michele continued to believe MSA was the most likely diagnosis and went back to her primary neurologist armed with as much information as she could find to make her case. Finally, he admitted she could be right, but he really wanted her to get another opinion.

He gave us a referral to a specialist in Dallas, but that clinic could not see her for 11 months. He also referred us to the Mayo Clinic in Scottsdale, Arizona, but they flat-out denied her request for an appointment. We had no remaining options.

It was now April 2022, Michele's 60th birthday. In honor of this milestone, she gave sixty presents away to her closest friends and family. I think she was considering that she may have an expiration date—one that was coming up sooner than expected. Until this point in life, she and I never gave that much serious thought to our mortality. Sixty was the new forty, they said. Michele had some big health problems, but we were dealing with them mostly, and she still looked quite young. You wouldn't know something serious was brewing.

In the meantime, I was seriously getting into CrossFit and feeling in the best shape of my life. CrossFit was my relief from all the stress of the last eight years. Minette was also enjoying CrossFit and just hitting her stride as one of the top women athletes in the world in her age group. How was Michele not among us? For so many years, it was the three of us taking on these kinds of experiences together. It almost seemed like Minette and I were getting to the best version of ourselves physically by robbing Michele of hers.

I did not want to consider MSA as her diagnosis. MSA is fatal. There was no hope if it was MSA. MSA has no foundation raising money for cures. No celebrities were rallying government agencies to conduct research. There were no experimental treatments. We were on our own. But after 37 years of experiencing Michele's uncanny intuition, I was afraid she was right again.

Taking the best view of the situation, Michele started thinking of how best to use whatever time she had left. At first, I didn't want to think about it or talk about it, but I realized I was wasting her valuable remaining time. So, Michele and I lived as best we could while she was alive, and we were together.

We knew it would be challenging to travel and visit people, but I was ready to give her any experiences she wanted. I had gained some experience while helping Keagan with his disabilities, so I was totally game to help Michele manage her disabilities, too. And maybe, oh, I hoped, just maybe, she had a lot more life to live than we thought.

───

A year earlier, Michele and I had packed up our little Airstream camper, which we called The Nest, and headed to Grand Teton National Park for a camping trip. We could never get enough of the mountains, and these didn't disappoint. We were both astounded by their beauty and expanse.

Using her cane, Michele could take short walks around the campground, which she was so happy to do. She also spent lots of time in her camping chair under the cottonwood trees. It was during unhurried times like these that she would process her situation through quiet reflection, prayer, and reading.

She highlighted nearly every paragraph in her old Bible, so she got a new one to study and mark up. She also reread *Heaven: A Comprehensive Guide to Everything the Bible Says About Our Eternal Home* by Randy Alcorn. I read aloud to her a John Muir book each evening by our little campfire.

These times made me realize that just being with Michele was my favorite part of life. We were meant to be together. Raising a family together. Worshipping God together. Running a business together. Summitting big peaks and adventuring in the mountains together. We both deeply appreciated God's handiwork—the wildflowers in the high country, lofty peaks, thunderstorms, and all the wildlife we saw. Even when I experienced something without her, all I wanted to do was tell her about it right away. When I summited a fourteener or hammered another mountain bike ride, I always looked forward to the eager, proud look on her face when I told her all about it. I had such a crush on that girl since the day I met her, and I never stopped wanting to impress her.

Now that she couldn't do as much, I still loved being around her just the same. It didn't matter that we couldn't backpack through evergreen forests or paddle board on mountain lakes; just sitting side-by-side under the Cottonwoods in the Grand Tetons was delightful. Her nearness was all that mattered.

After the April 2022 appointment with Michele's neurologist, the whole family got a sense of urgency for spending as much time as we could together. Michele mentioned how beautiful the Grand Tetons were, and Kailey got on it right away. She found a little group of log cabins in Jackson Hole, Wyoming, situated around a pond and a large grass field with a bonfire pit in the middle. There couldn't have been a better spot for our family. It took a lot of coordination to get everyone there, as it is far away from everything, but all our kids and their children were able to come that summer.

We had a little fox that came by each evening. Kyle and some grandkids got to feed it by hand. Some boys tried fishing in the pond. Sawyer, Kyle, and I bought lift passes and went mountain biking down the ski slopes. We played croquets on the lawn and enjoyed bonfires in the evenings, and we spent way too much time doing big puzzles together.

It wasn't easy for Michele to get around the grounds because she was now using an electric wheelchair, but she was willing to do anything to be with her family. By the time our week was over, I think all the kids and grandkids realized that this may be the last time they would get to do this kind of trip with their mom and their Marmee.

By the time fall came around after our big family vacation, Michele and I were spending every afternoon out on our front porch, admiring the North Range of the San Juan Mountains. I read aloud to her another John Muir story, My First Summer in the Sierra. It brought back so many memories of our years living at Angeles Crest and Bass Lake. We could still smell the fresh pine after the rain and feel the sharp bite of a winter wind. We could still hear the noisy calls of the stellar jay and taste the love in each of Michele's camp meals.

Like it was yesterday, we could remember the one time back when we dated, we took King Louis and Linda on the gondola from Palm Springs up into the snow. We wanted them to experience the fun and excitement of the mountains we both loved. At the top, we had them try cross-country skiing with us. Let's just say we learned that not everyone likes the same type of adventure, and when that happens, just change the plans (and get them warm. Try hot chocolate. Hot chocolate makes everything better).

We also recalled the misadventure we had during a trip to Colorado in 1992. We weren't as familiar with the Rockies as we were with our California mountains. One night, we innocently pitched our tent in a campground at Independence Pass near Aspen. This pass is only open in the Summer because snow blocks it most of the rest of the year. What we didn't know was that just because the pass was open, there was no guarantee of pleasant weather.

Later that night, a tremendous storm rolled in and dropped a lot of snow. That was kind of exciting and fun. A snowstorm in the summer in the high country! But then it turned to rain. It completely flooded our tent with slush. Like the true gentleman I was, I ended up sleeping in the warm car with one-year-old Sawyer and let Michele, Keagan, and Kailey enjoy the less-crowded tent in their wet sleeping bags.

We laughed as we remembered the time we took our Visiting Angels managers four-wheeling over Ophir Pass. Our annual leadership retreat was in Telluride, and taking Ophir Pass would cut off an hour of travel time. Plus, the pass is breathtaking. Everyone thought it was a cool idea except the managers—Katrina, Iva, and Chloe. Despite their fears, they agreed to try it and follow my car up and over the pass. Cut to them screaming and crying. It didn't help that there were cars lying in pieces at the bottom of the slope. With desperate pleas, they asked me to drive, but they didn't want to get out of their cars for fear they would roll backward off the cliff. After coaxing them out of the driver's seat, I took over maneuvering each vehicle, one at a time, the rest of the way, while the three of them walked to the top. They were not happy with me, but we got some splendid pictures!

After the stories, these conversations with Michele always turned back to admiration for the rugged beauty of the high country. From there, they flowed into discussions of how beautiful the mountains in Heaven would be and how much Keagan must be enjoying them. We pictured him whooping and running through those mountains with glee. Before long, we would both be in tears. We took comfort in knowing that those same Heavenly mountains were Michele's destination, too.

Michele loved her time working at Camp Soldotna the summer after her freshman year of college. She would often tell me how beautiful it was. On the central-western portion of the Kenai Peninsula in Alaska, the camp enjoyed access to rivers, lakes, mountains, and forests. It was exactly the kind of place both of us loved.

In the earlier days of her health decline, she mentioned wanting to go back to Alaska, and I was keen to see it myself, but we needed a vacation that accommodated Michele's limitations. The outdoor adventuring we did in the past was no longer an option. We decided a cruise was a good option, so we booked one for the spring of 2020.

The timing was not meant to be, though. Yep, you guessed it. In March, the growing pandemic shut down all travel. The cruise line gave us a voucher for the next summer, but that wouldn't happen either. It wasn't until August 2022 that we could finally go, and it was going to be difficult to travel by then.

For this vacation, we chose a fancy six-star cruise ship that held a maximum of 600 passengers. And fancy it was. They requested that passengers dress up for most meals. In the dining room, a string quartet played every evening. It wasn't a party boat, that's for sure. All the other guests were so elegant. They loved the fine dining and relaxing excursions. There weren't many excursions Michele could do, but we tried the easiest ones.

The crab feast was handicap accessible, but Michele didn't eat or even want to be near a single crab, so we did whale-watching instead. This required us to get on a fairly small boat. Small boats that rock back and forth weren't Michele's favorite thing, but the orcas were, so she toughed it out, and it was worth it. The whales came right up alongside the boat.

All the crew was so accommodating to Michele. We were waited on hand and foot. Thankfully, she could still stand up, transfer, and even take a couple of steps if she was holding onto something sturdy, which was a good thing because cruise ships aren't exactly wheelchair friendly.

Every door has a high threshold, so the crew can close off sections of the ship if they get flooded or damaged. Wheelchairs don't like high thresholds. Also, the doors close automatically and don't wait for wheelchairs to get through. And most spaces on cruise ships are tight, especially the stateroom bathrooms. In all fairness, we didn't make things any easier by choosing a balcony suite. We weren't about to have an interior stateroom on a ship, even though those were the only ones that were handicap accessible. We wanted to enjoy the gorgeous views from our own balcony.

One beautiful morning, we wanted to sit out on the rear deck for breakfast while the ship pulled away from port in Sitka, Alaska. We planned this entire event, getting up earlier than normal to get a good table. Michele needed lots of help to get ready, and her routine was pretty involved.

For one thing, she always wanted to choose her outfit for the next day the night before. I always just wanted to go to bed. But like many other things I learned as a husband, she wanted her outfit laid out the night before, and I wanted my wife to be happy and have a good night's sleep, so I learned to enjoy helping her select the outfit and lay it out the night before. It didn't matter in the least that she was going to change her mind in the morning.

That morning, I helped her get out of her pajamas and into her outfit for the day. I drained her catheter bag, brushed her teeth, and put on all the jewelry selections she desired for the day. Did you know you can wear multiple bracelets? On each wrist? And you can change rings on your fingers every day? Well, I didn't, but now I do. Oh, and don't forget that necklaces get tangled up overnight by some sort of jewelry goblin, so you really need to budget time each morning for untangling those babies.

One thing you really shouldn't do, though, is clean someone else's eyeglasses with your shirt. It makes them grumble. What they really want is for you to get a microfiber cloth and clean them extra well every time. I got pretty darn good at cleaning eyeglasses.

Fixing Michele's hair was a skill I never developed very well. Her hair was so healthy and beautiful. Almost every doctor she went to commented on how full her hair was. I appreciated those comments and her luscious locks, but blow drying, brushing, styling, and scrunching them were not among my curated talents. Choosing the right headband, scarf, or decorative clip seemed impossible. But doing Michele's hair became my favorite challenge in her morning routine. It meant I got to touch her and caress her cute little head.

Michele had given up makeup quite a while ago, mainly because she really didn't need it. She always had such naturally full eyelashes and a good complexion. And thank goodness for that, because I think having me do her makeup would've been traumatic for both of us.

Once Michele was all dolled up, we made our way to the back deck. This early, there weren't very many people we could rely on to hold the doors as we worked our way to this area of the ship, but I had allotted time for this inconvenience. It was just like when we lived in Los Angeles, and we had to allow for traffic on any travel plans. As planned, we were first to the dining deck, and we picked the seats with the best view as the ship was just leaving the docks at Sitka.

Picture clear, calm water reflecting the sun that's shining through breaks in the fog. Imagine sharp, snow-capped peaks of mountains poking out far above the clouds. Think of a postcard-worthy port town slowly fading into the background among a dense curtain of evergreens. This was her view as she sat down to breakfast. Simply stunning.

We were so content at that moment. All our troubles were far from our minds. We missed Keagan more than we could say, and we knew Michele was very sick. But we were with our two favorite gifts from God: the mountains and each other. We knew our lives (and deaths) were in God's hands, and we were not thinking about that right now. We were just enjoying each other and His creation. These were the moments we were so fond of. Just magical, simple moments we always cherished.

The breakfast buffet was overflowing with every delicacy you could want. Michele wasn't really minding not eating anymore, although I'm sure in this case, she envied everyone enjoying all the fine food. Before I ate, I prepared her breakfast. She drank a liquid meal called Orgain. She drank it with a straw because of difficulty swallowing. The only flavor options were chocolate, strawberry, and vanilla. These were her only selections for every meal. That morning, she chose chocolate.

Next, I got her pills out. She took a lot, but most of them were vitamins. The pill game was pretty fun, so much so that we played it several times a day. Handling the pills was difficult for her fingers, and she could only swallow one or two at a time, but she insisted on trying to put them in her mouth herself. The game started, and when she didn't succeed, I got to go retrieve the missing ones wherever they rolled off to.

The challenging part was that I didn't know for sure which ones I was looking for. And I didn't know for sure if she really dropped one. Sometimes she signaled a missing pill but hadn't really dropped one. She was so sneaky in this game. I could tell it was one of her favorite games because she was always laughing while I played it with her.

After she took her pills, she was all set. Then I ran through the buffet and grabbed everything in sight for myself. Full plate in hand, I sat back down with her, handed her the remaining Orgain, and said a little blessing over the meal.

I had situated Michele facing out across the stern of the ship, so she got the best view. (Well, I got the best view because I was facing her.) As I started eating, I gazed into her eyes and said, "Isn't this so beautiful?"

She nodded and sighed contentedly. I was staring into those captivating green eyes. We both had tears in our eyes. We were so content.

"Tell me all about what you see, and if anything changes on the wall behind you, I'll let you know," I said.

Unbeknownst to me, I said this right as she was taking a big swallow of Orgain. Laughter and swallowing don't mix for anyone, let alone a gal with MSA. Nothing went down the right pipe. Liquid chocolate came out of her mouth and nose rather explosively, completely covering the beautiful white tablecloth and her carefully chosen outfit. Her masterfully prepared hair got its fair share of chocolate, too.

Trying unsuccessfully to contain my laughter, I started mopping up the mess with my napkin, but I quickly came to a halt as she started her worst choking episode ever. Her eyes widened as the look on her face changed from laughter to fear. My heart fell into my stomach as time seemed to slow down. I thought she would not get through this one. Her panicked face told me she was thinking the same.

By this time, several passengers at nearby tables had turned their heads and showed concern. The wait staff came over to see if they could help. Just as one of the waiters had the phone in his hands, ready to call the medical team, Michele came through it.

Everyone was relieved she didn't need medical attention after all. I apologized to everyone, thanked them for their concern, and tried to clean up as best I could. Sitka was out of sight by the time we carried on with our breakfast, and I think our spectacle ruined the experience for other diners. Some of them left prematurely and didn't return. We certainly were no longer an anonymous couple on the ship. People seemed to keep their distance after that. A day or two later, I was sitting in the hot tub by myself while Michele took a nap in the room. I noticed a man I hadn't seen on the ship before hesitating as he walked past me.

"Excuse me," he said.

Oh great, I thought. He's going to bring up the choking incident. I turned to look at him, steeling myself for what might be an awkward comment.

"My wife and I have noticed how in love you are with your wife and what wonderful care you give her," he said.

I sat there staring at him blankly, caught off guard by his kind words.

"We realize it must be difficult to be on a ship in a wheelchair, but your relationship is just beautiful. We're traveling with friends, and we've all been commenting on it the whole journey so far."

I'm going to guess they hadn't been eating breakfast on the back deck that morning.

CHAPTER 11:

Questions in the Shadows

Shortly after our cruise, the Mayo Clinic called out of the blue and said they would see Michele after all. We hadn't expected this call whatsoever since they had originally turned us away. We figured it was because maybe her case was too vague, or maybe it wasn't really that serious. But since we still had several months until the appointment with the specialist in Dallas, we were happy to have an earlier consultation with the Mayo Clinic.

We scheduled a week of testing over the Thanksgiving holiday. When we arrived at the clinic, we finally felt like experts were involved in Michele's care. It was such a relief to know we weren't on our own anymore, trying to figure this out.

Every day of that week, she went in for multiple tests. Some were simple tests she'd done before, but a few were new ones. They tipped her upside down, scraped her shins, and made her wear an astronaut-helmet-looking thing to bug out her eyes. None of this was any fun, but Michele didn't complain. She wore her customary smile through every test.

While we were in Scottsdale, some good friends, Sheila, Greg, Lori, and David, came to have a fancy dinner with us at our resort hotel. These were friends who had worked at Angeles Crest Christian Camp with us. They lived in Prescott, Arizona, and were gracious enough to make the drive down to Scottsdale for a visit.

Michele found it increasingly difficult to socialize because her voice was so weak, and in a crowded restaurant, even with hearing aids, she couldn't hear. They were all shocked and saddened to see Michele in a wheelchair and unable to talk. We still had a great time, as these friends were all so dear to us. Good friends are just easy to be with. We all had memories of camp life that were wonderful to talk about. I leaned over throughout our dinner to repeat all the conversation about their lives and how their families had grown.

My dad and his wife, Joan, lived in the Phoenix area as well. My dad was in his eighties by then and struggling with mild cognitive impairment, so he had difficulty finding the right words to finish his sentences. The hotel we stayed at advertised a sumptuous Thanksgiving meal, so I made reservations for the four of us, plus my stepbrother, Rick, and Joan's daughter, Holly. The lot of us always enjoyed a delightful meal together when we came to town, and I thought we were going to top them all with this hidden gem of a spot for a Thanksgiving meal.

After the dinner with our friends, where Michele struggled with the ambient noise, I worried that the Thanksgiving meal might be too loud for her and my dad to have any kind of conversation, even though they'd likely be sitting right next to each other. Dad was always fond of Michele, and because of circumstances, he hadn't seen her for a long time. I knew he would want to sit next to her and have her all to himself.

But maybe we'd get lucky and be the only ones who weren't celebrating at home for the holiday. Maybe we'd be like the family in

A Christmas Story who resorted to going to the only restaurant open on Christmas, the Chinese food place. Only people in a hospital or coming from out of state for testing would go out to eat their Thanksgiving meal, right?

Not so much.

As we waited for a table, a hundred other people came in for dinner that night. The place was jam-packed. The ambient noise the night before was nothing compared to this. I knew the situation was shaping up to be trouble.

Dad, Joan, Rick, and Holly all showed up, excited to be together. As expected, Dad insisted on sitting next to Michele in her wheelchair. Joan tried to direct him to a chair at the other end of the table, but he wasn't having it. He stood next to Michele, frowning, unable to express himself properly, but we knew he was disappointed.

I spoke up and asked Joan if he could sit by Michele, but then Joan started frowning because now she couldn't sit where she wanted. Rick and I knew what was happening here and were chuckling quietly to ourselves. The seating arrangement wouldn't be the only awkward challenge of the evening, so the real fun was only just beginning.

My dad finally got situated and seemed content, but Joan was still frowning in her rather distant seat, preparing to be ignored by Dad for the rest of the meal. I got Michele settled in right next to Dad and gave her a little smile and nod to just let it happen. She and I had talked over the possibility of this dilemma beforehand. We knew if the restaurant was busy and loud, it would not work well for her and Dad to communicate, and we were pretty certain Dad wouldn't be aware that it would not work.

As we watched the crowds fill every seat in the restaurant, we got excited to see how funny this was going to be. Dad immediately turned his head and began asking Michele questions she couldn't hear. The conversation went something like this:

"Hello, Michele!" Dad said, turning to her and kissing her forehead.

Michele grinned from ear to ear, not so much from this endearing gesture, but to hide the laughter she wanted to let out, knowing what was about to happen.

"How are you feeling these days?" he followed up.

Michele heard the question but knew she couldn't say anything. One, because it'd be a very involved response. Two, because she knew she didn't have the breath and strength to answer. I politely stepped in to explain some of the testing she was getting, but Dad had zero interest in what I had to say. After about eight words of mine, he broke in because he just wanted to talk with Michele.

"I heard you went on a… a… somewhere… a trip… a ship," he stammered.

"A CRUISE, MICHAEL, SHE WENT ON A CRUISE!" Joan yelled across the table.

"Oh, yeah, a cruise," repeated Dad.

Again, Michele smiled back with no verbal response. She didn't really hear my dad, but Joan's follow-up was loud and clear, so she knew what he was talking about. Still, there was simply no way for her to respond; even in a silent padded cell, she would not have been able to project her voice enough for Dad to hear her.

Frustrated, Dad tried another topic.

"What's taken you so long to… be… no, to come… see me?"

Michele didn't hear this question in the slightest. She smiled patiently and looked at me for help. I started to answer on her behalf when Dad suddenly threw up his arms and napkin and yelled loudly, "For God's sake!"

People around us turned our way, perplexed. We were all seated just moments before, and no one had ordered anything; what could possibly be wrong at our table already?

Rick had already leaned over and smirked at me, knowing that this conversation would not work, and that Dad would not be aware of that. Michele and I had already completely prepared ourselves for my dad's response. The three of us just chuckled under our breath each time our eyes met over the rest of the meal. Michele didn't have to talk or offer any excuses. She just kept smiling and looking at me for reassurance. I gave her that and didn't crack any jokes while she sipped her chocolate Orgain drink for dinner.

The food ended up being terrible, and I paid a lot for it, but we got some great photos, and we didn't have to do the dishes. The live comedy, courtesy of my dad, was the highlight of the night.

That was the fun part of our Thanksgiving week in Scottsdale. On Friday, there was a big meeting with the lead neurologist at the Mayo Clinic. We were expecting another vague conversation, possibly even a range of diagnoses, as this was our fourth specialist. But when the neurologist and her intern came into the room, the intern seemed engaged, focused, perhaps even a little excited. Maybe they found something interesting for us! Something we never considered. Something treatable?

"You have Multiple System Atrophy," the neurologist said directly to Michele.

The announcement hung in the air like a cold mist. I shivered as it came to rest on my shoulders. Whatever last bit of hope we had for some good news drifted out of the room.

As they started explaining MSA to us, they found out quickly that Michele and I had done our homework and were very familiar with the symptoms and how MSA progressed. We had studied when a patient would typically get a catheter, a feeding tube, or a tracheotomy. When the neurologist explained that there was no treatment for MSA and it would lead to death, we knew that too, but it hit differently hearing it out loud from a skilled doctor. The neurologist and intern let us sit there quietly as tears welled up for both of us. My eyes wandered around the room, trying not to let the emotion overwhelm them. Could it be real? Was there truly no other path Michele could go down than this?

All Michele had been experiencing was exactly in line with what the neurologist had just told us. So, yes, it was real. This was the end of the line. We both knew it.

Michele felt some vindication in having guessed correctly what she was experiencing. Just like when her second twin was crowning, and she had to grab the chief of staff and yell at him to take a second look, she was right. She was relieved to get confirmation that she hadn't been overreacting to her symptoms. She really was sick. These last five years of continued decline and no effective treatments were taking a toll mentally. Now she had relief and a conclusion to all this.

The next question in our minds was how much time she had left. In the research we had done, some models showed a 5-year life expectancy, and some showed a 10-year life expectancy. With her being about four or five years into this, we wanted to know what to expect for her specifically.

I thought I should be the one to ask, but I could not get my voice to speak the words. I just kept sitting there looking around the room because I didn't know what else to do. Michele wanted to ask this question, too. I knew she did, and she was waiting for me to do it. I forced my gaze back down to my left to look at Michele, and as our eyes locked together, she reached over and patted my hand, indicating she wanted me to ask it.

With difficulty, I choked out the question, "How long does Michele have to live?"

"Months," the doctor replied. She was very prepared with her answer and sounded too sure.

"Could it be a year?" I then asked.

"No, definitely not. Not weeks, and probably several months, but not a year," she said.

If you had told me an invisible man slugged me right in the gut, I would've believed you. I could barely breathe. Now there was no holding back the tears; they were pouring off both of our faces. The doctor and her intern gave us their sincere condolences and quietly exited the room. There was nothing more to discuss.

That appointment seemed quick, and before we knew it, we were out in the lobby. We wandered down the hall, desperately needing a quiet place to cry. Michele's electric wheelchair felt so obtrusive as it kept us separated. I wanted to hold her, support her, and bear the weight of this unfathomable news, like I had done when I had to break it to her that Keagan had died.

But this damn wheelchair was in the way. It suddenly represented everything that was wrong and unfair about all of this. I wanted to kick it, smash it, destroy it, then scoop up Michele from among its ruins and carry her away from all the pain and fear and grief. Instead, I found myself just putting my face in my hands and letting the tears flow until I had none left to cry.

We were suspecting this prognosis, but with the expertise of the Mayo Clinic, a hospital that specializes in worst-case scenarios, we held onto some hope of a treatment. Now every ounce of that hope had evaporated in an instant. I ached like never before for my sweet wife. I felt completely helpless.

Months, just months, the doctor had said. "Did she really say just months?" I asked Michele over and over for a few days. How could Michele not be here in just a matter of months? Nearly 40 years of sharing our lives together in a fantastic marriage, enjoying mountain adventures, raising six children who gave us fifteen grandchildren, and now she would not be with me.

When we got back home, we canceled all other medical appointments and quit all the researching. There was no point. It was time to shift our focus to being present, cherishing the time we had left, and finding peace in every moment we shared. It was a relief to know what it was, how long she had, and what to expect. Yes, it caused her a lot of disappointment in knowing she wouldn't be here for everyone. I know she hung on to things she really wanted to do and see in life, still, like having Kassidy reconciled to her family. Her last full sentence to Kailey was not to give up on Kassidy. She brought up a few times the idea of me getting remarried. She wanted me to remarry someone who loved God. I told her I didn't want to talk about that part of the future. I wanted to be with her here and now, not thinking of a new life. She asked me not to forget her.

※ ※ ※ ※

Michele had a few dates she was looking forward to at the end. After the diagnosis around Thanksgiving, she had a target to make it to Christmas—one last special Christmas. After making it through Christmas and the New Year, she had her sights on her birthday, April 27th. As winter transitioned to spring, she was doubting she would make it, but she did. She made it to 61 years old.

After her birthday, she focused on our nephew's wedding. It was the last wedding of the cousin's club, and she was so happy to be around long enough to see all the kids married. But she and I sensed this would be her last trip to visit her family in Missouri. Some of them felt it too. When it came time for Michele to say her goodbyes to her two sons, her mother, her twin sister, her grandchildren, and her nieces and nephews, it was much more tearful than usual.

On our last night with the family, we enjoyed a very special moment with Minette and Linda in the living room. They played the song "Gratitude" by Brandon Lake. The chorus broke out into throwing up your hands and praising God.

Michele tried to lift her hands while that line played, but her arms barely lifted off the wheelchair. She knew the words already and whispered them with everything she had. Minette instantly saw what Michele wanted to do and lifted her arms for her, and we all sang loud and cried.

Even at this moment, we were thankful. Not for having to say goodbye to each other, but for praising God together. Not for being sick, but for belonging to Jesus. Not for losing Keagan, but for having a wonderful son. Not for a life cut short, but for a fulfilling life. Not for leaving behind family and friends, but for a chance to be in Heaven with Him soon.

When we lived in Southern California and throughout Michele's childhood, Disneyland was about as close to Heaven as you could get here on Earth. Our children enjoyed the anticipation of going to Disneyland as much as the actual day we got to spend there. Michele was always just as excited as they were. And it had a special meaning for us as a couple, since Disneyland was where we had our first date.

We lived very close to Disneyland for those five years we lived in the city, and we could often see and hear the fireworks that went off every evening. Linda gave our family annual passes as Christmas gifts a few times, and we used them frequently.

There wasn't really anything we didn't love about Disneyland. I loved the chocolate-covered bananas and Tom Sawyer Island. Michele couldn't go on any rides because of her vertigo, but she had more fun watching her kids delight in going on the rides than actually going on them herself, anyway. She loved the train that went through dinosaur land. The kids loved this too. What Michele truly loved most about Disneyland was soaking up all the atmosphere—

the magical lighting, the ambient sounds, the lively music, the plentiful decorations—and seeing so many people having the time of their lives.

As it became clear that her death was at hand, Michele used Disneyland as a convenient (albeit inadequate) metaphor for Heaven. She would say that waiting to die felt like driving around the parking lot at Disneyland looking for a spot to park before she could go in. This was it. She had already bought the ticket and arrived before the park opened. She only had to ride the tram to the front entrance, sit down just outside the turnstiles, and study the map to see all that lay ahead for her in the magic kingdom. The gates were just about to open.

The anticipation for Heaven was stronger than any despair she may have felt about death. She had more excitement about moving into eternity than fear. Her anticipation became my anchor, reminding me in my darkest hours that there will be eternal life. And though I knew I was losing her, God's peace lit up her countenance.

In her last months, Michele searched for everything she could find on Heaven. She bought and read or had read to her all the books there were about Heaven. Theological teachings about Heaven, stories from those who claimed to have gone there and returned, devotionals about our cherished rewards in Heaven. She watched movies about heroes of the Christian faith receiving their reward after their lives of trials.

Michele couldn't remember a time when she wasn't certain she would go to Heaven when she died. When she was young, she heard Jesus inviting her into His family, and she never questioned her destiny after that. She knew that if you're in Jesus' family, you don't have to worry one bit about getting kicked out. Throughout her life, she knew Jesus was in her heart, right by her side, listening to her, showing her how to live her best life, and guiding her toward who

He wanted her to care for and love. Now her lifelong journey of faith in Jesus was going to be realized. She embraced it as the next step in her life, knowing that what awaited her was immensely greater than anything she could imagine.

This deep faith was fueled by Michele's commitment to walking daily with the Lord. Whenever I hear pastors talk about healthy spiritual habits like having daily devotions, reading the Bible, and praying, I know they must have had Michele in mind as the example. She loved classic devotional books like *Stepping Heavenward*, *Streams in the Desert*, and *Jesus Calling*.

Michele always shared this learning with the rest of us. Throughout the house, she placed brightly colored sticky notes, index cards, and even posters that proclaimed the goodness of Jesus. Whenever she came across an inspirational quotation from a memorable sermon or a book on how to live a life that pleased her Savior, she would add it to the collection around our house.

These reminders were everywhere—taped to bathroom mirrors, cupboard doors, and kitchen appliances. When she ran out of places to tape them, she collected them in a box. By the end of her life, this box was overflowing with years' worth of wisdom, guidance, and support from countless sources.

Perhaps this is why Michele had such certainty of her destiny in Heaven. Everything she had studied gave her daily assurance that she was a beloved daughter of God. Michele loved Jesus, and He loved her. It was that profoundly simple and simply profound.

Several friends came to see Michele one last time. Michele started asking what they thought Heaven was going to be like for her. Have you ever asked someone that? It creates such a hopeful and heartwarming discussion. It delighted Michele to consider what others believed was just around the corner for her, especially after a long, difficult illness.

"In Heaven, you're going to be all done with this MSA," said one friend.

"Michele, you'll be able to eat a meal—a delicious, hearty meal—with no difficulty," said another.

"Yeah, it'll be a huge banquet with Jesus as the host—the marriage supper of the Lamb!"

Michele closed her eyes as a serene smile spread across her face. She hadn't eaten an actual meal for several years now.

"Soon you'll get to see Keagan and your dad and your grandma Schaaf," Kailey said. "And they'll be fully healed and whole. And so will you, and you'll be able to walk or run right up to them and hug them."

With this, tears of joy pooled up in Michele's eyes and rolled slowly down her cheeks. What a beautiful reunion she was going to have! When Michele asked our missionary friends, Steve and Arlene, what they thought Heaven would be like for her, they focused on the biggest delight of all.

"Think of how ecstatic Jesus is going to be to receive you!" they said. "He'll be there, arms wide open, eager to be the first to greet you. He will embrace you and say, 'Well done, good and faithful servant.'"

In that moment, Michele was light as air. Over the next several days, she unloaded her years of grief, loss, worry, and pain and replaced them with joy, hope, and anticipation of the greatest thing she would ever experience in life. She had this vivid picture of Jesus himself smiling from ear to ear with arms wide open, reaching for her with even his fingertips.

She pictured the Creator of Heaven and Earth expressing His utmost joy because she was coming to Him. Nothing else could compare to that. No other hope was greater. As much as the two of us dreamed of her climbing a majestic mountain again and paddle boarding in warm water with a beautiful sunrise peeking over the horizon, this reunion with Jesus was what she unquestionably looked forward to the most.

In Heaven with the Lord, Michele would find true rest. What a profound gift awaited her! She was ready for it. She was eager for it. But this doesn't mean she was without sadness. Although she was yearning for Heaven, she also wanted to stay here as a grandma, wife, mother, sister, and friend.

It's difficult to appreciate rest without the hard work preceding it. The degree to which you appreciate it may be tied directly to the amount of work or difficulty you experienced beforehand. Think of how great a vacation feels when you've been pushing it at work and juggling all of life's many stresses. Upon arrival, you stow your luggage and stroll out onto the veranda overlooking the gorgeous paradise below. You take in the unbroken expanse of beauty and recline in the softest lounge chair you've ever known. Now imagine what the true rest of Heaven would feel like after a long, painful, debilitating illness.

I'm not sure whether it's harder to die slowly or suddenly, but I think dying young is much more difficult than dying in old age. Younger people with terminal illnesses hang onto hope that something or someone will heal them, but the elderly usually know death isn't far away. Regardless of whether they're healthy, they know they are in the sunset of life. Often, they have lost many loved ones already, and it seems natural that they should go soon.

In our business of helping the elderly live out their lives in their own homes, Michele and I saw death often. Most of our clients had lived a full life and knew the inevitable was coming, especially once they needed hospice care. Hospice care typically begins when a patient has less than six months to live. Interestingly, hospice is a relatively new service; it began in England in 1967 under the direction of Dame Cicely Saunders. Only in 1978 did the first hospice care begin in the United States, in Oklahoma City.

Two months after her diagnosis at the Mayo Clinic, Michele was admitted to hospice care. She mentioned to several family members that she could feel her body was giving out, which wasn't easy for her to admit. Despite her struggles, she never considered giving up. She rarely complained or spoke negatively. Being with loved ones energized and contented her. Her family was by far her most valued treasure on Earth.

Michele poured her heart and soul into our children from the moment each one was born. Once we had grandkids, they became her most precious, endearing little loved ones. They called her Marmee, and she treasured that name more than any other role or title.

She had a special bond with Keagan's sons, Kai and Liam. We both did. I'm sure it's because of that extended time they lived with us after Keagan's accident. At first, it was just Kai, but a couple of years into their stay with us, Cheyenne and Keagan gave us that wonderful news: that they were going to have a second son, Liam.

We were ecstatic! We loved having little ones in our home, and we were glad we could help take care of them. It eased some of the burden on Cheyenne and Keagan while they tried to put their lives back together.

While they lived with us, we went on vacations together. We went to church together. Once Michele quit working, she would take the boys to the river in the summer to feel the cool water. She took them to the park to meet up with their cousins.

She also taught them how to be kind, considerate, and responsible children.

"Put away the toys you're finished with before getting new ones out," she would instruct them. It didn't seem to bother her that she had to repeat this ten times a day.

She helped Kai understand his responsibilities as an older brother.

"Liam looks up to you, Kai, so what do you always need to remember?" she would ask.

"Very careful I will be as a little brother follows me," Kai would recite.

Marmee was back in her element, taking care of those little boys as they grew up.

I experienced unexpected joy from being a grandpa. In fact, I wish I were as good a dad as I feel I am as a grandpa. When each of these two boys was trying to learn to sleep in their own bed, instead of being impatient like I was with my own children, I would put them down and play my harmonica in the pitch-black room for as long as it took to get them to sleep.

When I would come home from work, Liam would run up to me and say, "Grandpa, can I have an uh-uh-uh hug?"

If my hands were full, I would quickly dump everything and scoop him up because I loved uh-uh-uh hugs as much as he did. Marmee liked to snuggle, but I liked big hugs. His brother, Kai, liked them too, and so did his cousin, Louis, but Liam and I were the ones who started these hugs. I'm not exactly sure what "uh-uh-uh" means, but that's what Liam named them when he was a little older.

The hug involved me picking him up and squeezing him hard until he felt almost scared of how hard it felt. Then, I'd release him quickly, only to squeeze hard again, to the point of almost scaring him, then I'd release the squeeze and do it a couple more times. He'd always start laughing, not knowing if this was scary or fun. It was one of those uncertain-but-giddy laughs, the kind that escapes your mouth during a roller coaster ride.

Once Keagan and Cheyenne built their own house and moved out, our place felt so empty. It was unreal to suddenly not have their family in our home, sharing each day with them, eating dinner together. We did our best to stay close, though. Michele even kept a date with Kai and Liam for reading time every week.

When Michele started to have problems with balance and walking, she tried to downplay it for as long as she could. She just wanted to keep being Marmee for all her grandkids. Even after she became wheelchair bound, she wanted to love on all thirteen of them as much as possible.

When they came to visit, she would call them over, and they'd rush up to her chair, climb in it, and snuggle up to her. After the new year, 2023, her voice became very weak. The grandkids were all sad that they no longer got her squeal of excitement when she saw them. They'd still go straight over to her chair and give her a big hug, but they started realizing they couldn't ask her anything.

"Why can't Marmee talk so good?" Kai asked one day while I was driving him and Liam home after a barbecue at our house.

"Her breathing isn't very strong anymore," I replied.

"When will she get better?" he asked.

I hesitated.

"I'm sorry, Kai. She will not get better."

His eyes quickly teared up with confusion and hurt, and I felt helpless to shield him from the pain.

"Why did she have to get sick?" he then asked.

Kai's questions were now beyond easy answers. Some didn't have answers. That was one of them. I sighed deeply as I tried to think of what to say.

"What sickness does she have?"

Up to this point, Liam was letting his big brother ask the tough questions. He had been unusually silent. That day, after he hugged Marmee, he backed up from her, staring in wonder at her condition and why she wasn't talking like before.

Both of the boys, along with the other grandkids, had figured out that something was up with Marmee and were getting the severity of the situation.

"Does Marmee still have her smarts?" Liam finally asked, breaking his silence.

Before I could figure out how to respond, Kai found the question he really wanted to know the answer to.

"What's going to happen to her?!" he asked with obvious distress in his voice.

This was getting more difficult by the second. Should I be honest? How would an eight-year-old and a five-year-old handle the truth? Would it be too much for them?

Kai and Liam loved their Marmee dearly; I didn't want to break their little hearts. I desperately wanted to spare them from any grief, but I knew the truth was something we all had to face together. Taking a deep breath. I told them the brutal reality.

"She is going to die soon, boys."

Kai lowered his head and sat quietly, upset and stunned. Liam followed his big brother's lead. The three of us sat in silence for the rest of the drive.

CHAPTER 12:

When the Leaves Fall

February in Pagosa Springs is winter in all its glory. The frigid cold of January is losing its grip, but it is still cold enough for the snowpack to lie safely, covering everything in sight. Families like mine who love the winter aren't ready to think of spring yet. We're delighted with wrapping ourselves up in warm blankets and sipping on hot tea or cocoa or hitting the slopes on a bluebird day after a storm dumped ten inches of snow the night before.

This February was different. It felt bleak and barren. My mind drifted back to those black oak trees standing silhouetted against the fog like harbingers of what's coming. I could almost hear that stellar jay squawking from the distant past, another time when I felt Michele was slipping away from me.

Michele spent her winter days in her reclining chair. She couldn't do much at all anymore. She couldn't even talk on the phone or type out messages on her devices. Losing the ability to communicate directly with family and friends made Michele feel useless and disconnected. She had always been our family's communication hub.

That winter, I dosed out medications and vitamins, emptied catheter bags, bathed and groomed Michele, and answered her phone calls, texts, and emails. It was exhausting work, but I had help from caregivers, and we had established a routine that was working fairly smoothly. The expiration date that the doctors had given Michele the previous Thanksgiving was behind us by several months, and things felt like they were moving along with little change.

Then, one day out of the blue, Michele said to me, "I am tottering. My body is shutting down. I think it's time we called hospice to discuss the inevitable."

Nobody wants to call hospice. It feels like you're activating the final sequence, like you're announcing, "I'm dying! Hey everybody, look at me, I'm dying!" But it's also a time of uncertainty. You wonder, "What if once they look at me, they tell me I'm not ready, that I'm overreacting?" You don't want to scare everyone for no reason.

Nothing about Michele's health had significantly declined suddenly, but she felt a change. It was like her health was an hourglass, and it had been slowly draining for several months. In the beginning, there was plenty of sand in the top part, but now, almost without us noticing, it no longer looked like much sand remained. I made the call to hospice. It was agonizing, but I did it. We set up an appointment for the hospice team to come to the house and go over everything with us. As we waited for that appointment, Michele and I still questioned if we were overreacting. We were preparing ourselves to apologize to the team and then to our whole family for jumping the gun.

But on the day of our appointment, the hospice doctor and nurses did not brush us off or tell Michele she was overreacting. They were empathetic and comforting as they confirmed she qualified for hospice, which meant she appeared to have less than six months to live. They set up a thorough plan of care and discussed the entire process with us.

They helped us accept it was coming soon, that it was a reality, and we weren't being overly dramatic. We walked through how Michele was going to decline and how death is something we will all experience. It's a normal part of life.

There are a few moments in life that feel final. I remember finishing college and knowing I was closing a chapter. Starting a business and seeing it thrive after years of struggle—that felt like a finish line too. Even having your first child means everything shifts. Your old life is gone, and something new begins. The thing is, you keep living after all of those. You learn, you grow, and if someone asks you about it, you can tell them how it went. What it felt like. What would you do differently?

But death… death isn't like that. Nobody comes back from the dead and tells you how to prepare for it and what it's going to be like. Well, except for that one guy, Jesus. He's the only one. Michele understood and accepted her expiration date. She leaned on what the Bible says about death and what comes after. She trusted God and wanted to go through death gracefully, maybe a little excitedly even.

Visiting Angels allowed us to see many elderly people die peacefully at home. This was what Michele wanted for herself, so that's what we planned. I certainly wanted to honor her wishes, but I was more than a little intimidated by my role. Michele dying at home meant I'd have to do most of her final care, including administering medications.

The hospice nurse walked me through how to administer Adderall and morphine. I wasn't sure I'd have the courage to administer such potent drugs to Michele, but the nurse assured me they would be very helpful when the time came. Michele arranged everything—she wrote her advance directives and finalized her will and marital trust. She even wrote her goodbye letters to me and each of her children.

Being in hospice meant we wouldn't need a coroner's investigation or other legal proceedings after her passing. Our preparedness, in these ways, brought its own strange comfort. But even with everything in order, it felt like we could go on like this for a long time. Caring for Michele had become my daily rhythm. The extra work didn't bother me. It was simply our life now.

Then one Saturday morning in late May, Michele was laboring a little in her breathing. The night before, she wasn't quite her normal chipper self, sitting in her recliner, absorbed in her reading. She explained to me she felt a little unwell, like maybe she had a cold.

We decided she would stay in bed that day. This was the first time she did that. She never wanted to sit in bed or just watch TV all day. She liked her routine of getting up at a decent time, going through her morning grooming process, and getting out to her living room all dressed and ready for the day.

About midday, it was clear she was ill. I thought it was a cold, but she was struggling to clear her throat as she had little strength to cough. I called hospice to get their advice, and they said it could be a cold, but to calm her coughing and let her rest, they told me to give her the smallest doses of Adderall and morphine. This helped considerably, and I was grateful for the ability to make her feel better.

That evening, Michele opened those beautiful green eyes and looked at me. I needed that. I lived for our hearts to connect in our glances with each other, but throughout that day, her eyes had been struggling to make that connection with me. It seemed like she wanted to, but she was being pulled away. I was not thinking this was just a cold anymore, or that she would bounce back in a day or so. She was leaving this world. She was being summoned home.

I asked Kailey to come over to the house, and we started monitoring Michele's oxygen saturation. It was around 80 percent (a healthy level is 95 to 100 percent), so we asked hospice if we could give her some oxygen. They said yes and rushed an oxygen machine over to the house. If it really was just a cold, it was clear she needed help to get through it.

The next day, Sunday, she seemed to rest calmly. Kailey and I thought maybe she had stabilized a bit. I was giving her regular small doses of Adderall and morphine. She was on two liters of oxygen and her CPAP machine all day and night. On Monday, though, we had to increase the oxygen to three liters to keep her in the 80 percent range. The nurse said that was low, but OK for Michele right now. It wasn't awful yet. Kailey and I knew this was not looking good, but we didn't want to rush to conclusions. We didn't want to falsely alarm everyone in the family. Continuing to wait to give people an update, however, could end up being too late. It was clear there was no foolproof way to navigate all this.

We finally reluctantly called family members in Missouri. We told them we didn't know how long this would go on, but it was looking more and more like it was probably the end. Michele was not recovering; she was continuing to get worse. They discussed how they would or if they could travel to see her one last time.

Michele rested comfortably throughout the day on Tuesday. That night, I woke up several times to give her more medication. In the morning, her oxygen was dropping again, so we increased it to five liters. That was the maximum dose for the machine we had.

"Take her to the emergency room now!" Minette cried out when I called to give her an update that morning.

It took some time to convince her that it would not be wise. There was no reason to prolong Michele's life. Also, that would be against Michele's wishes.

When hospice first came over to set up her case, we had a long discussion about her final wishes and what treatment she would want. Michele and I spent several more days after that before we determined she would not go on a breathing machine with a tracheotomy. She was already on a permanent catheter. She had a feeding tube as well. We felt the trach really was the step that indicated you weren't making it. You wouldn't recover. Her quality of life would go down precipitously. She marked her shaky "X" on the Do Not Resuscitate (DNR) form and indicated her wish not to receive a breathing machine.

Kailey came back over to the house and sat devotedly by Michele's side, watching the oxygen monitor all morning. She jumped a few times in a panic as she saw the saturation dip down into the sixties. It was excruciating to have that machine essentially counting down Michele's end as if it were a clock on a bomb.

The hospice nurse soon arrived for her daily check-in and stayed. That made it clear to us that this may be Michele's last day with us. We then called everyone to come say their goodbyes. Sydney came over with her kids and Tad. Kailey asked Kyle to come over and bring their girls. Cheyenne brought Kai and Liam. Blake came by with Titus and Ezra. A few close friends were also there that Wednesday morning. "This is going to end soon, and it is going to be alright," the nurse told us. "Don't be alarmed, she is comfortable and with her loved ones."

But we were missing Minette and Linda. They, along with Kassidy, Sawyer, and Sullivan, were in our airplane flying to Pagosa Springs, trying to get to Michele as fast as they could.

Michele opened her eyes once, and I'm pretty sure she could see her loved ones gathered around her. That would've given her all the assurance she needed to let go.

Once, she responded to me touching her hand.

"You're being very brave, and we are all here with you, and we love you," I told her.

A few moments later, Kailey jumped off the bed.

"Her oxygen is at 50 percent! What do we do?!"

She did jazz hands like she touched something that shocked her. She was looking at me and the nurse. The distress on her face cut me to the core. Kailey knew there was nothing to do, but she was just reacting as someone not ready to lose her mother. How can you ever be ready?

Then the oxygen saturation dipped even lower. Michele took a short, shallow breath and stopped for a couple of seconds, then breathed again. We whisked the grandkids out of the room. A few of us started praying out loud.

Michele took one more meager breath. We waited for another, but it never came.

Kailey did not hold it together very well, and neither did I. We couldn't tear our hands away from Michele's. We watched as the color left her face from the top of her head down. I could feel her soul separate from her body as the color was fading. I stared at her for a while, trying to say goodbye. Actually, saying it was something I wanted to avoid. I couldn't get the words past my throat.

Weeks, months, and years of doctor appointments and tests, canes and wheelchairs, hope and heartbreak, uncertainty and fear were now done. Finished in a moment. Time had folded in on itself, decades collapsing into seconds. My mind swam through an ocean of memories in an instant, and I was right back in the cafeteria at Biola, staring into those emerald-green eyes. If only I could see them once more, bright with promise and eager for adventure.

Our plane load of family hadn't made it in time. They landed about 30 minutes afterward. When our texts came through saying Michele was gone, our pilot heard Minette's agony loud and clear. She banged the window of the plane so hard it broke a seal. It was awkward in a private plane with Kassidy, her new baby, and her estranged grandmother, aunt, and brothers. We'd hoped this event might lead to more communication with Kassidy, but it didn't.

We waited to call the mortuary until they drove over from the airport and had a few moments with Michele. I remember just standing there thinking I needed to be strong for my family, but I felt completely empty. I had nothing to say. This loss was too overwhelming. I was reeling over this conclusion to the last 40 years of my life.

I don't think it took long for the mortuary staff to arrive after we called them, but I can't be sure. Time didn't seem to move the way it should. As the hearse drove away, I wanted to watch it till the last moment. At the end of our street, it turned the wrong way to get out of our neighborhood. I saw it a few moments later, after it turned around and came back down the street.

It hit me that going the wrong way was a perfect exit for Michele. I pictured her waving goodbye to everyone as she flew away, and being so excited to finally see Jesus, she would've accidentally flown right into some planet and bonked her head clumsily. Then, she would've let loose that gut laugh as she redirected toward Heaven. For a moment, I stepped out of my suffocating grief, closed my eyes, and cracked a weary smile as I relished this scene. Yes, that laugh. I heard that laugh and felt a touch of peace. She made it! Michele was on her way to meet Jesus. She finished her life and did it with grace.

Reflecting on 40 years of life with her is delightful. Two people with individual goals and schedules who are trying to get along. We often pushed and pulled at each other. Sometimes for ourselves and selfish desires, other times for bigger purposes to help each other succeed in life. Marriage and parenting are only hard for the good ones. We worked at it hard because there was always a lot of 'us' that got in the way. Starting our own business and homeschooling demanded a lot, and we struggled through it as teammates. During the journey, it didn't seem very successful, and the results are still not final. But together, Michele and I were committed to the work. Even when we didn't completely trust the other one's decisions. We belonged to each other. I did not know where I belonged after losing Michele.

Since she got sick, every day was consumed with taking care of her. Now I didn't have to give medication to anyone. I didn't have to prepare liquid food for anyone. There was no one to bathe or groom. There was no one to read to anymore. I wasn't responsible for anyone's care schedule, so I didn't have to look at the clock constantly. House clocks were unnecessary. I hated the sight of them now.

I decided I needed to get away for a while. I took time away from work and went to a family condo in San Clemente, California. My niece, Reilly, and nephew Hudson came to spend time with me. So did Melissa and Joel. I really enjoyed having nothing to do, and I was thankful to be anonymous around town. The foggy mornings at the beach were almost as good as any afternoon thunderstorm in the mountains. Nothing was getting rid of the lump in my throat, though. After several weeks out of the office, I returned home. My heart was empty, and so was my home. I ate almost every meal out. It was too lonely to eat at home in the quiet all by myself. I hadn't been alone for four decades. Friends had stockpiled dozens of casseroles for me in the freezer, but I couldn't face sitting home alone. Meals had always been about being together.

Terminal illness is obviously very difficult for the person who's ill, but it's also a tremendous challenge for the caregiver. While they're not feeling the pain of the illness, they experience the emotional turmoil of watching someone they love suffer.

Even though friends and family looked at me as her healthy husband/caregiver, I felt like I was in the background, suffering alongside Michele. It was similar to Keagan. Sitting with him, not being able to help, was torture. Maybe it's like getting married. At the wedding, all the focus is on the bride. She does all the work, gets all the attention, and spends months on preparations. Her whole life as a young single lady culminates in this big event. But the groom is getting married too. He proudly stands next to her in the photos and in the background during the reception. After the wedding day, the groom takes on all the responsibility for the whole arrangement. He carries the burden now. For the sick person, death relieves their life's concerns, but the caregiver gathers up the pieces and does their best to continue on. And life must continue. In fact, life moves on quickly, whether we're ready or not.

For example, the spouse/caregiver is often in charge of planning a memorial service, which was true for me. Thankfully, I had help from family and friends. Michele would have loved to be there with everyone. My tired heart felt alone, even surrounded by family and friends—a fact I couldn't escape. I felt relieved that Michele rested peacefully, free from struggle, and that her joy was complete, but mine was not. Not in the slightest. My sadness was overwhelming. My loneliness was stifling. Once everyone went home, once the sympathy cards stopped coming and the concerned phone calls diminished, I was alone with no sense of purpose anymore.

I wandered around the house, feeling lost. Padgette was there, and as sweet a companion as she was, she couldn't come close to filling the void left by my wife. I wasn't mad at God. I was relieved for Michele. She and I had already worked through the meaning of all this for her. But I still felt like I was living in some alternate reality. Not knowing what to do, and having no one to talk to, I would walk up to our front door and look out the glass at the mountain view and say out loud, "Where are you, Michele? How can you not be here?"

Staring through the front door's glass, I saw a world drained of color. The bare trees stood like skeletons, their branches clawing at a pale, colorless sky. The grass was brittle and brown, and tumbleweeds skittered across my lifeless yard. In the distance, the mountains, once towering sentinels, were now mere shadows, smudged behind a veil of haze. The world outside was always so crisp and clear and full of promise. I had no desire to step into it now.

But I didn't want to stay in my house either. It had never felt so big and empty. My children, now grown, had not lived at home for years. The ghost of their laughter and footsteps haunted the surrounding silence. Michele's handwritten Bible verses clung to the walls like fading petals, their words vacant, their comfort dulled. Family photos in frames stood lifeless on shelves—smiling faces trapped in vague memories from ages ago.

I had nowhere to go. Nothing to do. My days of building and running a business were being carried on by others now.

Each day, I returned to the same window. The same bleak view. The same silence. The same ache. Our little corner of paradise in the mountains was nowhere to be found, and I had disappeared with it.

Slowly, I saw what was really out there. It was summer. The grass stretched high and lush, each blade a lush green that shimmered in the morning light. The dirt road, once swallowed by mud, now lay warm and dry beneath the sun's gaze. The air was still, calm—no longer howling with an angry wind.

But it was the mountains that had changed the most. No longer cold monuments to endurance or hardship, they were now alive with the promise of new adventures. Like steadfast friends, they hadn't turned away. They hadn't retreated. They had waited for me.

I cracked open the door and breathed in the soft, earthy fragrance of an approaching afternoon rain shower. That drew me through the doorway to sit on the porch rocking chair. Wow, the grass really was green and tall. The summer birds chirped and darted about as though thrilled to see me again. The trees surrounding the house swayed in a rhythm like friendly neighbors waving hello. I gave a nod to my mountains as the haze pulled back. God had put them there for me. I had a new appreciation for them.

I made plans for Kai and me to travel to Bali for his double-digit trip with Grandpa. I traveled to Missouri to visit family and go mountain biking with them in Bentonville. Kailey joined me on my porch to plan an epic backpack trip in the Alps and visit our missionary friends in Tanzania. I began having thrilling new adventures in many glorious mountain summers and snowy winters. I got to enjoy living alongside people again.

It felt like neither Michele nor Keagan was really gone. Their memories weren't fading away. The pictures in my mind of them distilled down to a few perfect images I love to recall. I often wish to update them on the wonderful things happening in my life now. Looking at my mountains reminds me that eternity does exist, and I will be part of it with them.

I've had dreams of Michele and Keagan. They were in the room near me, joining in with lots of people around us. They were just there in the room. People were talking. Keagan was working on some kind of project. They never interacted directly with me, but they were there. It felt very relaxed and peaceful, and everyone was happily occupied.

One morning, I was outside wondering what my day had in store. As I gazed at the peaks overlooking my house, I no longer felt any of the hardship or metaphors of endurance they brought into my life. These mountains shimmered with a new light, full of adventure and peace all at once. A crispness hung in the air, full of mystery. The trails beckoned, but not to test me. The peaks revealed a new range that lay beyond the ones I was familiar with.

MY MOUNTAINS

  I took a stroll down to the pond at the edge of my property to get a closer view. Kai joined me. There was much more water than I ever remembered. Trees had sprung up around it—tall, strong, and perfect for a rope swing. Everything around me felt more alive, more majestic. A sudden "Whoo-whoop!" erupted from a young man swinging on a rope and plunging into the pond with a splash that sent droplets dancing into the sunlight. I stopped in my tracks. It wasn't the yell that startled us—it was the voice. Kai's mouth popped open with anticipation. He bolted into the water, jumping on top of his dad.

  Back at the house, people occupied every chair on the porch. The yard and pastures were teeming with laughing children. No one was in a hurry as we reveled in each other's company and made plans for our next adventure. The next day, we packed up for a hike to a new peak, one none of us had summited yet. The sun was bright, the air cool and thin, the way it gets when you're up above 10,000 feet. Everyone was giddy, bouncing around with packs full of lunch and trail snacks. The little ones skipped ahead, and the teenagers joked and raced each other, and not one person complained. Not about sore feet, not about how long it would take. Michele, light on her feet, moved with a vitality I hadn't seen in years—no longer steadying herself, but thriving with every step.

  Halfway up, we reached a crystalline lake so clear and still it mirrored the sky—until the first splash. One grandkid jumped in, then another, and soon everyone was plunging into the water. Screams of delight and laughter echoed against the cliffs. Keagan slid down a glacier into the water, surfaced, and shouted something about how strange it was that the icy water didn't feel that cold. I floated on my back, watching clouds drift over the ridgeline, and quietly marveled that this moment—this joy, this mountain, this water—had been prepared for us. Not imagined. Not stumbled into. It was waiting for us.

We reached the summit by midday. There was no fatigue, just a satisfying sense of accomplishment. We spread out a delightful picnic—homemade sandwiches, fruit, and those pink and white frosted animal cookies Michele always brought on hikes. We sat close, inside a hole, in the scree stones to shield us from the wind, all of us munching our lunch without a care in the world. Nobody was in a rush to get back. Nobody was checking the time.

For our next adventure, we piled into old Jeeps and four-wheelers for a wild ride along cliff-hugging switchbacks and deep river crossings that sent sprays of water up the windows. But the engines never failed, and no one got stuck. We got lost—gloriously lost—on a side trail none of us recognized. But there was no fear, no frustration. Getting lost wasn't a mistake here. It was just another way to find something new. We laughed harder the more we didn't know where we were.

And through it all, Keagan led the way. Sometimes on foot, sometimes behind the wheel, sometimes standing still with a look of wonder on his face that told me he understood it, too. This was truer than anything we had ever known. This was what we were made for.

There was music. All kinds of fantastic music. But it was in the rustling aspen leaves, in the burbling water of the river, in the soft crunch of boots on a hidden trail. The clouds even joined in. The lyrics kept my eyes on the verge of joyful tears almost constantly. Here, He answered all my questions quietly, slowly, not with words, but just by being with Him. Being with Him and all those I love. It is peaceful. It is satisfying. It is mysterious. It is not lonely.

THE END FOR NOW

www.ingramcontent.com/pod-product-compliance
Lightning Source LLC
Chambersburg PA
CBHW071738150426
43191CB00010B/1620